IT'S PERSONAL

The Business Case for Caring

Lorna Borenstein

with Laurence Minsky

It's Personal: The Business Case for Caring

By Lorna Borenstein

with Laurence Minsky

Grokker Innovation Labs Press

© 2021 by Lorna Borenstein

Hardcover: 978-1-7359837-0-7

For every manager who wants to help their people thrive, and for every executive who wants to help their business soar.

Contents

FOREWORD

Putting Corporate Culture in Context

Libby Sartain, Former CHRO Southwest Airlines and Yahoo!

Libby Sartain is an independent director and advisor, working with companies on human resource issues or in an advisory capacity. With 40 years of experience in human resources, she is also an author and frequent speaker, using her HR leadership and management experience at companies in technology, transportation, and manufacturing. She led human resources at Yahoo! Inc. and Southwest Airlines Inc. during transformative periods. Both companies were among Fortune magazine's "Best Places to Work" during her tenure. Sartain now serves on the board of directors of ManpowerGroup, AARP, and AARP Foundation (Chair). She is the former board chair of the Society for Human Resource Management and currently is Chairman of the SHRM Foundation Board. She formerly served on the board of Peet's Coffee and Tea and Shutterfly, Inc. She chaired the compensation committees of all three public boards. She was honored in 2020 by NACD in the Directorship 100 as one of the 50 most influential corporate directors.

How timely for a book on workplace wellbeing to appear in the midst of a global health crisis (a pandemic), followed by an economic crisis (global recession), and then a social crisis (growing recognition of racial inequity). Never before has the concept of wellbeing been as important to us personally, as well as to employers who need healthy, engaged workers. Now more than ever before, employers need to find new and innovative ways to reach out, communicate, and provide value-added experiences for their people. Wellbeing is at the core of top performance individually and collectively: a healthy culture equals a high performing organization. Yet, accomplishing these goals seems to be more difficult than ever. That is why we need this book!

My forty-year career has focused on corporate culture and I have worked within and led two of the best people-centered, healthy corporate cultures during their formative years. I had the great fortune of being the head of HR for the first company to be named the #1 Best Company to Work For in America (Southwest Airlines in 1998). And later, to help Yahoo! Inc. make that list too. Like other enlightened and driven leaders in promoting healthy cultures, I was often challenged by my bosses to provide a business case for why we should spend our time, energy, and financial resources on building or transforming corporate culture, or to prove after the fact via metrics that our efforts were successful. A major contribution of this book is the way the author lays out how to build the business case for a healthy, resilient, and sustainable workforce, including how to make an impactful pitch to the team at the top. This approach will be useful to HR Leaders or any executives making an argument to invest in the wellbeing of their workforce.

As a leader in the HR profession—a profession I love—I experienced the evolution of the profession as we moved from administrative, to managerial, to the C-Suite, and the boardroom. The HR function has become as important to corporate strategy as Finance or Marketing, especially in our current crises. What has propelled this evolution is the understanding that no strategy can be delivered without the right talent and organizational capability. Talent always matters whether times are good or bad. During prosperous times, talent drives organizational growth and success. In times of crisis, talent will lead the organization through turbulent times and back to prosperity. In fact, I might argue that the bigger the crisis, the higher the need will be to focus on talent. That means we have to work harder to engage and retain our most valuable asset. Yet, our most talented workers are now also savvy consumers of work and opportunities available, so a talent brand is as important as a consumer or customer brand. HR is now part internal marketer and a brander of the worker experience to current and potential workers.

I have long believed that the relationship between employer and worker must be more than just a commitment to performing work in return for compensation. It involves trust. Employers are entrusted to provide an employee experience that shapes workers' futures, livelihoods, needs, and work-life wellbeing. The deliverables of HR to provide and employee decisions we make affect corporate capability and sustainability and create the day-to-day experience of workers and other stakeholders. The employee experience and the customer experience must be aligned and intertwined to deliver on brand promises. That trust cannot exist if the organization isn't performing well and returning value to its owners, workers, and all stakeholders. In the current environment, the problem is that no one knows exactly how to navigate through the uncertainty of a pandemic, so being transparent and creating trust is both difficult and extremely important. Because when trust isn't there or it is broken, workers always have other options.

With up to five generations of workers in your workforce at any given time, there can no longer be a singular approach to the pact made between employer and worker. While employers have traditionally set expectations, today workers are setting their own expectations for what they value from their employer. The crisis brought on by the global pandemic has only accelerated the situation with adaptation to remote work. This creates new challenges for navigating work-life balance and personal wellbeing. It creates more complexities in curating an employee experience that can be relied upon. It creates an even greater need for collaboration while finding ways to customize work arrangements to meet workers' needs and expectations. It requires organizations to demonstrate their own health and resilience through the turmoil. This book helps employers with that approach as it outlines the journey to bring caring, health, and wellbeing into your corporate culture.

We are now at a moment in time when human capitalism is rising in importance to workers, investors, customers, and communities. Environmental, social, and governance (ESG) criteria are an increasingly popular way for investors to evaluate companies in which they might want to invest. In 2019, Blackrock CEO, Larry Fink, wrote in his letter to investors that "Purpose is not a mere tagline or marketing campaign; it is a company's fundamental reason for being—what it does every day to create value for its stakeholders. Purpose is not the sole pursuit of profits but the animating force for achieving them." The Business Roundtable's August 19, 2019 statement redefining the purpose of the corporation, which committed to delivering value to all company stakeholders—customers, employees, suppliers, communities, and shareholders—was signed by 181 CEOs. This is an acknowledgment from these business leaders that delivering superior financial results isn't our sole goal.

It is time for corporate leaders, and HR in particular, to grasp this moment and run with it. I am optimistic that we will do so.

I worked with Lorna Borenstein at Yahoo! and knew her to be a brilliant people leader and marketer. Now she has created a company, Grokker, delivering wellbeing solutions via video to empower workers to take control of their health and happiness. The company embodies the concept of mass customization in that workers can make the experience their own, aligning with their interests, abilities, and goals.

This book, *It's Personal: The Business Case for Caring*, makes the case for why overall wellbeing of the workforce matters deeply to an employer. It evangelizes how to make it work and what the outcomes will be if implemented properly. An organization that embraces these principles will have more engaged workers, better retention, and an employee experience that can be customized to meet individual needs—and it will be a desired place to work for the best talent. But perhaps the most impactful outcome will be the sense of belonging and alignment to organizational purpose that can come about when the organization shows their care for workers as individuals. Belongingness is the holy grail of diversity, equity, and inclusion work, as it is essentially that feeling that comes from being part of something, such as a purpose or a cause. Social programs and wellbeing initiatives are powerful ways of creating an inclusive place to work. I invite you to begin your journey by reading this important book.

PREFACE: MY STORY

Thank you for caring enough to pick up this book. To me, health and well-being in all its forms—and truly caring about my employees as whole people with complex lives outside of work—is deeply personal. But it is also the key to success in business today no matter how you feel about it. While the rest of *It's Personal: The Business Case for Caring* will detail why caring is key, explain how to create a caring culture, and deliver on the title by showing why it is in the best interests of your business, let's start in this introduction by seeing how I came to that conclusion over the course of my first twenty-six years in business. You will see how I learned that genuinely caring about your employees is the single most important thing you can do to create a positive culture that will attract and retain top talent in competitive employment markets as well as get people to deliver above and beyond during downturns in your business when you need every ounce of productivity you can muster. What's more, I also learned that caring for your employees is the most important thing you can do to deliver results.

My health-and-wellness journey started six months after I gave birth to my first child, when my husband and I moved from Chicago to Toronto. I'd been hired by one of the top law firms in Canada to work on large corporate bankruptcy and insolvency matters. It was one of those firms that still had private offices with large mahogany doors that could actually shut. I had a 2,100 minimum billable hour requirement. This meant that I had to bill for 40 hours of working time each and every week, which required more like eight to ten hours per day if I wanted to take any vacation.

To bill this number of hours, one needed to actually put in at least twelve to fourteen hours per day, because not every minute was billable, especially as a younger attorney. After all, while senior partners could charge for thinking time, no one was going to pay for my twenty-six-year old thoughts. Other than on the weekend, the firm also didn't allow attorneys to work from home, and they emphasized face time as a measure of who was working the hardest. To be with my six-month-old during the work week, I had to choose between spending time with her before I left for the office in the morning and working late, or waking at 5:00 a.m. to leave for the office and then heading out early at 7:00 p.m. to get home by 7:30 p.m. and see her before her bedtime. I much preferred spending time with my daughter in the evening because I loved reading to her and putting her to bed, so I'd try to sneak out of the office at 7:00 p.m. as often as I could.

Since some of the senior partners were well known for swinging by a junior's office after 8:00 p.m. just to see whether the associate was still at work, sneaking out would involve placing my suit blazer over the back of my desk chair, along with a cup of hot coffee on my desk, and leaving the desk lamp on over an open file with an uncapped highlighter to make it appear to those passing by that I was merely in the restroom or in the library. I began keeping an extra blazer in my office on the hook behind my door along with an extra shirt in a clear plastic dry-cleaning bag so I would always have it handy, which had the extra benefit of giving senior partners the impression that I pulled all-nighters so frequently that I needed a change of clothes in my office at all times. When I asked some of the other more senior attorneys with children how they managed to stay on top of their billable hours and maintain a home life, they told me that I had to learn to live with less sleep and to plan focused family time for Saturday afternoons and Sunday mornings, and that way I could sleep in a little on Saturday and catch up on my work on Sunday afternoon.

Clearly, the firm did not maintain a caring culture. In fact, it all seemed frankly crazy to me. I was well paid, but the expectation of me to sacrifice my family life in order to bill outrageous hours in search of an eventual partnership felt off balance. I did not discuss this with my superiors or any partners because I did not want to be fired or considered uncommitted to the firm. Instead, I started quietly looking for another job that would excite me intellectually and allow me to work a ten-hour day and restore sanity to my life. (This approach of the "under the radar" job search is happening more than ever. I call it the silent revolution—younger employees voting with their feet without warning—which we will explore more deeply in chapter 1.) For me, it worked. I found a new job within three months at Hewlett Packard.

On my very first day of work at HP, a bell rang at 10:00 a.m. throughout the building, sounding vaguely like something from my old high school. Everyone began to slowly file downstairs to the cafeteria, where free bananas, hard-boiled eggs, warm beverages, and other healthy snacks were on display for all to enjoy. I chose a banana and followed the crowd, who were bantering and exchanging pleasantries about their weekends, past the unmanned checkout line and toward a table where three men were seated enjoying coffee. They invited me to sit with them, introduced themselves, and made me feel welcome. After fifteen minutes of chatting, with me mostly listening to their conversation and laughing along, we all got up and returned to our cubicles.

That same day, my boss stopped by my cubicle just before lunchtime and asked if I wanted to join her for a workout at the company gym. I was stunned. My boss, a very senior executive at the company, was inviting me to take an actual lunch break, even though I'd clearly had a midmorning snack break, and do something good for my health and wellbeing with her. She valued her health and mine and wanted to give me permission to take care of myself out in the open. I was elated and felt enormous gratitude for the opportunity to work at a company that cared about me. Not surprisingly, HP had very low voluntary employee turnover, and employees were tremendously proud to work at the company.

I am deeply grateful for my formative years at HP, where I was taught that trust and respect for the individual was paramount, and that open and honest communication was required if I was to succeed. Almost forty years after the company went public, the people-centric objectives established by founders Bill Hewlett and Dave Packard in 1957 in The HP Way,[1] were equally valuable to the pursuit of profit. It made me confident to ask for what I wanted and to speak up when I did not understand or when I disagreed. I believe it made me a better person, a better employee, and ultimately a better leader. Without my belief that voicing my thoughts would inure to my personal benefit at HP, I never would have asked to be seconded to work on a large Software and Services outsourcing project that changed the trajectory of my career. And without my belief that being heard was safe and critical to my success, I would never have reported being sexually harassed by one of the most senior executives at my division and had it handled with exactly the kind of dignity and respect for all concerned that should be the norm everywhere.

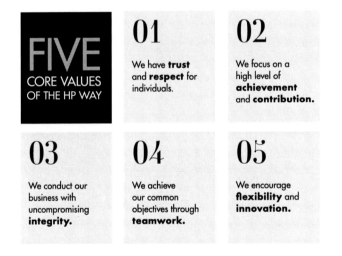

FIVE
CORE VALUES
OF THE HP WAY

01
We have **trust** and **respect** for individuals.

02
We focus on a high level of **achievement** and **contribution.**

03
We conduct our business with uncompromising **integrity.**

04
We achieve our common objectives through **teamwork.**

05
We encourage **flexibility** and **innovation.**

The five core values of the HP Way.

I also had the benefit of working for two of the fastest-growing and most iconic tech companies during the formative years of the internet. At eBay I learned the critical importance of community and how, in order for any marketplace to thrive, there must be a careful balance of power shared between the supply and demand forces. The seminal prerequisite to establishing the conditions in which a marketplace can exist and blossom is identifying the motivations of each side. As the first general manager of eBay Canada, I learned that to attract buyers to a new platform, I first needed to attract sellers, and to attract sellers, I needed to first earn their trust by understanding their fears as well as their needs, and then paint a compelling vision of an inspiring future where a nascent platform that began with the trading of Beanie Babies would enable the democratization of retail for all and connect small merchants directly with global buyers who would never step foot into their mom-and-pop brick-and-mortar locations.

A few years later, when entrusted to create a mass retail and specialty channel of new goods to expand eBay's US market beyond vintage and used merchandise as vice president of eBay's Apparel, Jewelry, Toys, Home, and Health & Beauty Division, I once again applied this motivations-and-vision construct to discover that addressing a corporate CFO's need to reduce the costs of excess inventory (in order to satisfy Wall Street analysts) was even more powerful in sparking action than speaking to a CEO's desire to grow revenue. Employers and employees are the parties in the workforce marketplace, and to attract top talent and retain them, we first need to understand them—both their motivations and their struggles—so that we can paint a compelling vision where they can thrive as whole people. A fair paycheck is simply not enough to satisfy today's employee; those days are over. For your business to succeed, you now need to make your individual employees feel authentically cared for. Because if you don't, they will leave you at the drop of a hat for someone who does.

At Yahoo! I got my first taste of the wonder that is subscription revenue while running the global online dating business Yahoo! Personals. I also had my first experience of reporting to a boss who made me feel great every time I saw him. This was back in 2004, when online dating still had a very big stigma attached to it, and everyone expected to meet their significant others IRL. The challenge was that people were struggling to find their soul mates, and the promise was that apps would remove the randomness of meeting someone by chance and put the relationship seeker in charge with proactive digital dating tools and the all-important digital photo. This too was a marketplace, but instead of Beanie Babies, people were hunting for love, companionship, and a "happily ever after."

What I learned from the outset at Yahoo! was that people mattered, work colleagues were friends, and teamwork was rewarded while sharp elbows were not. At Yahoo!, if you were loyal and drank the cultural Kool-Aid like I did, you were said to bleed purple, the color of our famous logo. That was me. I could not have anticipated how much the unconditional positive regard for and from my boss and coworkers motivated me. My second month on the job, I was sitting at my desk at 6:00 p.m. reviewing some financials when my desk phone began to ring. It was my boss, COO Dan Rosensweig. I was filled with an instant and ominous sense that I must have done something wrong. I answered the phone expecting the worst, and instead of presenting me with a problem or criticism, he told me what a great job I was doing and how impressed he was by my first few weeks at the company. I was relieved—elated, in fact—and grateful for his specific examples of things I had done well. He even asked me how my kids were doing and remembered their names and ages. This may seem like a small detail to you, but in that moment, he earned my loyalty, and I worked as hard as I ever have to deliver results for him.

In the months and years that ensued, when new entrants were attacking us from all fronts, and we needed to constantly innovate in order to survive, I gave it my all. This was easier to do within the confines of my Personals P&L than elsewhere in the company because I had direct control of all of the resources that I needed to shape the user experience, direct product and engineering, and market and advertise the service. But what I learned was that because my manager was someone whom I felt very connected to on a personal level, I did not want to let him down. Even when faced with corporate headwinds that necessitated across-the-board headcount freezes and budget cuts, I was prepared to give it my all and fight for Yahoo!.

The second lesson I learned at Yahoo! wasn't until after I took on the role of vice president of marketing and product marketing for the massive Search & Marketplace business. In Search, Google was the eight-hundred-pound gorilla with statistically proven algorithmic search superiority and ad relevance. When I first met Qi Lu, the head of Engineering for Yahoo! Search, a brilliant man who managed to get to work by 4:00 a.m. daily and never seemed tired, he explained to me that contrary to popular belief, Yahoo!'s search results were in fact equal to or better than Google's. I did not doubt his claims, but my team's marketing research showed that consumer perception of Yahoo! Search placed it as a clearly inferior experience to Google search. So how could both these assertions be true? If the quality is the same, how could the consumer perception be so skewed against Yahoo!? After more primary research, I was able to ascertain that while the natural search results (these are the bulk of search results that are shown down the middle of search results pages) of Yahoo! were at parity with Google's, the paid ads that appeared along the right rail on Google's search results pages and along the very top and the right rail of Yahoo! Search results pages were ranked by relevance on Google but ranked by highest bidding advertiser on Yahoo!.

In other words, the Yahoo! paid search results were far less relevant to the consumer's search query than Google's paid search results, and consumers did not distinguish between the paid and the natural search results. Therefore, to a consumer, Google search was perceived as much more relevant based on total page relevance. The brilliant Yahoo! Search engineering team had spent months improving the search algorithms to ensure that the quality of search results was as good or better than Google. Unfortunately, without understanding the perception of reality by the consumer, the as-good or better Yahoo! Search results were viewed as an inferior product to Google.

The lesson I took from Yahoo! Search was that the facts are overrated; only the user experience and user perception matters. If your employees don't feel that you care about them or don't feel that you offer sufficient opportunity for career advancement, then it doesn't matter what facts you point to, or how hard you try to explain that the personal development plans you've instituted are evidence of your serious interest in career development. In order to convince them that you care and are committed to development, you need the cultural equivalent of total page relevance. You can't argue your way into being an employer of choice. Instead you need to earn it and make sure you are in touch with how your employees are feeling about you. After all, we all know who won the search wars.

After Yahoo!, I accepted a role as president of what was at the time the largest publicly traded online real estate company, Move Inc. My experience being a Section 16 officer at Move Inc. taught me a lot about corporate governance, managing investor relations, setting expectations with the Street during a turnaround, Sarbanes Oxley compliance, dealing with activist shareholders, and the critical importance of the safe harbor clause when making forward-looking statements. But most importantly of all, the experience led me to a life-affirming pre-midlife crisis that resulted in my resigning and ultimately founding my own holistic wellbeing company. The company was going through the painful aftermath of the failure of the mortgage-backed securities market and the ensuing economic havoc of the housing market crash in 2008. I was plugging away at work but feeling burned out, uninspired, and trapped. A girlfriend asked me over coffee if I ever considered resigning. I laughed out loud at the question. Quitting? I had never quit at anything in my entire life. I'm the daughter of immigrants who taught me the value of hard work and perseverance, and the all-important value of the financial security that comes from achievement. Yes, I was unhappy, and, yes, I was going to work with a pit in my stomach as I helped the board of directors find a new CEO and replace many of the executive leaders that were resisting the turnaround. But the thought of quitting had literally never crossed my mind.

Then my girlfriend asked me the question that changed my life: "So, what are you afraid of?" Initially I scoffed at that, reflexively saying I wasn't afraid of anything but that I owed a duty to my employees and shareholders and board. But as I reflected upon the question more thoughtfully, I began to realize that indeed I was afraid of something, something so embarrassing that I am still a little ashamed to admit it today: I was afraid of what people would think. After all the professional and financial success I had objectively earned, I was afraid that if I left my job and had no title, no status, no RSUs, no invitation to the Fortune Most Powerful Women's Conference, that I would no longer be worthy. Fundamentally—and this took years of therapy to excavate—I was afraid that I was not loveable or worthy without achievement to prove it. This realization is what led me to resign and to very intentionally do so without a bunch of board of directorships lined up and without an EIR gig or new CEO role in the wings. I needed to purge my soul of the need to be someone and instead focus on just being me and seeing if that was enough. So, I changed my LinkedIn profile to chief family travel officer and told all the VCs and executive recruiters that I was taking a year off and not to call me or email me until that time was over. I honestly didn't trust myself to resist their calls and outreach and figured this was the surest way to give myself the time to free myself of the need to be someone and prove to myself that I had intrinsic value just because I am me. I traded in competitive half-ironman distance triathlons for yoga, I spent months learning how to be still, and I took my kids out of school for one to three months at a time and traveled around the world making up for lost time. In the end, I took off almost three years and transformed my fear of not being intrinsically worthy into the knowledge that while I'm not for everyone, the people I love love me for who I am and not for what I am or what I can do for them.

When we traveled, I didn't bring a nanny or have babysitters. Instead, I immersed myself in being with them. I even homeschooled my youngest daughter while traveling through southern China and loved every moment. What I did not love, was the reality that struck me while caring for my kids on the road. You see, back when I was working, I had childcare on demand, so I could go to the gym at 5:15 a.m. and be back for breakfast or go train with my triathlon team after work and come home to a prepared dinner and bathed kids. But you know what you don't have time for when you are taking care of kids in a hands-on way with no one to help? You don't have time to take care of yourself. I couldn't go to the gym or for a run or even make time to meditate or find healthy recipes to cook.

For the first time in my adult life, I felt like I had no time to care for my physical or emotional health, and I needed to do something about it. So, I took out my first-generation iPad and began searching for long-form video content to help me take care of myself. This was back in 2011, and there was very little premium video online. All I was finding were cats on skateboards, poor-quality videos of some woman in her living room trying to show me how to do a squat, and a few niche sites that had a very limited amount of HD fitness video classes. I was so frustrated. I wanted expert-led, premium video in a wide variety of topics to help me eat better, sleep better, move more, and stay flexible and centered, and I wanted to not feel so isolated and alone. I wanted community at the core and to feel inspired and uplifted. What I wanted did not exist. So, I did what any reasonable person would do: I went for a walk on the beach and yelled at my husband about how YouTube was broken and needed to begin producing long-form, premium wellbeing video content as a subscription to help people like me stay happy and fit.

While David agreed this seemed like a big opportunity, he didn't think it was something that would interest YouTube. Turned out he was right, so I came out of retirement and started Grokker in 2012 because of my personal need for expert-led on-demand video with community at its core to help me be a better me. But before founding the company, I decided upon two nonnegotiables if I were to do it: 1) I had to feel so strongly about the need for the business that I couldn't not do it, and that I would do it even if the business never turned a profit, even if it failed commercially. Simply put, I had to feel that creating it was something I just had to do, and that success would be in the journey rather than the destination. 2) I would only do it if I could create a culture in which I could bring my whole self to work, and where those around me felt the same. I had to create a uniquely human workplace that felt and was personal: where we emphasized fun and freedom, where we cared for one another as whole people, and where we shared our real-life struggles and supported one another because we cared about each other. I thought creating this culture would be the most difficult part of the business plan. But to my surprise and delight, more than eight years later, I work at a company that helps employers seamlessly integrate wellbeing into the lives of busy employees, and in a culture that welcomes the personal and makes every individual feel valued and connected while delivering stunning results.

I have learned that I cannot enjoy life nor live in integrity with myself if I am afraid of what others might think of me. And I have learned that creating a culture of caring, where people can show up as themselves and count on the support of others, is the single most important thing I can do as a CEO to secure the performance of my team and drive results at my company. And now, it seems that CEOs globally are awakening to the reality that caring for their employees is a business imperative. And that is why I am writing this book: because the time has come for us in the C-suite to have the courage and conviction to create a new kind of workplace and be secure in knowing that to deliver results we must care about the wellbeing of our employees, period. This book is the rallying cry to leaders who will be able to point to the book and the data in it to justify why creating a caring environment is corporate strategy and why culture matters most—not just because it is the right thing to do but because it is the smart thing to do.

I knew that I had satisfied the first criterion when I was moved to start Grokker with our mission to enable physical, social, and emotional wellbeing. In fact, the word "grok" literally means to soak in knowledge from another being so profoundly that you become one with them and changed by the interaction.[2] To be a Grokker is to be transformed by connection. I was less confident that I'd be able to achieve the second. Luckily, with a very clear vision of the cultural true north I wanted to work in and the careful selection of a founding team who shared this vision, I have had the unique pleasure of working in a high-performance environment that allows me and every other Grokker to be themselves and to take care of themselves. In 2020 Grokker was named a Fortune 100 Best Workplace. And now, the confluence of millennials and Gen Z entering the workforce, trends in health and wellbeing, and the increase in two-income families have generated a movement where employees are in the driver's seat and are demanding much more than a fair paycheck to attract and retain them. For the first time, there is a corporate imperative to create humane places of work that support employees' whole selves in order to deliver results, and employers are responding—even during the pandemic. In fact, 89% of employers have put measures in place "to ensure that people feel supported during this time."[3]

The world is waking up to the reality that work is personal and that there is a business case for caring. This book is intended to explain how we got here and what you as global leaders need to do to create a culture of wellbeing that will safeguard your company and allow you to thrive. It is divided into three key sections: 1) Building the Case; 2) Selling the Plan; and 3) Creating the Culture. Join me through the pages, and you'll gain the insights and tools you'll need to create a more effective caring culture in your organization. But let's start by looking at the human costs for employees and the financial costs for businesses of maintaining the status quo. It's an exploration that is sure to be well worth your time.

Section One:

BUILDING THE CASE

Chapter 1:

THE COSTS OF NOT CARING

Employers are in a bind. The world has changed, employee work expectations have evolved quite radically, and while our productivity and connectivity tools have advanced, most corporate cultures, benefits packages, and other key aspects of the enterprise operating norms have not kept up. As a result, we now have a fundamental mismatch between what employees need and what companies are providing. And it's costing big business billions of dollars each year. How? We'll get to that in a minute, but let's first look at the employee (and job seeker) mindset and the legacy business practices that are outdated or just plain ineffective. Needless to say, it is not a pretty picture. Despite Fitbits and Apple Watches, employees are dealing with conditions like high blood pressure, obesity, and depression. None of this should come as a surprise, considering that, according to the Centers for Disease Control, six in ten U.S. adults have a chronic disease, and four in ten have two or more.[3] As a result, many businesses—possibly even yours—could be in trouble and not even know it.

Look closer at the employee mindset, and the picture gets worse. Eighty percent of employed Americans today report that they're stressed out on the job.[4] More than 37 percent of workers report that they are sleep deprived.[5] And nearly one-quarter of employees report that they often or always feel burned out at work.[6] In fact, "employee burnout has reached epidemic proportions," reports Charlie DeWitt, the vice president of business development at Kronos, a workforce management organization. "While many organizations take steps to manage employee fatigue, there are far fewer efforts to proactively manage burnout."[7] It's no wonder millions of U.S. workers voluntarily leave their jobs each month.[8] This is literally burn and churn in the workplace.

As I mentioned in the introduction, I experienced burnout, but fortunately I had the resources to do something about it. While I am not alone in experiencing it, I realize that most employees don't have access to the same support and resources that I had. Just look at these three people who are considered "top talent" in their companies:

- Laura is a thirty-six-year old nurse in the Chicago suburb of Evanston who's pregnant with her first baby, a girl. She loves her job in radiology and has worked hard to build her reputation with the team. Putting her career on hold to focus on raising a family isn't an option. Not only does she find fulfillment in her work, she and her husband need to maintain two full-time incomes to make ends meet, and as a firefighter her husband is away at the station three nights each week. She wants to make the best of both worlds: find a way to care for her family while also working, willing to chase that elusive state of "work-life balance." But Laura has no family living near her, and the daycare she likes best requires pick up by 6:00 p.m. sharp, which she is afraid to commit to as she is often stuck in last-minute 5:00 p.m. meetings called by her single fifty-five-year old department manager. Laura is afraid of how she will be perceived if she needs to leave the office by 5:15 p.m. each day to pick up her daughter. She is also concerned about how she will have any time to take care of herself once the baby arrives and she can no longer make it to the private Pilates studio she loves for her twice-weekly 7:00 p.m. reformer class.
- Dan is a twenty-seven-year old software engineer in San Francisco. Considered a star performer, with meaningful product development experience at two different technology start-ups, he

and his partner are married and plan to have a family; both are focused on paying off their student loans and saving for a house. But Dan's commute has proven to be a challenge and, while he loves his job, after two years of taking the corporate shuttle over an hour each way down to corporate HQ and back, he's quietly considering relocating to Portland, where he can afford a house with a yard and work remotely for another tech company that offers surrogacy and adoption benefits.

- Barbara is a fifty-two-year old senior floor supervisor at a manu-facturing plant in Montgomery, Alabama, where she's worked for seventeen years. Her aging parents are beginning to need more of her time, and Barbara is now investigating elder care facilities that can both support her father with dementia and her mother, who at eighty-two is still spritely and social. Barbara has used up most of her vacation time driving ninety miles each way to the Birmingham area to collect her parents for doctors' appointments and facility visits. As one of only two women at her level, she is worried that if she misses any more work, her manager will ques-tion her commitment, and she needs the income to help support herself and her parents. She hasn't been sleeping well, has gained fifteen pounds, is now prediabetic, and has begun suffering from panic attacks.

Turn to your organization. If you look just below the surface, I am sure you will find similar stories of silent struggle. I bet that every employee has one story or another. In fact, pre-Covid-19, statistically three in ten of your employees were facing "material hardships," according to a study from the Urban Institute.[9] And I'm sure it's gotten worse since the pan-demic started. So, what is going on? Why is employee wellbeing at a boiling point, and why is it the employer's problem? And how did we get here?

First, the literal face of the workforce has changed dramatically over the last fifty years due to two main factors: "the extremely rapid growth in the participation rate of women; and the growing racial and ethnic diversity of the labor force."[10] In the 1950s the workforce was made up predominantly of white men who joined a company for forty years and earned a good living to support their families in exchange for total loyalty and an agreement not to bring their personal lives into work. Don Draper would hop on the train, briefcase in hand, donning his mac raincoat and fedora, and drink himself to oblivion each afternoon after delivering a brilliant new pitch to the client. He never asked for help, and no one ever encouraged him to seek it. The quid pro quo was that as long as he delivered results and remained loyal, he'd have a place at the firm, and no one needed to know his business. What's more, Don would leave the office at 5:00 p.m., have no evening work to catch up on or keep up with, and arrive home to dinner on the table with no household chores to perform.

But since then, we have experienced extremely rapid growth in the participation rate of women in the workforce. In fact, according to Mitra Toossi in the May 2002 edition of the *Monthly Labor Review*, "The factor most responsible for the earlier high growth rate was the rapid increase in the labor force participation rate of women, which stood at 30 percent in 1950 and increased to 60 percent by 2000."[11] When the norm goes from 70 percent of the workforce being men with full-time housewives to take care of the children, parents, community, and household to today, where only 29 percent of mothers are full time housewives and 71 percent are participating in the workforce with no one to take on the burden at home,[12] you end up in an environment where everyone is juggling a lot more, and the workplace is no longer immune to the realities of the whole lives of its workers. It is just a simple numbers game: the number of hours required to take care of house and home hasn't changed, but on top of this at-home workload, women now are working forty-plus-hour work weeks outside the home. Even if Don is willing to take on half of the household work and fold laundry each night, he and Mrs. Draper would still have four to five hours of extra work each day at home they didn't have back in the 1950s.

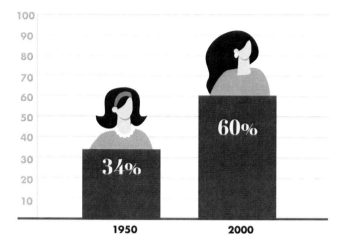

The percentage of women in the workforce in 1950 versus today.

While employees throughout the ages have struggled with attaining some form of balance between work life and home life, the line between the two has all but blurred today, and we're recognizing that and the battle for balance has been all but lost. True, technology has freed us to work with unprecedented flexibility, efficiency, and accuracy. Artificial intelligence (AI) and machine learning are changing the way companies understand and interact with customers; 5G technology is fulfilling the vision for truly connected cities; and voice technology and the internet of things (IoT) is making many of our workplace chores less cumbersome. But it has made our lives more complicated.

The goldfish is now actually winning

But since employees are now able to be productive and responsive 24-7, making it much easier to "burn the candles at both ends," they are more stressed when needing to meet their family obligations as well as work assignments. And the "always on" state of communication through multiple devices and platforms is putting all of us into a condition that writer Linda Stone calls "continuous partial attention."[13] Meanwhile, our average attention span has shrunk. In fact, today, the attention span of an average goldfish, which clocks in at a mere nine seconds, is longer than that of the average human, which is now at eight seconds, down from twelve seconds in 2000.[14] As a result, even the top employees are not bringing 100 percent of themselves to work—they are not fully engaged. It's no wonder that only a third of U.S. workers reported in a Gallup survey that they're involved in, enthusiastic about, and committed to their work and workplace.[15] Overall, this lack of engagement is costing employers billions in lost productivity.

The Goldfish is Winning

Due to "continuous partial attention," it's said that our attention span is now shorter than that of a goldfish.

Meanwhile, job candidates and employees for hard-to-fill positions are in the driver's seat when it comes to retention and recruitment. But it's not necessarily for more compensation, even with essentially stagnating wages. What they're seeking is the ability to address their entire lives—their whole selves—including the physical, emotional, financial, social, and community realities of their complicated lives. What's more, they want a sense of purpose and an ability to connect to their work and colleagues more meaningfully. Yet as far as we have come in the most technologically advanced era known to humankind, most employers are still not "getting it right." Yesterday's benefits approach—with its heavy reliance on smoking cessation programs, incentivized biometric screenings and health risk assessments, corporate gym subsidies, and the annual corporate step challenge—is simply out of date. Furthermore, the attempt to have health-care consumerism pave the way for people to shop around for the best medical treatments has resulted in cost-shifting with lower premiums for employers and higher deductibles for employees, leading to an extraordinary out-of-pocket exposure for employees at a time when an unfortunate diagnosis can deplete a family's entire savings.

I call today's approach part of the "biometric myth™," in which employer's efforts are not providing the results we were initially promised.[16,17] In the meantime, however, I just want to point out that it is putting additional stress on our increasingly time-starved employees to fully research and determine the best "bet" for their health-care insurance needs. And it could have an additional unintended consequence. Just as reminding smokers that smoking can kill them drives them to smoke even more as a way to relieve the increased stress,[18] I bet that reminding stress eaters that their diets are hurting them will make them eat even more. Employees do not need to be told what they already know. Rather, they need help managing and improving their lives as well as finding better opportunities to seamlessly fit healthier behaviors into their waking hours, the majority of which are spent at work. In other words, the benefits approach of yesterday is not showing caring to our employees. Instead, it shows that we care about cost cutting at the employee's expense.

Likewise, most workers can't even think about retirement when many of them are still repaying student debt—or still incurring it. Plus, they're saving for college for their children as well as supporting aging parents. It's no wonder that employees are unhealthier and unhappier than ever. The reality of day-to-day life is fast paced. Workers encounter demands from every direction—bosses, teammates, spouses, children. Are we making sure our employees can cope with this reality? As Dan Schawbel—partner and research director of Future Workplace and *New York Times* best-selling author of *Promote Yourself*—said, "Managers should promote flexibility, and ensure that employees aren't overworked, in order to prevent employee burnout that leads to turnover."[19]

In addition, the common practice of annual reviews is not meeting day-to-day opportunities to learn, grow, and create a dialog that helps both the employee and employer understand each other and hopefully make improvements in real time. Without a feedback loop that frequently shares what is going well and what is not—and with the loss of worker loyalty—we are witnessing a silent revolution where employees are quietly voting with their feet and leaving well-paid jobs for environments they feel are better suited to support their whole lives. And, often, we don't learn about what was wrong or missing until the exit interview, when it's too late—and only if the departing employee is willing to share. It's time for businesses to change—and the change is happening whether we like it or not. Before we get to the change, let's look at one more tectonic shift in today's workplace.

The workforce generational change

Compounding all of the workplace issues we have just cataloged, we're also in the midst of a key generational shift. By 2025, millennials and Gen Z-ers will comprise the majority of the global workforce.[20] For better or worse, these individuals grew up without experiencing a twentieth-century workplace—or the culture and attitudes it propagated. They are digital natives who don't remember the squeal of a dial-up internet connection, let alone the satisfaction of finding the perfect citation in the *World Book Encyclopedia* after hours of flipping through the weighty volumes while writing a term paper. Patience was not a necessary characteristic when growing up in a world where you could pick whatever TV show you wanted to watch on demand, fast-forward through commercials, and skip the library in favor of typing in Google queries and in a few clicks, finding supporting data for high school essays. They have always known women executives, and their benefits have always included 401(k)s and parental leave. Millennials and Gen Z-ers save their work not on a floppy disk, but in the cloud. Their interoffice memos have always been sent over email or Slack.

These young workers weren't conditioned to withstand the rigors (and let's face it, injustices) of corporate politics to just "stick it out" for their next pay raise or for a promotion. They graduated from kindergarten with as much pomp and circumstance as I did from college, and they received trophies for coming in eighth in their baseball leagues because no one is a loser anymore. They were raised to believe that they mattered and deserved to be listened to by well-intentioned parents like us. And they grew up in environments designed to make each individual feel truly unique and successful—yet under the constant fear of being a victim in the next school or workplace shooting—giving them an overriding drive for self-actualization beyond just earning a paycheck.

Moreover, they don't have the American dream, as it once was defined. They have seen their parents get laid off, particularly during the Great Recession of 2007 through 2009, and struggle financially between jobs. They've heard the stories of Social Security not being there for them and pension systems going bankrupt. As a result, millennials are the least engaged generation in the workforce. In fact, only 29 percent of them report that they are engaged while 55 percent claim they are not engaged, and 16 percent are actively disengaged.[21] With this lower engagement, they change jobs more often than other generations. About 21 percent of millennials report switching employment within the last year,[22] and 60 percent are currently open to finding a different opportunity.[23] More than 43 percent of millennials envision leaving their jobs within two years, while only 28 percent seek to stay beyond five years.[24] And only half of today's thirty-year-olds earn more than their parents, part of a downward trend in absolute mobility of children since 1940.[25] While half of millennials say they feel good about the amount of money they have for spending, less than 40 percent are what Gallup defines as "thriving" in any one aspect of wellbeing.[26]

The lack of engagement all makes sense. Not paid enough money to put up with an employer who doesn't meet their needs, and knowing that an employer could drop them at a small whiff of potential economic trouble, they are looking to join a company who will help them care for their elderly parents, pay off college debt, and live a fulfilling and meaningful life. In the end they're saying, "You're not paying me enough money to put up with all this without helping me figure out how to deal with life's stressors." In other words, if they don't feel you care about them and are helping them reach their goals, they are voting with their feet, and this voting is turning into a revolution. Keep in mind, when you picture a workplace revolution, you might envision an all-out attack. But this revolution is a silent one. It does not entail millennials and Gen Z-ers marching toward the C-suite demanding free doggie daycare or weekly massages. Rather, employees are just quietly leaving. You might not even notice it in your organization. But you can see this happening in companies everywhere. It's easy to poach the top talent out of places like Uber, McDonald's, and other established entities. While Uber[27] and McDonald's[28] are actively working to change their cultures (we wish them well and hope they succeed), others aren't, and soon these businesses won't have the talent they need to survive.

Employee turnover costs can be staggering.

Think millennials and Gen Z-ers are the issue? We've encountered the scorn for them in everything from articles and editorials to conference talks and hallway conversations. But they've been blamed long enough. In the end, they are not the problem. Quite the opposite: they are the answer. Why? Because they are shining a light on the opportunity costs that get in the way of businesses offering the benefits that truly matter. And while millennials and Gen Z-ers have simply started a workplace revolution, Gen X-ers and even boomers have learned that they can expect more from their employers and are now demanding the same. Those of us who built careers in the decades before the turn of the millennium can happily adjust to the new norms and enjoy the fruits of this progress. We are also in the position to make the changes, and we need to make them now, because, as an employer, we *do* have something—in fact, everything—at stake.

How do I know? Simple: because of what it's costing businesses to maintain the status quo. I'm not talking about the extremes such as the three executives of France Télécom who were sentenced to prison and fined thousands of dollars for creating a toxic work environment after thirty-five of their employees committed suicide.[29] Rather, I am talking about the little things that are costing businesses money but not showing the desired results as well as the business practices that could be impacting future viability. The examples are many. For instance, old school employee wellness programs were simply designed to help businesses save money by lowering the cost of insurance coverage. They focused only on the physical health of the employee as well as on tracking and monitoring employee behaviors. But while data can be used to benchmark, it doesn't enable or encourage productive action (and could cause increased stress among the employees). In fact, employee disengagement due to poor health costs employers $530 billion each year in the U.S., $280 billion of which is productivity losses (comprised of $198 billion in impaired performance and $82 billion in the opportunity cost of the absence.)[31] In other words, wellness programs are not actually saving money for employers but costing us in terms of lost productivity. These costs are substantial. As IBI (Integrated Business

Institute) president Thomas Parry, PhD, reports, "The cost of poor health to employers is greater than the combined revenues of Apple, Amazon, Microsoft, Netflix, eBay, and Adobe."[32] Clearly the wellness programs businesses are offering are not working to encourage employees to take the small, vital steps that could help them feel healthier, happier, and more productive and fulfilled.

Let's look at some of the other ways current business practices are costing the employer. Take the requirements for 100-percent utilization when it comes to billable hours (i.e., billing a minimum of forty hours a week). It may look like a good way to increase profits. And it might even work in the short term. But fatigued workers cost employers about $1,200 to $3,100 per employee in declining job performance each year,[33] so the returns will diminish while the culture of long hours remains the same. These long hours also encourage employees to remain glued to their workstations or desks, a problem since physically inactive employees are two times less productive and produce lower-quality work.[34] By contrast, employees who are vigorously active at least once per week are more productive and have an average of eight to ten fewer sick days than those who are physically inactive.[35] Walking meetings might sound much better at this point, but we don't even need to go that far. To start, what we need is to give employees the tools, support, and structure they need in order to perform at their best. This no doubt varies by company, but employers who heed the demands of millennials and Gen Z-ers and do what it takes to make sure their employees feel that their work-life balance is being achieved will be issued the ticket to the promised land as it relates to optimal employee productivity. While we will get to examine the tools and support employees require more fully later, we first need to explore one more bit of bad news.

The crippling cost of employee turnover

As I mentioned earlier, employees are silently leaving companies that don't meet their expectations for supporting their wellbeing. This turnover can cost up to 30 percent of an employee's salary. Let's break it down: For an employee with a salary of $45,000, the average cost of turnover comes out to be approximately $15,000, including "productivity costs" that come from lost institutional knowledge, the time lag to find a replacement, and the time it takes for the new employee to become fully productive. What's more, the average cost-per-hire for companies is $4,425,[36] so you are losing on both ends. Need more? Let's look at what it takes to calculate the cost of turnover to your business. First, you should determine the costs of the lost productivity of the employee who has decided to leave, which can be as much as 75 percent of his or her salary during the search,[37] since the manager would eventually need to bring in someone else—or have others work overtime—to make up for this lost work. Also, in this category: any costs involved with the separation. Then you would need to determine the costs of either hiring a temporary worker or forcing others to work overtime to cover the responsibilities of the former employee while the position is open—or the havoc that it wreaks during poor economic times when the business has a hiring freeze. Next you need to calculate the costs for recruiting the new employee, including placing advertising, screening resumes, interviewing candidates, and checking references, as well as the cost of an outside recruiter should you choose to use one. Finally, there are the onboarding and training costs of the new individual, including the costs of the lost time by teammates helping the new person get up to speed. Take all of these costs and add them up. That's your per employee cost. Then multiply it by the number of employees who need to be replaced in a year, and you have the total annual costs of employee turnover in your organization. It's a lot of work, but it should be eye opening. While some turnover can be healthy, helping bring in new ideas and energy, too much can sap the profits from an organization.

You can also calculate the estimated cost of employee disengagement in your business. Using a formula provided by LinkedIn,[38] which draws on research from Gallup for their numbers,[39] you should first estimate the number of actively disengaged employees in your enterprise. How? By multiplying the total number of employees by the disengagement rate. If you don't have this number, start with industry averages. I cited 16 percent earlier in this chapter, and Gallup claims its 17 percent, so we can use that for now. Therefore, for a business with one hundred employees, sixteen to seventeen of these workers are actively disengaged. Then you need to calculate the cost of the actively disengaged employee, which Gallup says is 34 percent of their salary. To determine a baseline cost without knowing which employees are actually actively disengaged, simply multiply your organization's median salary by 34 percent. Once you have this number, you can multiply it by the estimated number of actively disengaged employees in your enterprise to estimate the total cost to your organization.

There's one more cost, and that is with the perception and value of your brand. While I called employee departures a silent revolution, there's one place where they're not being quiet: social media. Just as today's smart businesses are turning their employees into brand advocates by arming them with sharable content, disgruntled and disengaged employees are taking to social media to tell their stories as well. While we might hear about the videos that go viral of restaurant workers showing how their employer's food is actually prepped, there's much more chatter among private networks, not to mention the comments on Glassdoor and elsewhere, such as the Yelp employee who posted an open letter to her CEO on her blog.[40] These posts, in turn, can affect your ability to attract skilled employees and might mean that you would have to pay more in total compensation to attract the skill level you need. What are your current and former employees saying about your company online?

Another way to think about it: your brand is a badge to your potential recruits and employees. It implies the level of quality you expect in a new hire and the level of performance you expect on the job. There are plenty of stories of people who receive two job offers and take the lower-paying one—even substantially lower—because the chance for growth was more apparent, the environment felt more comfortable, the culture seemed more supportive, and/or the chance to make an impact or contribution was more immediate. Workers know that the badge your brand provides, for good or bad, will stay with them on their resume and can help them long after they've departed from the company, and it becomes part of the calculus when deciding whether to take a job or stay with a current employer.

What's more, in today's era of growing consumer activism, how you treat employees—and others in your pipeline—can impact your transactions, revenues, and profitability, for good or bad. People shop with their values. All other things being equal, they will pick the stronger brand, and one of the factors that contributes to the brand perception is how a company cares for its employees. Yes, if you have a weak brand, you can compensate and generate improved transaction levels with discounts and price cuts, but a race to the bottom in pricing is not a sure way to reach the top in revenues, profitability, and customer loyalty, let alone stay there.

The bottom line: what you're not doing for your employees—the cost of not caring—could be costing your business. We need to accept that we're operating in a new world, with new players, new rules, and new stakes. Sure, we must look at benefit packages, but it should go beyond wellness programs. We must also look at employee attraction, retention, and engagement programs in a new way. We might even look at "alumni" programs for former employees to keep them feeling within the "family" and not poaching employees nor badmouthing the experience. And the business must authentically care. What do I mean by care? After all, caring means something different to everyone. It's complex! Finding the right formula for you takes work. Each company is different. But, rest assured, we will explore steps you can take to find the right one for you in chapter 2.

In the meantime, you might say your organization is already caring. And it might be doing so on a one-to-one level between the managers and their troops in the trenches. I know you care, because you're reading this book. But is the entire culture—and the employee value proposition, including benefits package—of the company structured to ensure a fully caring environment? Who is put first: the customer, the employee, or the shareholder? As we will explore more deeply in chapter 2, there used to be a balance between all three of these stakeholders when deciding business priorities, until economists began saying that the role of the organization is to optimize profits for the shareholder, period. Back in the 1980s, leading investors would look at the condition of the corporate headquarters, and if the perception was that management invested a lot of money in it, shrewd investors would not invest in them. But crappy, broken furniture is not a way to motivate a workforce. Luckily, today, investors are also realizing that all three of these stakeholders matter. After all, as I mentioned above but is worth repeating here, if you don't have happy employees who ultimately deliver the customer experience, how can you ultimately have happy customers?

What's good for workers is good for business

Today, enlightened senior leadership teams know that they need an amazing culture to attract and retain talent—it's simply essential to results. And the facts back it up. Since 1998, the companies on the Fortune "100 Best Companies to Work For" list have consistently outperformed the S&P 500 stock index by a ratio of almost two to one. Wellbeing is now front and center as a business imperative for industry-leading, high-performance companies: Business Group on Health/Fidelity reports that "85% of employers now consider employee wellbeing to have a meaningful role in their business strategy, up from 78% in 2019."[41] As Ryan Picarella, president of WELCOA (Wellness Council of America), a membership-based, not-for-profit that helps members create caring and compassionate organizations, told me: "Stress in organizations that don't care about their employees goes up substantially. Depending on the type of job, employees are more accident prone, and more days of work are going to be missed. And in some of the bigger companies like the Apples of the world, they spend millions if not billions of dollars on innovation and creativity. If you have high levels of stress, you will have more cortisol in your blood, which basically shuts down the innovation hub in your brain and the fight-or-flight, reptilian part your brain takes over."[42]

So, you might now be asking, "What does it mean to bring back balance?" My short answer: focus less on balance, and look at life more holistically. Recognize that work is a part of life. Artificially trying to separate the work self from the home self simply does not work. For most employees, the other parts of their life come first, particularly since the start of the Covid-19 pandemic. Start by considering your employees not as workers or staffers, but authentically as "partners" and "team members." The reality is that forming bonds between colleagues is critical to forming happy, healthy, productive teams. Then make a firm commitment to ensuring the wellbeing of your employees. Do the right thing, not just to attract and retain the best of the best, but to make the world a better place. Finally, look at corporate benefits in a new and different light. Be sure to include health and wellbeing, personal finance, and skills and career development programs.

Let's start with health and wellbeing. The opportunity here is to help employees manage their health and wellbeing in new and better ways, to understand their challenges, and to deliver creative approaches that make it easier for your employees to meet out-of-pocket expenses and get healthier in the first place. With personal finances, we have the opportunity to help people manage debt, repay college loans, plan for their children's college, plan for how to help them care for their aging parents, and perhaps even look to their retirement. And for their career, you have the ability to nurture better leaders, create new opportunities for your employees, and build the skills they'll need for success tomorrow. Want more details? Stay tuned. We'll help you create your vision for your reinvigorated corporate benefits package in chapter 7. In the meantime, I have some good news for you.

As I mentioned above, these advancements have already begun by many forward-looking organizations. Employees are telling us what they want, and it turns out that what they want is not only also good for us as workers, it is good for our businesses. Today, as both employers and employees are connecting the dots between health and job performance, workforce programs are undergoing a massive reboot, so they actually do more than help employees manage their health risks—as well as potentially reduce insurance costs for us. Employees truly want more. They want to improve their wellbeing by addressing every area of health, in ways that work for them, according to their unique challenges and goals. But they will never achieve these goals if they're in the wrong environment. If you want to enable measurable behavioral change, and increased workforce productivity, then keep in mind that it all starts with delivering on an authentic commitment to employees' holistic health.

Just think of it this way: employee health, engagement, productivity, and retention are all firmly interconnected, and it is high time that employers figured out how to start taking better care of their employees by assuming a larger role in keeping them happy and healthy. At the same time, your employees aren't waiting. Rather, they are taking back the power. This is what I call the Human Connection Movement™ in the workplace, which is fueled by a growing desire among employees to feel more connected to one another and as a result, better connected to their jobs. But many companies today are in danger of either not seeing this new power balance or refusing to acknowledge it.   When confronted with the rebelling townspeople who had no bread to eat, Marie Antoinette is supposed to have replied, "Then let them eat cake." Today, many managers are about to become the corporate equivalent of Marie Antoinette. In other words, a clueless response or ignorance, will doom you.

On the other hand, if you create the type of environment employees want to work in and provide a human workplace that focuses on supporting the employee's whole self, people will truly want to work for you. You will also end up with healthier employees who take fewer sick days and show up to work "ready to go!" Well, here is the good news. The solution to this epidemic is actually inexpensive, uncomplicated, and scalable. However, it does require the desire to create a more human workplace that invites employees to show up as their whole selves. It also requires a little bit of courage on your part. You see, to create an authentic environment, you must be prepared to listen and to lead by example. And be sure to execute with the urgency of knowing that lives are at stake. After all, as Barbara Brooks Kimmel, founder of Trust Across America, points out, "Toxic workplaces literally make employees sick, while constructive workplaces have just the opposite effect."[43]

The good news is that if you uncover anything not to your liking, you can always change it. In fact, you'll see that it is not that hard to change, and most likely the work even within your company has already begun. We're entering the next phase of the revolution, the phase where we join it to improve our cultures and our business results. What these new enlightened benefit programs look like will be covered in chapter 7, and how to gain acceptance within the organization in chapters 5 and 6. Right now, it's time we learn to take our medicine. But what is it and how will it help us succeed? We will deal with that in the next chapter.

Using Habits Based on Your Corporate Values
to Show How You Care

A Guest Perspective by Caryn Marooney,
General Partner, Coatue

The information contained in this should not be considered investment advice from Coatue, and Coatue may or may not hold positions in the companies referenced in this article.

As I mentioned earlier, people shop their values. So do workers. Let's explore this idea with Caryn Marooney. She's been a key player in values creation and employee delivery at Amazon, Facebook, Netflix, Salesforce. com, and many other companies. She is currently a general partner at Coatue, one of the largest technology investment platforms in the world. Here's what she has to say:

"There are so many fundamental mistakes people make regarding corporate values. To start, they go through these values exercises. They spend a lot of time. They get lots of feedback. The founder may or may not be involved in it but generally agrees with it. They bring their people with them on the journey. They write down the values, put them on a poster and their website, and, feeling like they're done, then they go back to work. But it's never going to make a difference if your values are just put someplace. You need to actually live them. Employees are hungry for a sense they're living the values they have professed to matter. And it's the everyday habits that end up being the things that make the values come alive. These habits, traditions, and celebrations need to be thought out to fully support the corporate values.

"One example I always think about is Amazon. I remember we were launching the Kindle, and everybody knew you'd never order room service if you are an Amazon employee. You just don't spend money. Amazon is about customer service and margins. It was ingrained into employees by the desks made from doors that were still there. If we care about customer service and keeping margins a certain way, that trickles through everything we do—from the littlest things to the biggest things.

"Another example: If you walk into a Facebook office, it feels true. They would always say, 'We are not done. Never finished.' And the office itself wasn't finished. It was beautiful, but it wasn't finished. Then if you go into a Google office, you see colors and beanbag chairs and lava lamps. There's a sense of fun and exploration. As for traditions, one of the things Facebook would celebrate was your "face-versary," which meant the length you had been at the company. It was a big deal. They would be celebrated during the Q&A with Mark. It was really meaningful to people. Everybody knew their face-versary. And the point was to celebrate. Apple, on the other hand, places the design and user experience above everything else. It creates a difference. But you also don't have an argument internally at Apple, whether or not it's an open culture. If you value an open culture, don't go there. Apple actually has a very secretive culture. Apple's headquarters is interesting in the physical design. It's built like an oval. When you walk around the building's inside track, there are almost no chairs or sitting areas other than the cafeteria, because they want you to get into a conference room if you want to do some work. But at Facebook, it's the world's largest open room.

"So, the things you do and celebrate every day—the habits—are really important: Do they showcase your values? Do they reinforce them every single day? And do we create behaviors around them? Because the external world is not going to acknowledge them. They are not something the external world does or should care about. So, how do you create the celebrations, habits, and rituals that are unique to your culture, are meaningful, and establish what you believe to be important? Keep in mind, it can't happen overnight. It takes a very long time to build something that's meaningful.

"Values are incredibly helpful, because the one thing every company needs to do, whether it's really small or really big, is to be able to move quickly when required. Imagine a ship that can turn quickly and one that can't because it has to tell everybody on board why they're turning. But if the values and behaviors are aligned, then you have the ability to turn the ship versus having to reexplain every time. If you aren't living your values, it is actually incredibly exhausting and takes a lot of time to bring people along internally and externally. And every value has a trade-off. If there's no trade-off, it's not real. That's a constant trade-off, and it's reflected down to the office. It is not that one is better; it is just that they are different. And your brand is just the external expression of your company's culture and values.

"At my agency, we had this problem that when everybody shared good news, we got people always trying to show off. It came to the point where they were not helping each other. And nobody was really listening, because it was kind of boring. So, instead, we decided to share our lessons learned every week from the week before. You could only talk if you had something go wrong. We were trying to showcase in that ritual that mistakes happen. You're not trying if you're not making mistakes, and if you don't hide them, you actually help other people. And we found that people listened to these things because they wanted to avoid them. It helped in this culture of being not afraid and of quick learning. We had to celebrate it every week. It couldn't be a fake one. At first, I thought it wasn't going to be successful. It had to be a real lesson learned. And this one habit really helped establish the culture.

"The trap that I've seen is when the old timers in companies— whether it's five people or fifty thousand—miss the 'good old days.' In any company that continues to grow, there will be some group of people that miss them. It is really hard to celebrate the culture and the values without the storytelling being about these good old days. One of the most important things for these companies to do is to celebrate the new talent and the new viewpoints, or else they get stuck. You can maintain the same values— and the old stories are how you communicate the culture—but you need these outside viewpoints, experiences, and expertise, and you need to have new stories. Otherwise, people get stuck. You can romanticize. People long for the good old days. So, you have to honor the founding stories people really love to hear it. But then you've got to find a balance. And you have to take the founding stories that convey the values and make them relevant and important to today.

"There is no such thing as a cookie-cutter culture. A great culture doesn't look like somebody else's culture. Google is different than Apple is different than Amazon and so on. And these companies have really interesting cultures. Don't try to be like them. We couldn't be like them if we wanted to. It is not who we are authentically. Show me the list of how to develop a great culture, and it is the habits. Otherwise, it's pretty greenfield. I'm really excited about what great culture looks like from the bottom up, because somebody is going to chart the next thing."

Chapter 2:

EMPLOYEES ARE CONSUMERS

We all know that the longstanding employment compact between employer and employee has crumbled. But what many employers do not recognize is that it has been replaced by a new one penned by the employee. While the employer killed the previous one, many still expect workers to respect their part of the old bargain. To understand how we got here, let's start with a short story. The roots of it date back to right after World War II. I bet you can even picture this workplace. Some of the most evocative impressions come from that era, the images of the late 1950s and early 1960s. It's easily evoked because it is actually not that far away, whether you experienced it firsthand, binge-watched *Mad Men* or *Marvelous Mrs. Maisel*, or grew up on the reruns of *The Dick Van Dyke Show*, *I Dream of Jeannie*, *Bewitched*, and other classic shows on Nick at Night or TNT. Close your eyes, and I bet you see high-powered men in business suits and fedoras and well-coiffed ladies sitting behind rows of desks or switchboards. We might even be able to recall the smell of cigarette smoke and hear the jingle jangle of ice in highball glasses as well as the clickety clack of typewriters, mimeograph machines, and high heels.

During this period, the predominately all-white men exchanged their individuality and productive hours for the reassurance of knowing that they would earn a fair wage and a higher quality of life than their parents, live comfortably even during retirement due to their generous pensions, and never experience unemployment during their thirty working years as they'd always work for the same employer and be a 100 percent loyal company man. Women, except the young or the unmarried who provided clerical support in the offices, managed the homes, cooking, cleaning, raising the children, and fully supporting their husbands' domestic comforts. Ray Kroc, founder of the McDonald's franchise system, wrote in his book *Grinding It Out* that he preferred to hire married men, because he got two employees for the price of one.[44] In exchange for lifelong employment at a fair wage that would enable them to fulfill the American dream of home ownership, a car in the garage, two kids, and a BBQ in the yard, these men in fedoras and gray flannel suits would not bring their personal lives into the office, despite the cracks displayed in Cheever and Updike novels or movies and plays like *The Man in the Gray Flannel Suit* and *Death of a Salesman*. These loyal "company" men would show up to work every day from nine to five—never bringing in their personal problems or questioning authority—and their employer would take care of them in return, period. That was the social compact.

This workplace—the entire world—was indeed a different place. It was a time marked by the rapid growth of the suburban middle class as a result of the postwar economic boom and the merging of Fannie Mae, the Federal Housing Administration, and the Veterans Administration-insured mortgages, which as part of the GI Bill, created a post-World War II home ownership boom that drove home ownership up from 43.6 percent to 61.9 percent between 1940 and 1960[45]—combined with the Veterans Administration–insured mortgages created by the GI Bill after World War II—helped to create a postwar building and home-ownership boom. Other, more modest incentives—most notably the deductibility of loan interest from federal income taxes—further advantaged owners over renters. While employers of the 1950s and 1960s weren't concerned about gender and racial equality, it was the pinnacle of employee health-care and pension benefits as well as the extreme uniformity of the workplace.

To understand how we got there, we need to go back to the 1700s in France and the production of their war weaponry. Lieutenant General Jean Baptiste de Gribeauval, as part of a series of innovations, standardized the components used in their weaponry, so spare parts produced at different arsenals could be interchangeable.[46] When Thomas Jefferson, who was then ambassador to France, learned of this innovation, he brought it back with him to the United States. The idea spread to Eli Whitney, who obtained a contract from the U.S. government to manufacture muskets based on this approach. While Whitney was reportedly not very successful as a gun manufacturer, he employed the concept when he invented the cotton gin and, with its success, became the popularizer of using standardized parts to enable mass manufacturing. Over time, and in particular with the building of the transcontinental railroad, this standardized manufacturing approach, coupled with the military command structure, was adopted as the most effective method of managing employees and widely spread across the continent.

As a result, military "command-and-control" thinking, with its emphasis on top-down management coupled with ever-greater efficiency, set the approach and structure for business at the start of the industrial revolution, an approach and structure that has remained the prevalent use case in business today. But like any approach and structure, there are trade-offs and perhaps a shelf life to how long it can last. It made sense to have assembly lines and production areas where tasks were routine and repetitive. However, the world of work has changed dramatically in the last twenty-five years with emergent technology, the digital revolution, and the birth of the gig economy, and it continues to change at rates that are objectively faster today than ever. Machine learning and the promise of artificial intelligence are rapidly taking over many routine and repetitive tasks involving large data sets. But where these technologies are not advancing quite as quickly as previously feared is in the nuanced areas of assessment and decision-making. What we need today more than ever are creative problem solvers. We need people who can think on their feet. And especially with an increasingly distributed workforce, we need workers who are able to collaborate without being collocated. The era of command-and-control management is arguably over—not just because employees want it to be, but because the complexities of today's businesses mean they cannot thrive using an outdated approach created for the manufacturing of munitions by the French military in the 1700s.

Meanwhile, up until the 1940s, most people, let alone workers, didn't have health insurance, which was "invented" at Baylor University Hospital in Dallas in the late 1920s. Occupancy rates were low, as people avoided hospitals at all costs because they couldn't afford using them. An official there "noticed that Americans, on average, were spending more on cosmetics than on medical care"[47] but also recognized that the small amount paid for cosmetics was within their daily means, while a hospital stay was not. They offered a group plan to area teachers for fifty cents per month, which was not noticed out of their monthly pay. And, thus, Blue Cross Association in Texas was born, and with it, health insurance as a benefit was founded.[48] Soon other Blue Cross Associations were started in other states as well.[49]

Health insurance, and other employee benefits, became commonplace in the U.S. after two things happened during World War II: 1) the National War Labor Board froze worker salaries even though there was a severe labor shortage and 2) "the federal government ruled that money paid for employees' health benefits would not be taxed."[50] In other words, offering health insurance, which was relatively cheap, was used as an incentive to recruit and retain a skilled labor force. It was a way to boost overall compensation without giving raises. Soon every major employer started offering it. Then, during the economic boom years of the 1950s and 1960s, health insurance became a standard part of the employment contract to help attract employees. The benefits also kept improving, so employers could continue to stay ahead of their competitors in the war for talent.[51] But once the economy hit the skids—just as insurance costs kept increasing along with insurance company profits—employers started looking for ways to cut back. By the 1980s, unable to eliminate health insurance benefits altogether and desperate to reduce the annual cost of providing medical health care to their employee populations, employer-sponsored physical wellness programs such as smoking cessation, health risk assessments, and biometrics screenings became popular offerings.[52] Ironically these early wellness programs were sold to employers by the very same companies who were offering the insurance coverage. And these programs became a standard part of benefits packages as well.

There was one more area during the heyday of the employment social compact where employers expanded employee benefits: retirement benefits through their pension plans. "The American Express Company established the first corporate pension in the U.S. in 1875."[53] And while the banks, railroads, and such then-leading companies as AT&T, Eastman Kodak, General Electric, Goodyear, Standard Oil, and US Steel soon followed, they did not take off as a standard employee benefit until the 1940s, when labor unions started requesting them too.[54] But by the late 1970s, companies wanted to eliminate them, and they lobbied for the establishment of 401(K) plans,[55] in order to shift financial responsibility to the employee.[56]

Social responsibility is good business

Finally, there was one more major shift in the thinking of employers that helped rationalize their cutback in benefits. The date can even be exactly determined, because on September 13, 1970, Professor Milton Friedman published "The Social Responsibility of Business is to Increase Its Profits" in the *New York Times Magazine*.[57] In this relatively short article, Friedman proposed that the only responsibility a business has is to its shareholders and that any notion of a broader social responsibility was tantamount to socialism, which would result over time in the destruction of the free market. Prior to this paper, business leaders thought they had a responsibility to three key stakeholders: 1) the owners of the company; 2) the employees; and 3) the greater community at large.[58]

Friedman, however, wrote that "in a free-enterprise, private-property system, a corporate executive is an employee of the owners of the business. He has direct responsibility to his employers."[59] Friedman also argued that the "doctrine of social responsibility" was dangerous and flawed as it involves the acceptance of the "socialist view that political mechanisms, not market mechanisms, are the appropriate way to determine the allocation of scarce resources."[60] While more a political document than anything grounded in true economic theory, giving many a tool to justify their own selfish instincts, Friedman told the business world from his academic perch, that acting upon good intentions in the near term would have devastating long-term economic consequences. And business leaders ate it up.

Ironically, with the benefit of nearly fifty years of hindsight, the captains of modern industry who penned this new 2019 definition of corporate responsibility have proven that Professor Friedman got it wrong.[61] The new statement in effect cements the idea that blindly caring for shareholders to the exclusion of all other stakeholders, including employees, is what destroys capitalism. It is not shortsighted to believe that all people "deserve an economy that allows each person to succeed through hard work and creativity and to lead a life of meaning and dignity.' "[62] In fact, caring for all stakeholders, including employees, is the way to secure a free market for all. It is a bitter irony that Friedman's own admonition that well-intentioned CEOs would destroy capitalism if they cared for anyone other than shareholders has been soundly rejected by the very CEOs who are now fighting to save capitalism by reshaping employer-employee relationships. When CEOs of the world's largest banks, manufacturers, health-care providers, and airlines coalesce around the concept that what a corporation owes its employees is on par with that of its shareholders, we all need to take note.

This statement, by the way, was produced by the forty-five-year-old Business Roundtable, which, as they mention on their website, applies "CEO expertise to the major issues facing the nation. Through research and advocacy, Business Roundtable advocates policies to spur job creation, improve U.S. competitiveness, and strengthen the economy."[63] Just to give you a historical context for this ground-shaking change, the revised statement of purpose diverged materially from the various versions issued over the prior twenty years. And for the first time in its history, the 181 CEOs who signed the statement rejected the principle of shareholder supremacy and adopted a new "modern standard for corporate responsibility" that acknowledged employees as a key stakeholder. "The American dream is alive, but fraying," said Jamie Dimon, chairman and CEO of JPMorgan Chase & Co. and chairman of Business Roundtable, regarding the new take on corporate responsibility. "Major employers are investing in their workers and communities because they know it is the only way to be successful over the long term. These modernized principles reflect the business community's unwavering commitment to continue to push for an economy that serves all Americans."[64]

Underneath it all during the 1950s until today, there were also the stirrings of social and political change. We had the civil rights, women's rights, LGBTQ+ rights, and disability rights movements. Whether business leaders admit it or not, these diverse voices make enterprises stronger. You can't innovate, recognize blind spots, see trends, create the new, and build upon the strengths of others without these diverse viewpoints. It's hard to understand why many businesses put themselves at such an obvious competitive disadvantage for so long, even with the realization they emphasized uniformity and conformity. Today, half of the workforce is comprised of women, and we are making great strides with other forms of diversity in the workforce, and it's benefiting all of us.

Don Draper is dead

Not to beat a dead horse, but of course the world has changed in other ways as well. As I mentioned in chapter 1, workers of all races and ethnicities are realizing that for the first time in recorded history, they'll not achieve the same level of wealth as their parents.[65] They know the employment contract is dead. And, stated again, people are willing to exchange a lower paycheck for a higher standard of life. Combined with all of the other changes I listed above, this is not your father's work environment. Don Draper is dead. So, who replaced him, and what do they want?

The workplace does not look like Don Draper's era. Your wellness programs shouldn't either.

Let's take a deeper look at our emerging workforce, Gen Z. Born between 1997 and 2012,[66] they are racially diverse. In fact, only 52 percent of this generation are Caucasian. Of the remaining, 25 percent are Hispanic, 14 percent are African American, and 6 percent are Asian.[67] They're not as patriotic as older generations, they want to feel that they have a purpose, and they embrace social change.[68] They are, as Jean M. Grow and Shiyu Yang describe them, cynical, pragmatic, and independent,[69] more so than millennials. Clearly, they are not going to put up with a disappointing work environment. So, what do they want and need? My short answer: ask them! They know what they need and desire. Find the workers you want to replicate and look into their needs. Paternalism is dead. There are so many ways to get the needed input, from surveys and focus groups to suggestion boxes.

But the ask must be sincere. And authentic follow-up must be assured for employees to believe you, open up, and fully participate.

"Caring and curiosity are pretty tightly aligned. And asking questions is the root of curiosity," Zander Lurie, CEO of SurveyMonkey, told me. "It doesn't always mean you're going to meet the demands or requests of the respondent, but, at a minimum, it's going to inform you with data about what the people you're trying to serve want. And if you ask the right questions with the right frequency in the right mode of the people who are serving your customers, and you get an overwhelming response, it would be strange to not meet them where they are. If your employees feel heard, it usually leads to better outcomes."[70]

In the meantime, beyond any specific benefits, my research indicates that employees want to experience three key senses at work: purpose, belonging, and balance™ (I call it PB^{2}™ here). If you provide a human workplace that focuses on the whole self of the employee rather than on "recruitment," people will want to work for you. But if you don't, they will have alternatives beyond just going to work for a competitor. Millennials and Generation Z are entrepreneurial and can easily jump right into the flourishing freelance, gig-economy scene. Technology, which has enabled employees to work from anywhere, has also made it easier for professionals to go out on their own. While there are many inherent challenges to working as a freelance consultant, it can become an attractive option to those who don't want to "deal with the corporate nonsense." They are focused on forging ahead and developing their careers. If your company fits within their plans and helps them achieve their goals, great. If not, they're gone. Some are even ghosting their employers and just stop showing up, rather than providing the niceties of a two-week notice. After all, why should they provide the courtesy—which used to be part of the employment contract—when they've seen their parents get laid off at the drop of a hat? Rather, it's off to the greener territories as soon as possible, charging ahead.

In other words, you have to commit to employees and develop a culture that supports them if you want employees to commit to you. Word will spread as a result, and candidates will come to you. So how should you "commit to them"? It's simple: Listen, Link, Live™:

1. **Listen to your employees.** Understand who they are and what they need, both the big things and the small. As I said above, ask them. The best example of this is SurveyMonkey. Because surveying people *is* their business, they take listening to their employees seriously. To find out what's going on, SurveyMonkey conducts an employee satisfaction and culture survey very quarter. But even more importantly, they listen to their employees every day. They'll ask them little things like, "What coffee brand should we put in the kitchen? And big things like, "What health benefits matter most to you and your family?" Now think about the ways that your employees can give you feedback. After all, I bet you are already thinking about how you can give *them* feedback through their performance reviews. It's easy to get started. For a small step, simply nest your curiosity into things you're already doing, such as adding a five-question survey to the end of your annual employee reviews. As a bonus, when you connect to employees and understand what they want, you can better define your mission. (And if you want more on SurveyMonkey's approach, just stay tuned to the guest perspective at the end of this chapter. It's with Zander Lurie, their CEO.)

2. **Link your culture to your purpose.** Employees need to feel that they intuitively understand the connection between your company's mission and its culture. As Caryn Marooney alluded to in her guest perspective in chapter 1, link your inside worker-facing world with your outside brand. To be believable on both sides, they have to match. Nobody links the internal and external better than Pinterest. With their mission to connect everyone in the world to the things they find interesting, they have employees give seminars on the things that they find interesting. And

every year they host "Knit Con," a two-day event in which their employees teach each other cool new skills. The topics range from hula dancing to wine tasting to coding. Knit Con helps Pinterest employees connect back to the company's purpose and mission. You can also share customer success stories every single week that tie back to your mission. Here at Grokker, we share quotes from our users every single Tuesday to let our employees know how people are benefiting from our solutions. Whatever you do, let your people know how you're living your corporate mission.

3. **Live your values.** Values aren't just posters you put up on the wall. It's the way you operate every day. I bring up my company's values in the first job interview, because cultural fit is as important to me as skill. As we saw with Caryn Marooney's examples, living your values will result in the product and the service that will delight and sustain our employees and our customers. Freedom, for instance, is one of our five values at my company. To bring this value to life post-pandemic when in-office work is once again the norm, everyone can work from home on Wednesdays We also give employees the freedom to take care of themselves and their families, because we trust them. You, too, should look at your corporate values and create opportunities for your employees to live them. If one of your values is for "community," for example, ask yourself how can you embrace community at work? Perhaps you create a "Give Back Week" where employees get designated days to make a huge impact within their communities. They can walk, volunteer, donate, play games for a cause, whatever. You can leave the specifics to them, as long as you give them the opportunity.

Having employees share their passions is one way to help them experience their company's purpose and mission.

More thoughts on purpose, belonging, and balance

As you can see, if you listen to your employees, you will learn what they want and value in a workplace beyond pay—information you can use in crafting your corporate values and in bringing your current values to life. Whatever you do, you must also link employees to the company's mission, providing the sense of purpose they're seeking. And, finally, you have to personally live the values. It's not enough to listen and talk about purpose if you don't live your values in your policies and your actions. Authenticity is key. Express who you are and provide the habits to express them, and everyone will feel a sense of purpose, belonging, and balance.

You conduct market research with your consumer or customer prospects. Why not conduct it with your employees and prospect audience as well? Millennials and Generation Z-ers look at the world, including careers, through a consumer lens. They are first and foremost concerned with developing their own personal brands, and in many ways, they inherently understand branding better than many old-school corporate leaders. But it goes beyond just these two cohorts. As Deloitte points out, all "workers share the same basic marketing-funnel journey: We consider opportunities, evaluate potential companies, commit to working for an organization, and the company then either earns our trust and loyalty, or we seek a better opportunity."[71] And as the former OpenTable CEO Christa Quarles told me in a recent interview, "Your employees are no longer employees. They're volunteers. They are there because they want to be there."[72] I also believe that taking this approach can also help us "win back" some of the talent out there who are working as consultants. #freelancelife doesn't have to be true. Look at their conversations, glean the insights from them, and you can appeal to this elusive, but valuable employee base—people who understand what it takes to run a business and can think like a business owner.

Of course, an employee-centric culture should put a premium on wellbeing. But if your workforce isn't aligned around the same health-and-wellness values that resonate with your top talent, you risk losing the battles of attraction and retention. That's why building a culture of wellbeing is so essential. Fortunately, your workforce wants to work in an amazing culture, and you can start creating it today. Believe me, it's an initiative everyone wants to get behind and support—and now's the time to make it happen. But keep in mind, the definition of "wellness" has changed dramatically over the years, particularly as it relates to employee health-and-wellness programs, and employee expectations have changed along with it. In fact, the modern definition of "wellbeing" more accurately describes an all-encompassing approach to multidimensional health people are now aiming to achieve. For instance, the Global Wellness Institute (GWI) defines wellness as the active pursuit of activities, choices, and lifestyles that lead to a state of holistic health.[73] In 2014, they published the first Global Spa & Wellness Economy Monitor, measuring the size of the global wellness economy—industries that enable consumers to incorporate wellness activities and lifestyles into their daily lives—for the first time. And it's huge. In

2017, the market size of the workplace wellness economy was determined to be $47.5 billion (note that it was $43.3 billion in 2015, for a 4.8 percent average annual growth rate). But keep in mind, says GWI Report for 2018, "valued at $48 billion, the workplace wellness market is small in comparison to the massive economic burden and productivity losses associated with an unwell workforce and widespread worker disengagement."[74]

The best way to promote and reinforce workforce wellbeing—to really bring it to life—is through a formal benefits program. As we've discussed, today's top talent considers wellbeing benefits as more than "perks," especially when they know their programs are designed to make their lives better as opposed to being used as cost-cutting, tracking, or surveillance tools for the employer. Wellbeing programs are an essential part of bringing purpose, belonging, and balance into the employee experience. And practically nothing demonstrates "we care for our workforce" more clearly than offering HR-sponsored, employee-centric wellbeing resources and activities that are customized for your diverse and dispersed employee base. This means offering holistic programs that incorporate all aspects of an employee's health, including fitness, mental health, sleep, nutrition, and social and financial wellbeing. Plus, one more thing: People often want more out of work than the paycheck. People want to enjoy it. Their work is part of who they are and should bring them satisfaction and identity. Because of this, employees value relationships with coworkers and managers as well as a comfortable work environment. In fact, employees who are socially connected in the workplace are seven times more likely to be engaged in their jobs. Unfortunately, only 30 percent of employees report that they have a best friend at work.[75] Among the remaining 70 percent, "only 8% were engaged, 63% were not engaged, and 29% were actively disengaged."[76] And, in a survey conducted by the National Business Group on Health, just 34 percent of employees strongly agree or agree that their employer actively encourages social interaction among employees.[77]

Social connectedness, especially within a corporate environment, is essential for wellbeing and one of the strongest predictors of it.[78] Since we're spending more of our time at work than ever before[79]—it's employees' home away from home—we want that time spent to be meaningful, especially since many will spend more of their waking hours at the office than in their actual homes. Research shows that employees who are socially connected in the workplace have higher overall feeling of wellbeing, are better at engaging customers, and produce higher quality work.[80] And with an increase in the sense of community, life satisfaction and overall happiness also increases.[81] But forming these bonds does not happen over a gin gimlet after a round of golf anymore. Rather, it happens during work as part of the workday. Bonds are formed at the office coffee bar, during small group walks around the parking lot after lunch, at the midmorning team video meditation breaks, during Friday afternoon online happiness hours, and as part of virtual weekly company meetings. I'd like to point out that employees who have access to these types of wellbeing programs are likely to report having good relationships with their coworkers.[82]

Before you act on your findings, though, think it through. Take some time. I get it. You find a window and you want to act on it immediately, but the resulting approach will be purely tactical and possibly piecemeal. Rather, your wellbeing solution needs to be integrated and aligned with your mission, vision, and values. Aon talks about hard-to-get digital talent and the importance of appealing to their interests by taking a holistic approach in designing what is commonly referred to as the total employee experience.[83] I think this should be the case when trying to reach any type of employee. Your employee-related solutions should ideally be seamlessly aligned and working together, from your compensation and benefits to your corporate culture, from your onboarding to your celebrated company rituals. And it all needs to lead up to one very big promise: your employee value proposition (EVP).

Just creating an EVP will give your company a competitive recruiting advantage. According to AON's UK Benefits and Trends Survey 2019, only 24.5 percent of companies say they have a clear EVP, although 51 percent are currently planning on developing one.[84] Employers with EVPs report that they have a positive impact on recruitment, employee engagement, and retention. Meanwhile, "84 percent of the world's top 100 most-attractive employers (according to college students) have an EVP."[85]

What's your employee value proposition?

In the academic world, value propositions can be reduced to a mathematical formula: value equals the functional and emotional benefits, including the identity badge value of using a certain brand, divided by the physical and time costs or pain of obtaining those benefits. The higher the benefits in relation to the costs or pain, the greater the value. The employee value proposition essentially works the same way. In the employee contracts of old that we had discussed previously in this chapter, benefits included dependably growing salaries and rich insurance and pension plans. The costs or pain were the forty-plus hours per week and loss of identity (i.e., "sucking it up").

But, as we've discussed, millennials and Gen Z-ers don't want that value exchange. However, as I mentioned earlier, people are seeking purpose, belonging, and balance in their working lives. To help, I invite you to use the PB^2 framework as you develop your employee value proposition. Purpose, belonging, and balance are part of the experiential benefits, the numerator portion of the equation. Of course, the financial package (including salary, 401[k], and other compensation) and benefits package (including health, wellbeing, dental, disability, and paid time off) need to be competitive too. Other points include career development and brand badge value. Note, I didn't explicitly say culture and values, because they inform everything else.

When thinking about financial compensation, keep in mind the long-standing Two Factor Theory of Motivation developed by Frederick Herzberg, which established that while low salary can contribute to job dissatisfaction, it does not contribute to job satisfaction. Rather, factors such as achievement, recognition, advancement, growth, and responsibility are what create job satisfaction.[86] In fact, Herzberg concluded that experiencing meaningfulness of the work itself increased work satisfaction. While it is important to offer competitive compensation packages to prevent job dissatisfaction, it is critical to create conditions where employees can feel a sense of impact and achievement as well as be recognized if they are to feel satisfied at work.[87] Meanwhile, Herzberg's research also found that dissatisfaction could stem from poor relationships with supervisors and peers, which can be counterbalanced by a feeling of belonging among colleagues at work. Upon closer examination what becomes clear is that the softer areas of corporate culture are not nice-to-haves but are corporate imperatives in a new world where employees are in the driver's seat demanding more than a fair paycheck but a sense of purpose, belonging, and balance. As a result, you also need to think about the costs—the pain—to employees, which becomes the denominator, to determine what you can minimize.

While this formula might sound theoretical, this model can help you think about how you want to convey value or at the start, create your employee value proposition. You should also think about the value you want recruits to bring to the company. Then you need to sum up your EVP in a way that is clear, catchy, and differentiated, particularly with those in your category. An example, from Yelp: "We believe in giving our employees the tools and resources to keep them healthy, wealthy, and wise. Whether it's unlimited snacks, or health-care benefits, we believe happy employees are successful employees."[88] Morningstar, which we'll more about in chapter 9, "is a place where talented, driven people can grow."[89] And Trader Joe's proclaims, "We prioritize the development of our crew members. We don't pigeonhole crew members into 'only running the register' or 'only stocking the shelves'; our crew engage in a variety of tasks and hold a range of responsibilities—running the register and stocking the shelves, of course; also merchandising, creating signs, accepting deliveries, demoing products, and engaging with customers."[90] Honeywell's states that "you can make a difference by helping to build a smarter, safer and more sustainable world."[91]

Of course, it's not having a clear, compelling statement that makes the difference. Rather, it's fulfilling on the promise that truly matters. We'll look at how to best create and actualize a culture of care in the final chapters. But next, let's take a deeper look at this new generation of workers in chapter 3. And, in the meantime, I have a treat for you that can help you understand the case for caring from someone else who makes it personal.

♥ ♥ ♥

Connectedness, Culture, and Curiosity: Some Thoughts on Creating a Truly Caring Work Environment

A Guest Perspective by Zander Lurie,
Chief Executive Officer, SurveyMonkey

We've already heard a little about SurveyMonkey, the need to feel connected at work, and the importance of listening to your employees, which requires curiosity. Let's now bring them together as we hear from Zander Lurie, the chief executive officer of SurveyMonkey. Zander also serves on its board of directors, which he has been a part of since 2009. And previously he was senior vice president of entertainment at GoPro, and has served on that company's board of directors since 2016. Prior to GoPro, he was SVP of strategic development at CBS Corporation, via its acquisition of CNET Networks, where he served as chief financial officer and head of corporate development. Zander began his career in the technology investment banking group at JPMorgan, leading equity transactions and mergers and acquisitions in the internet sector. He holds a JD and an MBA from Emory University, and a BA in political science from the University of Washington. He also cofounded the California-based nonprofit organization CoachArt, which serves chronically ill children and their siblings. For me, Zander is also one of the most thoughtful, caring people I've encountered in a professional environment. He connects with employees at all levels, reaching out to congratulate them on their successes and supporting them when times are hard. In other words, he really walks the walk. Now let's hear his thoughts:

"The workforce we're trying to attract today, and the skill sets of really talented workers, particularly at a technology company, are very different than the skills sets of executives from thirty years ago. Most of the technology wasn't even created back then. So, you have to start with recognizing that the key employees that make this place special are different. They grew up differently, and their educational background is different. And they are more important today to your overall business than employees were thirty years ago.

"On the other hand, exclusive patents, contracts, and supply chains are much less important. These used to serve as large moats around a company. But companies can now get to some semblance of scale with a fraction of the capital you needed thirty or fifty years ago. You can treat your people differently in a place where you know your revenue is rock solid. The media business is a good example. *Friends* had a contractual commitment with NBC. They couldn't take their talents to ABC or elsewhere. Sports rights are usually locked up for ten or twenty years, so they're truly monopolistic assets for a company. Same with a seventeen-year patent on a pharmaceutical drug, where nobody else can make it. Maybe in a world where you had these types of assets, you didn't need to treat your people well. But not many businesses have them anymore. Even the media world has been totally upended by technology, and now there are endless distribution outlets. If you treat an actor, director, or writer poorly, they can go to Netflix or somewhere else.

"To appeal to the new workforce as well as inspire and motivate them in what is the most competitive labor market for human talent in the history of the world, especially in Silicon Valley, New York, London, and other major centers, the employer must now present a very compelling employee value proposition. If you don't or can't create a differentiated experience for employees, the cost is high. You will lose your key talent. Since it's incredibly expensive to recruit, your business is almost destined to fail. The best starting place is to be curious about what is important to them. I'm a forty-six-year-old straight white guy and can't begin to imagine what the optimal benefits package is for our diverse and global employee base. For me, to just intuitively feel that I'll know everything about the environment to create and the benefits to offer would be pretty arrogant. The advantage of being curious is that you're more likely to create a really special organization for employees to do their best work. And if you hire well, have a good strategy, and don't lose employees, you've really got a better chance of succeeding.

"I think as a CEO, you articulate your corporate value proposition both in terms of how it's good for the business and for our employees; if you do a good job, of course shareholders will be the beneficiaries. Basing all of your decisions on what's best for shareholders is not a path to victory. If we spend a thousand dollars on paid marketing ads, it'll drive short-term revenue, and that may or may not be the best way to spend the next thousand dollars at your company. But maybe you need to make more longer-term investment decisions for the health of your business. If you invest in health care, in employee resource programs, or in enabling people to have more time off with their new baby, you can reduce recruiting costs and the dislocation costs when we don't have the right number of engineers, salespeople, or others. By supporting employees, they will feel more connected to work and feel more supported, so they'll be less likely to leave.

"There are decisions CEOs make that set the company up for long-term success. In many ways, it's like buying insurance or setting up your portfolio for tough times. SurveyMonkey went through tough times when the previous CEO, Dave Goldberg, suddenly passed away from a heart attack. I stepped in at a time when there were a lot of tensions and unhappy people. We were fortunate enough that Dave built up years of goodwill, so many employees kept us afloat until I came in and was able to re-invest in our culture. But if you run roughshod and people only stay because the company is very profitable or they make lots of money, they will leave as soon as you hit hard times. So, not having a bank of goodwill is pretty troubling.

"Everything starts with our values and culture. When I welcome new employees, I talk about my family, how I got to SurveyMonkey, and our strategy, mission, and values. I joke that printing companies are killing it because every company is making posters about their values. But ultimately your values are what governs who you hire, how you pay, who you promote, and who you fire. And it starts with the executive team. You've got to be vigilant about rooting out the guy (sorry, but it's often the guy) who's interrupting women, who's not paying fairly, and who's promoting by unfair mechanisms. You've got to spend the time prioritizing diversity in the recruiting process and making sure you have inclusive policies for folks at work. You really have to do the hard work and it's expensive. You have to acknowledge you are going to spend more time and money on the stuff that you once thought was confined to HR, because it makes your business better, your teams stronger, and drives long-term value for shareholders.

"We're in a fortunate position because SurveyMonkey's core product is software which helps organizations solicit and understand the opinions and sentiment of the people we're serving. One of the reasons the SurveyMonkey brand is beloved is that it is associated with asking opinions. If we've learned anything in politics, culture, sports, and entertainment or even in the workplace or your kids' school, people want to be asked their opinion. They want to have their voice heard. And, SurveyMonkey software is in this elegant position of sitting between a human being asking another what she cares about.

"We are constantly trying to pull out nuggets from our customers. When we were using panels for research, we had a male-female option. But we realized that there is a meaningful size of the population that doesn't identify with one of those two gender boxes. As a result, we were not delivering a representative panel when there is only a male-female choice. Moreover, you're actually offending a good number of people when you don't offer nonbinary options, so we added that option too. And it was a nontrivial amount of engineering work to feather that into all of our products.

"A SurveyMonkey core value is 'Stand for Equality.' There are very few things that are as easy to execute and have a super high payoff than striving for gender parity with your board of directors and executive management team. If you get male-female parity, the data suggests that you're going to be a lot more diverse in all the other areas too. And diversity is simply good for business. You have a greater chance of designing products that are liked by the whole world. If you have a diverse team creating your products, you have a better chance marketing to women and underrepresented minorities. It's not like we are a boutique investment bank with twenty clients. We have seventeen million people who use our products. So, I'll be damned if ten white guys are going to figure out what the world wants. And I know I am in a position where I have more influence now because of our brand, scale, and balance sheet. If I can help make our company a more diverse, inclusive, and fair and our customers then share that message with other companies, maybe humankind will advance a tiny bit.

"We also want to have fun and we want to make sure that people are getting noticed for great work. We celebrate the milestones along the way. It's not about the finish line. It's about the journey. We make sure you celebrate the birthdays and have fun.

"We ask ourselves: is this just a poster or are we actually employing initiatives that demonstrate our commitment? For instance, we have half a dozen employee resource groups that we put real weight behind. The executives show up and have money to spend on programming outside speaker's events. We definitely ask ourselves if we are just checking the box or if we are actually putting time and money and our reputation behind it. We want to make sure we're not just glossing over stuff, that we're actually doing it.

"I've never been CEO of another company, but it does make it more fun to be in the job if you care and other people know you care. I know I want my family to know I care about them. I want my friends to know I care about them. And I want the people who work around me to know I care about them. It might be a bit of a security thing for a CEO, but I feel that maybe I'll be at my job longer if I believe the people around me care. And to me that's a good investment in the business."

Chapter 3:

WELCOME TO THE PERFECT STORM

Most often, when Gen Z is written about, the focus is on the fact that they are the first generation of internet natives, and as such, their digital views and behaviors are different. What is less written about is how this generation has less trust in and enthusiasm for brands and has greater interest in exploring their own passions. This is because their childhood was vastly different from the ones leaders and managers experienced. To understand just how we can move forward in the new work world order, let's take a deeper look at this new generation of workers, which I briefly described in the previous chapter.

Theirs was a generation raised to believe that they were special, and their parents kept them sheltered, carpooling them from activity to activity, constantly surveilled, while pressuring them to achieve some greater life purpose. They received trophies for coming in eighth in their soccer tournaments and were lauded for even mediocre report cards. They engaged in no-cut sports as well as martial arts and STEM-based extracurriculars that gave them enormous confidence while teaching them to expect that grown-ups not only paid them attention but owed them their undivided attention whenever they requested it. They grew up deciding what the family did on weekends, what they ate for dinner, and what they watched at any time with the advent of on-demand TV. They developed a sense of entitlement and with it a deep-seated need to feel in control. What's more, they grew up being constantly compared to their peers who were learning to read by the age of five, being tutored in Mandarin and coding in multiple languages by the age of seven, and being wedged into a much more conventional set of accelerated expectations in the increasingly competitive high school AP and college admission process.

Operation Varsity Blues,[92] which uncovered a broad criminal conspiracy that bribed prominent American university athletic coaches into extending offers of admission to children of affluent families who did not play the competitive sport into which they were recruited, was the perfect manifestation of just how important achievement was to this generation and their parents. They began resume building by middle school with their parents' full participation and grew to expect sacrifices would need to be made, as well as shortcuts taken, all in order for them to get ahead. They were bred to achieve like a generation of thoroughbreds competing for a limited number of starting gates.

At the same time, they grew up bombarded with social media as a primary means of interaction, and this had three key developmental impacts: 1) an increased cynicism when evaluating others derived from the innate understanding that the person you hold yourself out to be is apt to be no more real than an Instagram filter, 2) a shorter attention span,[93] and 3) a need or perhaps compulsion to be constantly connected.[94] As a result, this generation also became the most anxious, multitasking, and productive one yet.[95] It is interesting to note that the "brains of multitasking teens and young adults are 'wired' differently from those over age 35."[96]

And then, the Great Recession of 2008 hit, and the foundation that had been so perfectly laid for these young hopefuls came tumbling down. They saw their parents get laid off for the first time, and the lifelong promise and expectation of the perfect life path blew up in their faces. The companies where their parents had toiled so hard to gain status fired them in mass layoffs, homes were repossessed, pensions disappeared, and money saved for college tuition dried up. Gen Z was still largely in elementary school at this time—or not yet in school or even born—and so they spent the rest of their childhood with less financial prosperity than the previous immediate generations, and as a consequence they have turned out to be less motivated by money than by meaning.[97] They also learned early on that companies do not offer loyalty and therefore employees do not owe it either.

These young workers now think in terms of stints, not careers. They want to know what you can do for them over the next six months to a year. After that, if they don't feel invested in your company and that they are thriving, they are happy to quit and go try their luck at another employer without hesitation because, to them, employers are largely fungible. In fact, one of the key differences between these younger groups and Gen X-ers and boomers is that they are driven more by fear of missing out on something better down the road—classic FOMO—than by fear of making a mistake. Just watch how they handle a new TV remote compared to a fifty-year-old. They have no fear of pressing every single button until they figure out how to work it, while the fifty-year-old hesitates, afraid that if they press the wrong button the TV will freeze and be irreparable, as was the case in the early days of television when the electronics were far less sophisticated and user friendly. We are all products of our environment. Older workers are afraid of losing a good thing. Younger workers are afraid of missing out on the next great thing. They fear that by becoming complacent or not demanding enough, they'll end up mediocre as opposed to fulfilled and living their best life because they believe that is what they deserve.

This is a central tenet of managing younger employees: you have to make them see that if they leave your employ, they will be missing out on the greatest opportunity available to them for the next few years, and then you have to back that message up with action. A completely separate yet important aspect of these younger workers' lives is the massive amount of stress and anxiety they experience.[98] While many experts have theorized on the origins of this, what most agree on is that these younger workers are suffering from greater reported levels of anxiety and depression than ever before,[99] and that they are prepared to discuss it and treat it with talk therapies, mindfulness, and medication.

Stress has reached epidemic proportions in the United States, and employees are now looking to their employers for help managing it. While on the one hand the relationship of trust that had existed between employers and employees has eroded, employees are now demanding their employers help them with their social and emotional problems because the lines that separate work from personal life have become blurred, and employees are no longer willing to pretend that they are not suffering.[100] In 2019 we saw a massive increase in companies investigating mental health and resiliency programs to offer to their workforces because absenteeism and presenteeism caused by anxiety and depression was estimated to be costing employers $16.8 billion.[101]

And then in early 2020, the world was struck with COVID-19 and the global coronavirus pandemic which sent millions of employees home to shelter in place as the worldwide economy went into recession. Corporations were forced to lay off or furlough millions of employees over video conference while struggling to stay connected with their employees who were scared and at home, unsure of when the virus might strike their family as well as whether they would have jobs to return to when the crisis abated. The fiscal and medical threats to life and livelihood on the heels of the shift in the workforce power dynamics and generational evolution as previously discussed have culminated in the perfect storm, and we now need to rethink how to restructure from here on out.

Caring amid COVID-19 and beyond

As I write this, I am sheltering in place at home in Northern California, where I have been social distancing with my husband for five weeks during the global COVID-19 pandemic. The experience has underscored even more the need for caring as an employer because my entire Grokker team and those of all of our global corporate clients are also experiencing this crisis. As a result, all preexisting norms have been broken, and what has become clear is that this experience will permanently change how we work, how companies perceive the criticality of the bond between employee and employer, and why almost overnight the importance of caring for the whole person in order to keep them safe and motivated has been broadly embraced by corporate leadership. Working from home while we try to contain COVID-19 is also inculcating new habits and demanding new accommodations, and the challenges of working within this new reality is both undeniable and profound.

Leading a company—a workforce—in the midst of a global crisis is a learn-as-you-go and trust-your-instincts (and hope-to-not-screw-it-up) endeavor. It's certainly not something I learned how to do in college or law school, and there's been nothing quite like the COVID-19 outbreak in my professional career to prepare me for this. As with the novel virus making its way around the globe and wreaking havoc on financial markets and, worse, on the physical and emotional health of many, there simply is no such thing as "business as usual."

Everyone is asking the question, "What am I supposed to do?" It's a question with a million variations, and with just as many answers. For business leaders, this level of uncertainty makes responding to both the strategic and tactical difficult, because we can no longer rely upon our historical experience or pattern recognition with any degree of confidence. Without a crystal ball, figuring out "What's next?" is a moment-to-moment challenge. Take, for example, the madness over the Paycheck Protection Program (PPP) Loans. The application process was confusing, at best, particularly for small businesses without easy access to the expertise required to submit a timely and accurate application that would fall squarely within the requirements of the CARES Act.[102] And the aftermath? While history is still being written, as more funds are being made available while funds already awarded are being rescinded,[103] and investors hotly debate the morality of accepting government funding as well as the risks of being sued,[104] it is too soon to tell the outcome.

Most companies don't have the luxury of time to sit around and pontificate—they must act so that their business can survive. Most cannot wait on federal funds to arrive before deploying tactics to stay in business and thus turn to the perfectly Vulcan concept of societal decision-making: "The needs of the many outweigh the needs of the few or the one." Otherwise stated, the call is to take whichever actions and make whatever sacrifices are necessary to enable the company as an entity to survive the crisis in the long run. But the key to knowing what your company needs to do to survive depends upon where your company falls along the 3-Tiered Stratification Model.™ While this model can help provide direction to any business model going through disruption, here is how it works using our post-COVID world as the example. First, you need to identify your tier:

- In the top third are organizations that thrived during the crisis or market disruption, primarily because their industry has become an "essential" category, like telehealth/digital wellbeing, that is required as a result of the pandemic or because they are offering an innovative product or service that's meeting a new need or burgeoning market created by the pandemic's impact on lifestyle, like DIY at-home hair coloring or preprepped family meal kits. Sales are accelerating and, with new habits in place, they are planning for growth after the pandemic.

- Middle third organizations are companies that do not yet know how much they will be impacted long term by the pandemic or other market disruption. They have not seen benefits from it; in fact, it has likely hurt their business sales moderately to significantly. However, what is unclear is whether the hit to their sector will be quite temporary, meaning just a few months, or long term, meaning several quarters to a year. These businesses are characterized by taking a conservative or wait-and-see approach. They may have instituted certain cost-reduction measures or have put significant controls on operational expenditures to provide air cover while things play out but have not made fundamental changes to business operations or personnel.

- Organizations in the bottom third have experienced massive hits to revenue and sector-wide demand as a direct result of the novel coronavirus or other market disruption. They're struggling to find relevance and, aside from suffering short-term losses, are seriously assessing the long-term impact of the status quo and do not anticipate a rebound of their market until, for example with COVID-19, people are free to once again travel, gather together in groups, return to school, work, go to the mall, and resume daily life without being tethered to their residence. Beyond the most obvious examples of bottom-third industries would be products and services one does not need when one spends the majority of their time at home, such as dog walking, car rental, and gym memberships.

If you work for a company like Instacart whose business is unable to keep up with new orders and is consequently looking to poach talent from anywhere it can to fill the *300,000 open roles* created by soaring demand for home delivery resulting from the pandemic,[105] then you are in a Tier One company. If you are somewhere that may have instituted a hiring freeze in a particular department like Google recently announced,[106] but there are no widespread layoffs, you are likely in a Tier Two company. And if you work for a company like Kohl's that just laid off 70 percent of its 122,000-person workforce,[107] you are in a Tier Three enterprise. Once you have identified the tier your organization fits into at this point in time, you can determine how to move forward and lead.

It is, of course, easiest at a Tier One company. The focus will be on recruiting and retaining top talent as well as on managing growth while minimizing burnout through holistic wellbeing. Surprisingly, the next easiest place to know how to move forward is at a Tier Three company. When demand has disappeared and it is clear that an industry is facing insurmountable market headwinds, cash must be conserved. In these cases, there is no alternative to mass layoffs or furloughs, plant closures, and expense slashing. The only choice is the manner in which this is carried out and the degree of empathy shown to the newly unemployed. Can benefits be extended, can resources to assist with outplacement and filing for unemployment be made available, and can access to emergency rent funds or food be provided? Can any of it be made less scary, and can the stigma of having been let go be minimized through strong, supportive communication?

Knowing how to lead at a Tier Two company can prove the most challenging of them all. The employers here may wonder, "Do I talk openly to my employees about the uncertainty we are facing as a company or try to merely paint a rosy picture in hopes that no one worries? Should I share a vision of the future and explain the milestones we need to achieve together as a team, acknowledge that while there is risk, there will be great rewards and enlist employees in this shared goal to get people to commit and stay?" Another option is, of course, to stick your head in the sand, say nothing, and pretend no one notices. Or perhaps hope that everyone is too afraid to look around. But the truth is that your top talent is never afraid to look around, and the Tier One companies are out there poaching, so beware.

At one California-based Tier Two company, the CEO told employees that while it was unclear how long it would take them to emerge from the current slowdown they were experiencing, no one would be fired. The CEO would take no compensation for up to two years to cover all salaries at the company if need be. That put everyone at ease, even though there would be no bonuses. In exchange, the employees were asked to stay focused, keep doing great work, and have faith. Such bold action has a powerful emotional impact. It says, "We are in this together." It says, "I believe we are going to make it, and I am putting my money where my mouth is."

How we lead in times of great uncertainty says a lot about our character. Hold on to your humanity and trust your instincts. You got this. The threats to life and livelihood brought on by the COVID-19 pandemic will permanently change how we work. Not only do we now need to rethink how to restructure from here on out, but we need to decide and reinvent how to support our employees in the new normal.

3-Tiered Stratification Model application to markets and businesses

Now let us dive a bit deeper into the 3-Tiered Stratification Model and examine its application to all markets and businesses. But to get there, first, let me explain more in depth the farming metaphor that inspired me when I first developed the model. As an avid tomato gardener and CEO who has spent eight hours on a Sunday lovingly removing aphids by hand from twenty-four plants to rescue them from an infestation—the only proven method—I can tell you that caring for my garden has helped me tend to my team far better. Depending on the stage of my company, we have benefitted from changes in approach, and my team has required different kinds of support. Therefore, rather than simply labeling companies in the 3-Tiered Stratification Model by a number, there is an additional, far more nuanced and instructive tripartite naming convention:

- **Harvesting hypergrowth**—Thriving companies with accelerating sales and a growing customer base are much like farmers whose crops are both ripe for market and in high demand, like golden raspberries in the summertime. Reaping the rewards of meeting customers' needs with a perfectly timed product or service, harvester companies face the enviable challenge of trying to keep up with demand—while simultaneously remaining ready to jump on new opportunities that extend their market leadership and drive further growth.

- **Pruning for growth**—Companies in this stage are cautiously removing extraneous aspects of their business that are impeding their ability to succeed in the future by paring down to the strategic core from which growth is possible. Like farmers tending to fruit trees in an orchard, they need to ensure they do not overcrowd or overwater, and most importantly that there is sufficient sunlight reaching each tree to enable photosynthesis to occur.

- **Ploughing and preparing the soil for regrowth**—Much like commercial farmers who aerate and fertilize the soil between crops while patiently awaiting the changes necessary before attempting to begin anew, companies facing overwhelming market headwinds or in turnaround mode must reassess strategy with an objective point of view, and then watch with hyperfocus in order to know exactly when conditions will once again be favorable to sow new seeds and drive the regrowth.

Now let's take it a step further and examine the longer-term approach to managing workforces and morale depending upon your present situation. Every company will have important decisions to make related to its personnel and what kind of resources will best help it organizationally in order to either harvest, prune, or plough while anticipating and hopefully meeting the shifting expectations of employees.

3-Tiered Stratification Model™

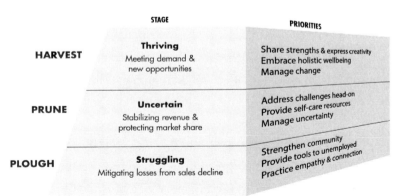

STAGE		PRIORITIES
HARVEST	**Thriving** Meeting demand & new opportunities	Share strengths & express creativity Embrace holistic wellbeing Manage change
PRUNE	**Uncertain** Stabilizing revenue & protecting market share	Address challenges head-on Provide self-care resources Manage uncertainty
PLOUGH	**Struggling** Mitigating losses from sales decline	Strengthen community Provide tools to unemployed Practice empathy & connection

A brief overview of how to apply the 3-Tiered Stratification Model to your business.

Harvesters: Managing in an environment of abundance

Whether in a postpandemic world or not, Tier One Harvesters will emerge as industry leaders but should take care not to become complacent. The innovation and agility that enabled them to get their product or service to market, combined with the good fortune of perfect timing, spurred massive sales growth and brand equity in an otherwise ailing market—but this may not have staying power. As new entrants begin copycatting or introducing their own even more innovative or disruptive solutions, the creativity that helped garner that initial Tier One success will be even more critical. Rarely does the first mover stay on top unless they are masters of innovation as a culture and the continuous cultivation of talent, as we learned from MySpace, Netscape, Kodak, and one of my beloved alma maters, Yahoo!.

For Harvesters, the challenge lies in sowing the cultural seeds and establishing the practical conditions and freedoms that will continuing fostering employee creativity from the start. Look at examples like Google's 20% Program, introduced back in its start-up phase, which gave employees the liberty to work on any passion project of their choosing for up to 20 percent of their work time,[108] or Genentech's Give Back week, which for a decade has provided employees with a dedicated week during which they are encouraged to devote themselves to working on causes they care about.[109]

In addition to investing in your people and the initiatives that are meaningful to them, Harvesters in hypergrowth would be wise to prioritize projects that cultivate and promote leadership while showcasing the exclusivity of being a member of the so-called in-crowd. This can range from providing access to unique opportunities such as early manager development training, onsite celebrity speaker series, employee mentorship programs, inspirational destination team offsites, and consciousness-raising digital resources such as on-demand "mindfulness for performance" video programs and the like.

Naturally, when it comes to attracting and retaining talent, to Harvesters it will always seem like you are unable to hire quickly enough and are constantly behind in filling open roles. The good news is you can and should be able to recruit the most in-demand talent, assuming your employee value proposition is aligned with employee expectations and you have strong word-of-mouth referrals from your existing workforce.

Pruners: Focusing resources to cultivate a more certain future

Unsure how long it will take to accelerate growth—and taking an optimistic, wait-and-see approach—Pruners have a focus on stabilizing revenue and might be freezing headcount to cautiously conserve cash. As these companies stay transfixed on improving business results, they should absolutely have a compelling long-term vision that is well communicated to employees and in which each individual understands and can articulate how his or her role contributes to securing the desired future corporate outcome.

Pruning companies may learn too late that you can't ignore things like employee stress and burnout when resources are scarce, specifically the hardships associated with short-sighted parental leave policies or less-than-adequate childcare or eldercare support benefits. Employees will quit or be unproductive due to emotional health issues if you fail to consider what kinds of support your people are going to need to make it through when they are expected to make do with less and stick it out. Empathy is essential to your bottom line when you cannot just throw money at the problem, although as I hope you have learned in managing modern employees, empathy is pretty much always a requirement, and cash is no longer a substitute for caring, period.

Forward-thinking employers in every tier, in fact, will keep these benefits on the docket or start rolling these out as the demand for talent to be productive and to keep churn to a minimum due to the high associated costs are very real irrespective of where you sit on the continuum during a downturn or a recovery. What's more, in a hiring-freeze environment, retaining your talent is mission critical, as you are not allowed to replace the headcount you lose, even if they leave of their own accord. Now isn't that a sobering thought, as well as a compelling reason for treating employees extremely well and investing the effort to figure out how to retain them?

Managers in Pruning companies need to ensure that their existing team's needs for flexible benefits are being met with solutions that help them manage their everyday lives (and are available at relatively low cost), like flexible work hours, extra paid leave, professional development/educational reimbursement, networking opportunities, and small-group volunteer projects. In addition, introducing low-budget voluntary ad hoc employee groups (e.g. moms, runners, sci-fi fans) to develop a strong sense of community and creating a wellbeing program that suits people's real needs are both strong signals that management cares. Investing in inexpensive culture-boosting ideas is a particularly smart strategy to entice the employees you need most to stay with you over the long haul.

Don't underestimate the power of strong leadership and flexibility to retain employees during a time of uncertainty. Great things can happen with a positive outlook and a sense of freedom. A recent Randstad study found that 61 percent of people would be willing to accept a lower salary if a company offered a great benefits package[110]—and this speaks volumes about what really matters to today's workforce and what it takes for an employer to meet their expectations.

Ploughers: Reimagining the fundamentals for what's next

Focusing on the basics while waiting on a sector or market turnaround, Ploughers cannot rush into their reboot. But they do have the potential of infinite blue skies ahead if they can just weather the storm and reemerge— possibly stronger than before. This is akin to grapevines that have been stressed by drought conditions and are known to actually produce the most delicious wine, albeit at a much lower yield, because through surviving the ordeal they develop far greater character. Likewise, Ploughers, having experienced hard times, may have massive morale issues as well as unsettled and anxious employees, including those on furlough. It takes time—and management support—for a Plougher's remaining workforce to develop the kind of resilience that leads to long-term survival and the strength to thrive anew.

As a Plougher, you will have both the enormous power and potential to connect with your workforce, even those furloughed, and ensure they know that you care about their health and wellbeing, and that you will be a transparent communicator that can be relied upon. You must take this responsibility seriously and earnestly, as once the bond of trust is broken, you will not be given a second chance. Conversely, if you are a good shepherd of this trust, you will be rewarded with sincere and lasting loyalty the likes of which have all but vanished from the modern workforce. That's why Ploughers need to focus on identifying their best talent, coming up with ways to train them for next steps, and retaining them through regrowth. Adding new talent may rely on articulating to candidates your goals for success and showing commitment to cultivating a healthy culture and future.

With benefits, while it's probably a requirement to cut costs and find more affordable options—and reach for low-hanging fruit—it is critical to still try and help people feel their best and even more in control of their everyday lives. Rank-and-file employees at a Plougher are likely overwhelmed with fear and anxiety and are greatly in need of a steadying force to make them feel that it will all be all right in the end, no matter what. Offering EAP and on-demand wellbeing resources to help alleviate stress and anxiety will help maintain a sense of empathy and connection. The key is to offer something that reaches everyone and helps even those who may soon no longer be on the job. Proactively reducing the stigma employees who are furloughed or laid off are feeling and retaining a sense of the relationship bond that will otherwise be abruptly severed are especially important if, as a Plougher, you'd like to be in a position to rehire people when the time is right to begin the turnaround, and/or you want to avoid your corporate name having been tarnished by your handling of the downturn.

So, what are some examples of what employers can do? Recognizing that the days of corporate gym subsidies or on-site yoga instructors are now behind us just like lunchtime highballs and ashtrays, here are a few that were implemented during the stay-at-home orders during the pandemic:

- A large media and entertainment conglomerate created a company-wide event that connected employees around emotional health, helping to alleviate anxiety. Having furloughed a large number of employees, with the remainder working from home, this organization kicked off a company-sponsored Grokker activity to help everyone stay healthy and remain engaged and connected while sheltering in place. As a matter of fact, they specifically didn't want to call this initiative a "challenge" in order to keep the focus on pursuing wellbeing, not on competition or prizewinning. One of their focus areas was emotional resilience in which the participants explored video content related to gratitude, positivity, productivity, focus, and stress relief.
- One company launched a challenge in which their participants shared their daily at-home wellbeing activities by posting photos with captions of themselves with their family members working out, doing yoga, or cooking together.
- Another ran a "Healthy at Home" initiative that provided employees with resources to help them create and share a variety of home-based routines to feel their best.
- A fourth company hosted a daily five-ingredients-in-under-thirty-minutes healthy dinner recipe challenge.
- Yet another held group "Mindfulness Moments" scheduled at set times during the week where they watched stress-reduction and resiliency training videos together and discussed how they were feeling before and after the video.

I am inspired by these and so many other creative acts of corporate caring. Like those running healthy-at-home challenge examples, many others were also less focused on physical movements alone and requested holistic content to support their employees with resilience, burnout, time management, mindfulness, and balancing the demands of working parents and caregivers. For all of the tiers to move forward in the new world, what must be underscored is the importance of ensuring we are supporting employees with what they need, when they need it and how they need it, rather than relying upon what perhaps worked in the past.

♥ ♥ ♥

The End of Shareholder Capitalism and the Start of Something Better

A Guest Perspective by Susan Schuman,
Executive Chair, SYPartners

Over the past twenty years, Susan Schuman has built and led SYPartners, a firm that consults to many of the world's most visionary leaders to help them transform their businesses. She's worked alongside Fortune 100 CEOs and their teams to imagine the future they want to create and to build their strategies, cultures, and human behaviors to make their vision a reality. Her clients have included executives at AARP, Ascena, Blackstone, Coach, Facebook, GE, IBM, Oprah Winfrey Network, PPFA, Starbucks, Target, Weight Watchers, Viacom, The CW, and many others. Prior to SYPartners, Susan was the general manager of Studio Archetype, one of the first premier web design firms in the U.S. She also ran her own marketing and product strategy consulting firm, and spent seven years at Apple, where she was group manager of Worldwide Product Marketing. Susan is also vice chair of the kyu collective and sits on the boards of ViacomCBS, Wheels Up, IDEO, and IDEO.org. Here's what she has to say:

"We were founded to help companies go through episodic, once-a-century transformations at what used to be considered epic scales. But transformation and change are now a constant, and it is now about helping companies build the capability and capacity to constantly change.

"We believe that a company can't just transform its business in a vacuum; it has to transform its culture at the same time. And we believe that 'process' doesn't change people; *people* change people. Keith, my business partner, and I came from Apple, so we understood human-centered design. So, starting from day one, there has been a human element in everything we do. It's made it natural to consider a wide range of human needs and impacts as being necessary—beyond shareholders.

"We also realized that companies recognized as being great are that way because they're great companies on the inside—and that great companies on the inside will become great companies on the outside. If you look back at some of the great companies like Hewlett Packard and IBM, you'll see that they grew up in a multistakeholder scenario where they thought about more than just the financials. So, we asked ourselves: how do you make a great company? We found that you have to have a great leader—not just in terms of driving financial results, but a leader that can balance and drive both performance and humanity. We also realized that when we are transforming companies and their cultures, we're helping the leaders undergo their own personal transformations. You can't bring out the best in others until you bring forward the best in yourself. You can't fully activate or transform a company to pursue a new future until you create conditions for the teams inside that company to thrive. And you can't have thriving teams without thriving duos, which are twosomes of flourishing individual humans.

"We've been successful because we believe that transformations have to be leader led. At the end of the day, you have to find leaders who either have the propensity to believe in or already believe in the power of unlocking humanity in their organization, and have a deep desire to create conditions for human flourishing.

"To lead in a multistakeholder world, the role of the CEO is going to need to shift. They're going to have to create new value for all constituents, not just extract value from their existing assets. They're going to need to distribute power without creating chaos, while also creating new governance structures that unlock the potential in their people. They're going to need to exercise their own creativity—and the creativity of their people—to find new ways forward. And they'll need to create conditions for human flourishing. It used to be that leaders' primary responsibility was driving performance—and maybe the most enlightened among us would then focus on the humanity of our organizations once we hit our performance targets. Now, both performance *and* humanity need to be design principles for the organizations that are going to thrive. The market demands it, employees are demanding it, and it's the right thing to do. The conditions for people to thrive and succeed so they can bring their best work, their best selves to bear at work, are the responsibility of leadership. We create those conditions. And if we don't get the balance of humanity and performance in our own orgs, we can't expect to deliver it for our other stakeholders.

"Culture is just as important as the financials because it's what will make you a successful company in the future. Boards and leadership now have the responsibility to bring culture and people into the equation for the long-term viability of a company. Historically it was only about shareholder value, and now it is about multistakeholder value. Culture and people are no longer an afterthought. I am on the board of a large public company, and we spend as much time on the culture and the people as we do the strategy and the business. We do it because we also know future success is going to be about talent.

"I think the pandemic shines a light on all of these shifts even more. Every CEO we're speaking to now talks about the fact that their company is not going to go back to the way that it was. They can't just restart with all the same assumptions. There is going to have to be a "new" new. CEOs will have to really think about the future they want to create as well as the strategies, ways of working, and behaviors needed to get there. And it has to be from a human perspective because it's going to be about how fast people can change their behavior. It's about building the capability within our people and company to continuously transform, and the way you build this capacity is through empathy and understanding the whole human— because now more than ever they are bringing their whole life to work with them. The leaders who don't believe in a culture of caring will, over time, find that they will no longer be able to lead into the next generation and will be replaced by those who lead holistically. Even during periods of high unemployment, we will still have a war for talent. If you want to get the right talent, you are not going to hire just any talent. You want to hire the right talent for what you need to do. And they're still going to be choosy, because they want to believe that the company they're joining is one that is both caring and human led.

"How are we different at SYPartners? We help the CEO find the belief and desire within themselves to lead their company in a new and a different way that is from a humanity-based, not just a financial, perspective. And we help them tell stories about the future they want and bring those stories to life in a way that allows them to then build the belief in others. There are a lot of management consultants who come in, and they start with fear that bad things are going to happen: their role is to minimize the potential of bad things challenging the current state. We come in and ask leaders instead, What's the vision of the future? What do you want to become? What's that future you want to create? Even if they don't know how to create it or how to articulate it, we can help bring that out from them. Sometimes CEOs have the future in their heads but don't know how to get it out. We helped them do that. Then we help them bring their leadership in line with that, reconnecting them to their core so they could build a future from there. Some leaders want their leadership team to be a part of helping craft that future, so it becomes a shared vision. That way, they are actually much more willing to lead it, and they become much more of a coherent team to go out and execute it together.

"A new vision and strategy have to work their way all the way down into the organization. A lot of times, they are activated at the top but never get deep into the org. Part of infusing them all the way down into the org is by reimagining your process, structures, metrics, and rewards to make sure they are also getting aligned to the new vision and strategy. A lot of times CEOs think, "Oh, I changed the top; I've got everyone in agreement; I've communicated what we're doing; I'm good to go." They don't realize that the systems down to the Z level of the alphabet have to reinforce that new direction. For large enterprise companies, these systems can be massive. Some send in a change management team, and they try to change all the systems, but that takes so long. Given we're in an era now of constant transformation and change, systems are going to continuously be out of whack. The next evolution is going to be on how we can change the systems with much more agility than we have in the past, to adapt with ever-evolving vision and strategy.

"Grappling with the transformation of our companies and organizations today is a bit like playing with a Rubik's Cube—it's not enough to solve for one side of the cube; you have to align all the sides in order to be successful. Leaders must now see that everything is multistakeholder and must think about all of their constituents. As a CEO, you have to think about all of those things in a way that you have never had to think about before. As you look around the table, you now have to look at the individual, almost in 360 degrees—not just the job they do, but their whole lives, which is why I think creativity, humanity, and caring are going to play such an important role."

Chapter 4:

HOW SHOULD YOU CARE?

If there is one overarching piece of advice you should keep in mind as you choose how to demonstrate care for your employees, it's that you need to do so in a way that's consistent with your culture and values. Employees have highly refined BS meters and will sniff out an impressive-sounding but unrealistic platitude no matter how prominently the words are hung on the office walls. Enron, a company that failed in 2001 due to fraud that sent multiple executives to prison, had "Integrity" listed as one of its corporate values. But they clearly didn't live this value. You see, a company is just like any other organism. It is alive, and its component parts are employees, who will naturally do whatever it takes to survive and thrive. Employees will quickly figure out what it takes to succeed at your company by observing what is rewarded and what is not, taking these cues from watching their manager's behavior and their colleagues.

I bring this up because corporate culture is what happens when management isn't in the room. If your new-hire training espouses the importance of teamwork as a value and Teamwork posters are hung all over the cafeteria, but once on the job the imperative of hitting top-line revenue at all costs—and pitting employees against each other for the biggest haul— is what determines bonuses, reviews, retention, and promotion, you can be sure that in spite of all attempts to promote helping others out, your employees will not take the time or effort to live the value of teamwork because doing so will hurt them in their Darwinian search for corporate survival. If there are no instilled rituals, financial rewards, or embedded social incentives encouraging teamwork, then it's not a real company value; it's a false PR message or a pipe dream. So, your teams will prioritize revenue at all costs, and be rewarded for it personally, while your corporate culture suffers.

So, if you want to embrace caring for your employees because, as we have discussed, it is critical to your corporate success, you need to find a genuine way of expressing this care so that it fits into how you do business, or else it will amount to nothing but hot air. According to research published in the 2019 *Harvard Business Review* article entitled "The Leader's Guide to Corporate Culture," culture change is essential to ameliorating corporate performance.[111]

It is possible—in fact, vital—to improve organizational performance through culture change. How? First, leaders must become aware of the culture that operates in their organization. Next, they need to define their aspirational target culture. Finally, they must master the core change practices of articulation of the aspiration, leadership alignment, organizational conversation, and organizational design. Leading with culture may be among the few sources of sustainable competitive advantage left to companies today. In other words, to be successful today, leaders must stop regarding culture with frustration and instead use it as a fundamental management tool.[112] Since every company culture is different, what I will outline for you next is an effective five-step framework to help you and your team derive your way of caring for your employees.

Step 1. Be authentic

As the CEO or a leader in your organization, you need to start by modeling a culture where you can bring your whole self to work each day. Too often, we play the role we believe we should be playing—the hard-nosed executive, the buttoned-up lawyer, the gregarious deal-closer. But we are more than our job title: we are sons, daughters, spouses, partners, parents, and friends. You need to lead by example and show up as human. It may be as simple as telling the truth when you leave the office early to catch your daughter's soccer match or take your son to his orthodontist appointment. I was on a conference panel recently on how to support women in the workplace who are saddled with #TheSecondShift, working after work to take care of children, parents, community, and households. A fellow speaker encouraged the execs in the audience to "parent loudly" and model for others that it's okay to have a family and need to attend to children's games and skinned knees. The audience applauded. You see, showing up as your authentic self as a frontline employee is risky business—you have no clout or influence, and you certainly have no air cover to protect you from the judgment of others. Senior leaders are the only people who can show up as their true, authentic selves and give employees permission to do the same.

Several years ago, my mother was diagnosed with cancer. I had to find the best treatment option for her and personally take her to Arizona for her surgery, and then move her from Montreal into my home in Northern California for her six-month course of chemo and radiation. This was a very big event in my life, and I didn't want to pretend otherwise. In the past I would have simply donned my work body armor and shown up with a smile without divulging the truth of what was happening at home. I would have been afraid of what people would think—was I burdening them or being too personal?—and I would've worried that my commitment to work would be questioned. But this time I chose to share with my entire company what was happening with my mom, and why I would be away for several weeks, and how I was feeling: sad, scared, distracted, and determined. After I returned from her surgery and settled my mom into my home, I began taking her to her chemo appointments and kept the team at work up to speed on how things were going for her and for me. My colleagues were amazingly supportive, and on weeks when my mom was feeling better, she would come to my office on occasion for lunch with my team. Everyone was happy to see her, and it felt natural to have her with us. My mom's cancer brought many of us at work a little bit closer because I was vulnerable and very real with what was going on in my life, and they were empathetic and supportive. Thankfully, my mom made a full recovery and is five years cancer free. She recently relocated permanently to live near me and still visits me at work from time to time. Not having the additional burden of carrying this secret and being able to speak about it with friends at work was enormously helpful and made it feel a whole lot lighter.

Imagine if every employee in your company felt comfortable enough to share their personal struggles at work. Imagine how safe a workplace that would be. Then imagine the strength your employees could derive from the understanding of colleagues and managers, and the relief at not having to pretend everything is fine when going through a serious life event. Imagine how much more committed and loyal they would feel to the company and their manager.

A few years after my mother's cancer scare, my youngest daughter began to experience very serious anxiety and depression. She was only fifteen, and it was the scariest time of my and my husband's lives. Once again, I shared with my team what was going on at home and how we were striving to help her cope with the help of psychologists, psychiatrists, educational consultants, autoimmune specialists, pediatricians, teachers, counselors, and communities of parents who had been through something similar with a child. Sometimes at work I would need to leave in the middle of a multiperson meeting to take an urgent call from my daughter, and no one asked any questions other than, "Are you okay?" The ability to be myself through such a trying period and feel like I could still be myself at work was a gift. What I didn't realize was that unbeknownst to me, this gift was benefiting other people at work as well.

One day in the spring of 2017, Chris, my head of engineering, came to see me. He said that Chad, one of his best developers, seemed out of sorts, his productivity was significantly impacted, and he was exhibiting signs of what he suspected might be depression. He asked me if I'd be willing to speak with Chad to check in and see if he was okay. I met with Chad, and he shared quite freely how he was feeling lethargic, hopeless, emotionally erratic, isolated, ashamed, and unable to will it away. Having experienced the devastating impact of depression on my daughter, I recognized all too well the familiar symptoms. I asked Chad if he thought he might be depressed and asked him if he would be open to seeing a psychiatrist or psychologist to help figure out what is going on and to help him cope with it. I explained some of what I had learned over the years with my daughter's struggle and the importance of having a toolkit of strategies to use when going through emotionally exacting times. I also offered to be a sounding board as he explored what could be done to help him with his own mental health, and to meet with him weekly to simply chat and provide a safe space where he wouldn't have to explain himself or feel defensive. As I shared with his manager at the time, "As one of the keys for Chad to not feel alone, he needs to know he has people at Grokker who care deeply about him."

A midwestern family man to the core, Chad had been raised to shake things off stoically and, prior to Grokker, had never been exposed to the West Coast world of open dialogue around mental health. But he had heard me share my daughter's journey over the years and decided that in spite of the stigma, he would give it a shot. I reached out to my network of mental health professionals, and along with Chad's own persistence, we found him a fantastic doctor in Dubuque. He began seeing the doctor and eventually tried a highly effective medication that—along with Chad's hard work involving mindfulness, physical exercise, social connections, and faith— helped Chad overcome his depression. What's more, just a few months after the onset of his depression, Chad began advocating for the destigmatizing of mental health with his friends, family, colleagues, and community.

Today, Chad's Facebook timeline is littered with comments thanking him for sharing. The words most commonly used are "brave" and "courage." Chad's bravery for coming forth elicited shares from dozens of others about their own struggles and those of loved ones. Creating a work environment where showing up as yourself is encouraged affects peoples' lives in meaningful and even permanently positive ways. I don't save many notes that I receive, but this one is on my phone and serves as a constant reminder of just how important it is to make work personal and be authentic so that those you work with never feel alone:

"Lorna, I know I've said this before, but thank you so much. Your help through my depression was what I needed, and I think we've been trained by the world to expect that once the workday is over, our relationships with our bosses are over. I, and everyone else at Grokker and elsewhere in your life, are blessed that that is not the case with you. You are the embodiment of 'it's personal,' and I know I would be worse off never having known you. Today, the weight on my shoulders is light, I'm not overwhelmed, and I'm optimistic again. I had a scheduled therapy appointment this morning, and I didn't need to make another one, at least not in the immediate future. So, thank you a million times over. I love you and am forever in your debt."

Pinterest employees have a saying: "Be yourself, not your selfie."[113] My friend, former head of finance at Pinterest, Natalie Fair, embodied this principle when she faced down her personal fears to tell the CEO, board, investors, and all of Pinterest's employees that she wanted to leave finance to build a new social impact division at the company. "Authenticity and speaking your truth goes a long way," Natalie told me. "When we're feeling comfortable, that's the time to do that uncomfortable thing. It's a big part of leadership." Had Natalie not felt confident approaching her boss about her desire for a change of focus, she would have simply left to pursue her goals elsewhere. Her CEO would never have seen it coming and would not have known why. Moreover, the cost of replacing Natalie would have been high, and a smooth succession would have proven impossible. But, fortunately, the relationship Natalie had with her manager enabled her to show up authentically and share her thoughts about a change of career path with him. This was personally important to Natalie, and the culture at Pinterest gave her permission to be authentic without worrying about her loyalty being questioned or upsetting the natural order of things. The culture at Pinterest, as it turned out, was critically important to the company retaining a top executive and facilitating an easy transition that did not hurt the business. As my friend Kay Mooney, the former head of transformation at

CVS Health, likes to say, "Companies can do good and do well at the same time." (For more from Kay, look for her Guest Perspective in chapter 5.)

Pinterest's business is a community based upon shared passions, and the company weaves the authentic nature of these roots through their employee interactions and workplace design. Nowhere is this better exemplified that at Knit Con, Pinterest's annual two-day internal conference, where employees teach each other about their personal areas of passion, which I mentioned in chapter 2. In 2019, CEO Ben Silberman said: "We recently held our fifth annual Knit Con with 250 employee-teachers around the world, dozens of guest speakers and over twenty Pinner- and creator-led classes. Little known secret: within the walls of Pinterest sit employees who are also experts in beekeeping, survival, ultramarathoning, kickboxing, and water coloring, and Knit Con is where they share their skills with their colleagues and friends—a practice we affectionately call 'knitting.' It's where classes like disaster preparedness, watercolor painting, and jiu-jitsu are explored. By bridging online ideas to offline action, Knit Con is essentially Pinterest in real life."[114]

I believe that this is exactly how you live the company values and connect your employees to a larger purpose they can be proud of. Pinterest states, "Our mission is to bring everyone the inspiration to create a life they love."[115] With Knit Con, the company ensures that as Becky Cantieri, chief people officer at SurveyMonkey, puts it, "Your insides match your outsides."[116] By the way, this sets up the conditions for setting up the second step in deriving a framework of caring at your company.

Step 2. Inspire others to action

You cultivate followership by demonstrating leadership. Remember, the poster will end up in the trash; telling people to follow you is not enough. Show people a future they want to be a part of by painting a picture of where you're headed and how you're going to change the world. Inspire them with that common vision by showing them how they can be a part of it. When they see the impact that they can personally have in manifesting this new reality and feel inspired to join the journey you are leading, they will make the choice to act. You literally need to inspire them to action.

Caryn Marooney, who we first met in chapter 2, believes that "if you get people to love where they are going, they will help you figure out how to get there."[117] The beauty here is that you do not need to have all of the answers. You just need to set the vision and draw a picture of a future where your employees want to see themselves, and then you can trust them to help make it happen. When you trust your colleagues, you don't need to know everything, you just need to know where you are heading. Now, effectively communicating a vision of the future that will resonate with your employees is difficult, so let's examine a messaging framework developed by Caryn that makes it easier. It's called the R.I.B.S. Test: Relevant, Inevitable, Believable, Simple.

RELEVANT

Is your vision relevant to the group you are targeting with your messaging?

INEVITABLE

Does the future state you are espousing feel like something that will actually happen?

BELIEVABLE

Will your employees believe your company will achieve your goal?

SIMPLE

Is your messaging effortlessly repeatable, natural, and sticky?

A framework for effectively communicating a vision of the future that will resonate with your employees.

R is for Relevant. Is your vision relevant to the group you are targeting? It can't just matter to you and your C-suite, it must matter to the specific individuals you need to inspire with your future vision. If you need your rank-and-file employees to buy into your cultural vision, it must be meaningful and relevant to them. At Grokker our company vision is to "advance the personal pursuit of physical, emotional, and spiritual wellbeing." No matter how little time you have in your day, no matter how in or out of shape you are, no matter your age, gender, geographic location, or job, Grokker is here to help you be a better you, regardless of your abilities or constraints.

That vision resonates with frontline employees as well as execs, because we all struggle to find the time and motivation to take care of ourselves. We are all so busy and overrun with demands on us from work, home, and community that the idea of someone actually trying to help us live a happier, healthier life is a universal desire. It is relevant.

Now if we apply the same messaging framework to corporate culture, we can take any company's values and run them through the Relevance test. At Grokker we have 5 Values: 1) It's Personal, 2) Fun, 3) Freedom, 4) It's the Results that Matter, and 5) the Enthusiast (our user) is at the Center of the Grokkerverse. Let's take the first value and break it down. "It's Personal" has two aspects: the first is that we as employees know one another as people not just as coworkers. We share our trials and tribulations, like my mom's cancer; we celebrate life events and support each other through challenges; we are real, and it is personal. The second aspect of "It's Personal" is more nuanced: It means that we treat one another like family in our professional pursuits. We care about each other's success at work and want to actively help one another be the best we can. This also means that we give each other the benefit of the doubt and assume others have the best of intentions and are acting in our best interest.

At Grokker, when you provide constructive feedback, it's always done privately, and it is appreciated by the recipient who acknowledges that the provider took the time to give feedback because they care about you and about the company succeeding. So if a colleague presents a new marketing plan that feels lackluster, or comes across as overly negative or critical in a meeting, or releases a new feature that lacks sufficient polish, you are encouraged to care enough about the other person to take the time to pull them aside and let them know that you appreciate how much they value delivering their best and that you want to point out to them how in this specific instance they seemed to come up short. It is precisely because your colleague's trust that you are trying to build them up rather than tear them down or make yourself feel smarter or more important that this form of personal feedback works so effectively. The appreciation for the feedback and sense of ownership by the team to help one another thrive is what inspires people to share.

The side benefit is that we always give one another the benefit of the doubt. If someone loses their temper in a meeting, our instinct is to ask if they are okay rather than be defensive or combative. My former head of engineering would at times be prone to what you might call crankiness. From time to time, we'd hear him express this grumpiness quite fully in our exec meetings, and rather than respond in anger, we'd generally acknowledge that Cranky Chris was present (truly a term of affection) and one of us would go check on him afterward to make sure he was okay. Not surprisingly, we are also very quick to apologize and to take responsibility for our mistakes, which makes it a safe place to be yourself. "It's Personal" is relevant to everyone, and we use the language with one another all the time.

Every new employee also goes through conflict-resolution training that I still personally teach once a month. The premise is that we are going to have times when someone's actions hurt your feelings or create sufficient upset that if left unaddressed could lead to permanent resentment. As a company that deeply values personal relationships, we cannot afford to let issues fester, and so we provide a model for how we clear conflict. In fact, leadership is tasked with modeling this conflict-resolution behavior so that it becomes the norm for all. One key to the model is that it assumes good intentions on the part of all parties. Another is that no one is expected to apologize. Rather, the goal of the exercise is to simply ensure the discloser is heard by the receiver who presents back what the discloser felt and experienced so that they understand the discloser's experience. Otherwise stated, it is a connection exercise.

When you feel connected to another person and understand how they experienced the interaction, but without any judgment, it is easier to feel empathy. So, while the exercise does not request any sort of apology, I have never witnessed a clearing that didn't end up with several given freely for inadvertently causing harm. Even when we need to confront one another, and perhaps especially then, it is done through the lens of this foundational "It's Personal" company value. What's more, this conflict-resolution model inspires employees to clear the air when necessary and to do so in a way that keeps everyone safe.

I is for Inevitable. Does the future state you are espousing feel like something that will actually happen? Can your employees see a world in which it can happen? This tests how much wind is at your back in manifesting the new state of being versus how strong the headwinds opposing your vision may be. The stronger the tailwind, the easier it is for your employees to sign up to your vision because it fits into a worldview they buy into as the natural evolution. Back at eBay in the fall of 2000, I was at a leadership meeting where our CEO, Meg Whitman, shared her vision of eBay generating $3 billion in revenue by 2005. At the time, eBay's revenue for the prior quarter was just $97 million, so Meg's goal implied a 50 percent revenue growth rate per year for the next five years. This was a massive BHAG, but inside the company, we all felt that while this was an aggressive goal, with the tremendous growth in e-commerce we were expecting, it was indeed where we were headed. A giant digital shopping platform that was going to democratize commerce for everyone was going to emerge. It was exciting and exhilarating and even a little bit scary, but we all saw a world in which this was going to happen, and I for one wanted to be a part of it. There were many factors that contributed to the inevitability of this outcome, so it wasn't merely a wish or a fantasy, but rather an ambitious outcome we were working hard toward. This inspired so many of us to action and kept us working nights and weekends in furtherance of the goal.

B is for Believable, which is something of a truth test. Once everyone agrees on a future state that looks a certain way, the question becomes whether your company will be the one to achieve it, or more specifically whether your employees believe your company will achieve it. To be believable, they need to say, "Yes, I can see this is you." As Caryn Marooney cautions, this step takes a very long time, and you must keep at it, striving to make it believable until it is so. An example she gives is how long it took for people to believe that Facebook would reach beyond college campuses and become a global social network bringing people together, or how long it took for Google to believably be the one to organize all the world's information. In your own work creating an enduring culture of caring at your company, you will never be done convincing employees to believe that you will deliver on your promises.

S is for Simple. Your messaging must be repeatable, natural, and roll off the tongue without any effort. Too many compound words or run-on sentences are not going to help your message stick, but a punchy and clear phrase will. Think of this as needing to meet the ten-year-old elevator pitch test. Can you speak your future cultural vision aloud in the time it takes to ride up an elevator to a meeting? If you can't, it's too long. Furthermore, if my ten-year-old niece Dani is listening to your pitch in the elevator but cannot understand and repeat it back to you after hearing you, it's too complicated. Today's ten-year-olds are pretty savvy, so don't dumb down your message, just pump up the resonance. By applying this R.I.B.S. framework, you should be well positioned to have future state messaging that your whole organization will rally around and be inspired to bring to life.

Judy Elder may not be as well known as other popular visionaries like Bill Gates or Elon Musk, but as the head of the consumer division of Microsoft Canada in the 1990s, she was renowned in the Canadian business community as a dynamic leader who inspired others, particularly women, to meet challenges head on. Judy always urged women to be proud of their ambition, to reject barriers, and to simply "make stuff happen." Judy passed away suddenly in March 2002. After visiting the funeral home to say goodbye to Judy, my friend Colleen Moorehead, then president of E*TRADE Canada, and I headed to a bar to toast our dear friend and console ourselves. After an emotional day, we decided that the best way to honor Judy was to keep her legacy alive by creating a way for other women to hear Judy's voice on the empowerment of women and learn from her example as a leader. We enlisted a small group of Canadian female leader friends who joined together to establish The Judy Project,[118] a five-day, annual forum to educate and motivate rising female business leaders.

We didn't know exactly how to make it happen, but we had a strong vision of a future where up-and-coming women in business could be lifted up and made more skilled and confident in their careers. We painted a picture for Judy's partner, David Powell, and with his blessing we approached Roger Martin, dean at the Rotman School of Business at the University of Toronto, about creating a leading executive forum designed to support and prepare women for executive leadership and the C-suite—a program sponsored by corporate employers keen to invest in rising female leaders, and where the memory of Judy Elder would inspire others for decades to come. Dean Martin found the vision we messaged Relevant (meaningful to the objectives and prospective students of the business school), Inevitable (programs that focused on advancing women in business were going to happen), Believable (we could pull together the financing and clout to make it a success in partnership with the university), and Simple (fostering the next gen of female business leaders was easy to grok).

The Judy Project launched in April 2003 and now, nearly two decades after her passing, Judy's vision continues to galvanize a new generation of women leaders.[119] You can read all about the genesis of the project from idea to institution as well as words of wisdom from lecturers and participants of the program ranging from Prime Minister Justin Trudeau to Shelly Lazarus, chairman emeritus of Ogilvy & Mather, in *The Collective Wisdom of High-Performing Women: Leadership Lessons from the Judy Project* by Colleen Moorehead.[120]

Step 3. Create a safe space for employees to give and seek support

We all want to always appear confident at our jobs, which can hold us back from seeking support when we need it. As we have all discovered with the benefit of experience, it is a sign of courage, not weakness, to ask for help, and your willingness as a leader to show vulnerability can bring colleagues closer and create a community bond. But without assurances that seeking and lending support will inure to your benefit at the company, no one will take the risk of appearing vulnerable.

At most companies not only is strength rewarded, but vulnerability is actively discouraged. So, you must try doubly hard to create a safe environment for employees, and what's more, you need to reward them both for seeking support and for giving it. At Grokker, we introduced the weekly High 5. We put Post-it Notes and a Sharpie in the break room next to an empty glass fishbowl and invited employees to nominate any colleague who had helped them solve a problem, accomplish a goal, or just made their job easier that week. Then, at the weekly company meeting, we read these High 5s out loud and randomly pick one from the fishbowl as the week's High 5 and give both the nominator and nominee a ten-dollar gift card to their favorite coffee shop. By creating a company practice that gives a weekly shout-out to employees who help others and who receive help, we are reinforcing the importance of giving and seeking support. Some companies are now employing a similar principle by introducing the compensation practice of crowdsourcing micro bonuses based upon colleague feedback. For example, Cisco has deployed a social recognition program whereby employees can receive more than ten awards annually valued at twenty-five dollars each when nominated by colleagues.

Beyond making it acceptable and encouraged to ask for help, we need to openly discuss our business failures and in fact institutionalize and reward the open examination of what went wrong and why in order to create cultures that learn as opposed to cultures that punish mistakes. Prior to their sale to Symantec, the leaders at theft protection company LifeLock were facing repeated rejection on their path to selling the company. They decided to be brutally honest with each other in their prep meetings, recognizing that no one gets everything right the first time. While it was uncomfortable at first, the new culture of transparency gave the team permission to share immediate feedback on whether a pitch worked or didn't, eventually leading to a successful sale.[121] "I think vulnerability is the most powerful tool in any leader's arsenal," former LifeLock CEO Hilary Schneider said to me. "I spent a lot of time trying to pretend I wasn't vulnerable in the workforce, and I found that the more authentic I am, the more people connect."[122]

At Outcast Agency, an iconic Silicon Valley PR firm cofounded by Caryn Marooney during the dot-com boom, the importance of personal wellbeing as a survival skill became apparent in 2001 when the stock market crashed, and Outcast's clients were so severely hit by the recession that they lost 70 percent of their clients in one day. As a result, Outcast had to lay off more than half of their employees and cut back to a skeleton team. Caryn and her cofounder, Margit Wennmachers, felt that for the team that remained, it was important to say, "It is our job to be as healthy personally and professionally as we can, so we can bring these (laid off) people back." And within eight months, they had hired back half a dozen of the employees they had let go.

Another lesson from Outcast that helped them thrive despite strong headwinds was inculcating the daily practice of sharing lessons learned above celebrating success. "I think we all feel we are secretly failing, and we are supposed to hide that," says Marooney. But by sharing lessons learned, you can turn that on its head and make it completely normal to examine every outcome by starting with, "Ok, here's what wasn't that good." By debriefing with an eye to sharing what was a surprise, what worked previously but didn't this time, what we thought was going to be great but wasn't, and what may have changed, we can teach our teams how to learn faster. What's more, we can teach our teams to get comfortable with failure, and that builds incredible resilience, so when they fail instead of feeling ashamed and justifying, blaming, or burying the outcome, their reaction becomes, "Oh yeah, that happens. Here's what can I learn from it," and quickly move on to "Now, what's next?!"

By embracing and modeling the purposeful examination of lessons learned, you can create a culture where it is safe to take risks counterbalanced by curiosity and accountability. Just think: if you can encourage people to be curious about why something went wrong as opposed to being worried about being found out as fallible, you will fundamentally change the mindset in your workplace for the better.

Step 4. Make it personal by sharing your own life story

Oftentimes, leaders choose to hide big life events from employees, such as caring for a sick parent or even taking on a new commitment as their kid's soccer coach. They don't want colleagues to assume their personal obligations will take away from work performance, so they hide it or downplay it, creating a barrier that inhibits close connections. But it's personal, so why pretend otherwise?

My friend Juliet de Baubigny was a top venture capitalist at the iconic firm Kleiner Perkins Caufield & Byers (KPCB) before leaving to cofound Bond Capital with Mary Meeker. When her young son was diagnosed with type 1 diabetes, Juliet saw an opportunity to employ her network to make a difference. She founded a nonprofit called Beyond Type 1 with Nick Jonas, Sarah Lucas, and Sam Talbot, reaching out to colleagues, friends, celebrities, and family to share her personal story and seek support. Within the first year, Beyond Type 1 had amassed over five hundred thousand Facebook followers, raising awareness and donations toward a cure. By sharing her personal travails and galvanizing forces around an otherwise devastating situation, Juliet created a public victory. It all started with having the courage to share.

The truth is that if you can encourage people to bring the outside in by holding the door open for them, you will build a far more successful business because your employees will show up as their whole selves. The trick is that you have to model this behavior first.

Step 5. Give employees permission to take care of their own wellbeing

Airplane safety has the right idea: you should always put your oxygen mask on first before helping others. If you don't make time for self-care, you won't be able to bring your best to work. When employees see you giving yourself permission to take time for wellbeing, they will feel comfortable to do the same, resulting in healthier, more productive employees.

As a busy entrepreneur and mom, I stay centered with a life mantra I created called the 8-3-3-1 Stability Framework™. My recommendation actually has four interconnected parts: sleep, exercise, nutrition, and fun. If you think of your life as a tent with four flaps, and all of the flaps are staked to the ground, your tent is stable. So, even when a storm hits, your tent remains upright. Should one flap come loose, your tent will flutter in the wind. But if two or more of your flaps become untethered, it's unstable, and if the wind begins to bluster, your tent is apt to be tossed about and collapse. To prevent my tent from being tossed around and collapsing, I apply the 8-3-3-1 Stability Framework to my life—and it's what I share with people I mentor.

What does 8-3-3-1 mean? For me to feel grounded and emotionally balanced, I need eight hours of sleep a night, three nutritious meals a day (I can't live on PowerBars, although I've tried), three sweaty workouts, challenging yoga practices, and/or meditation sessions per week, and one fun thing to look forward to each week with friends or family. For me, this is nonnegotiable. Those are my flaps—and for me, they create connectedness and stability.

The 8-3-3-1 Stability Framework™

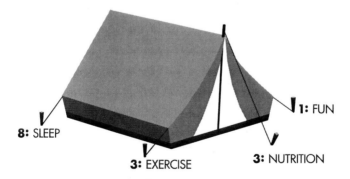

My strategy for staying centered. What is your 8-3-3-1?

If I am traveling and miss my workouts but am still sleeping and eating well and have something fun to look forward to, I know I will be okay. But if I miss more than one of these key balancing elements at a time, my life will fall over. So, I check in weekly to see how I am doing and adjust my priorities accordingly. I often will be found squeezing in a twenty-minute yoga workout at the office in plain sight during weeks when I feel slammed, and this is a key to how I manage my life. I suggest that everyone find their own "nonnegotiables" that you must do to maintain your own wellbeing and create your own 8-3-3-1 equivalent, so you have a simple way of staying on top of the fray. Your numbers can be different, but look at it this way: if you have more than one flap that isn't properly staked to the ground, you'll have an early-warning system and know what to pay attention to in order to feel your best.[123]

And to grant your teams permission to care of themselves out in the open, I would invite you to examine what kind of visible weekly rituals you host or could host that would allow your teams to both mingle socially and emphasize wellbeing. Instead of drinks after work that go unattended by late-working employees or those with children who need to get home, try a "forced break time" every Thursday afternoon at 3:30 p.m. for thirty minutes. This can be anything from a wine-and-cheese tasting to a small Halloween costume contest. The key is for the time together to not involve work priorities but just to be about connecting and/or doing something good for yourself. That's what we do at Grokker each week, and we've found it to be essential for our mental health and for employees to get to know each other as a community. Or how about organizing a weekly Wednesday morning walk around your office neighborhood. Instead of gathering for a third cup of coffee, invite everyone to meet in the lobby and just take twenty minutes to walk outside and get some fresh air. You'll find the group grow over time, plus creativity and energy will rise upon their return. Our engineering team goes for a twenty-minute group walk together after eating lunch each day, and it has become a much-loved and well-attended ritual that is often the only form of exercise they may engage in that entire day.

♥ ♥ ♥

Flipping the Wellness Paradigm

A Guest Perspective by Ryan Picarella,
President, WELCOA (Wellness Council of America)

So now that we talked about what you need to understand and do—building the business case for caring—let's look at how you should sell-in your plan for creating a more caring environment at your organization. We'll start with building the pitch, with valuable ideas that you can use even beyond the scope of my book, in the next chapter. But before we move on to that topic, let's hear from Ryan Picarella, president of the Wellness Council of America, better known as WELCOA, a nonprofit organization that seeks to improve employee wellbeing and create healthier, high-performing organizational cultures. Ryan helps create holistic wellness initiatives for organizations and communities that improve the lives of working people in America and around the world. He brings a deep interest in human connection, culture, and psychology, and his career spans human resources, organizational development and wellness programs, and product design. Outside of WELCOA, he serves as an advisor on the Healthier Workforce Center of the Midwest, on the International WELL Building Institute advisory group, and on the board of directors for the Gretchen Swanson Center for Nutrition. He has a master of science in industrial and organizational psychology from the University of Tennessee at Chattanooga as well as a bachelor of science in psychology from Northern Arizona University. Let's hear what Ryan has to say:

"Organizational wellness programs were originally created to reduce health-care costs—that was the promise insurers made to their customers and was why insurance companies began buying wellness companies. The thinking was, 'If you do this today, you're not going to incur cost tomorrow.'

What we have learned is that we are just treating the symptoms and not actually getting to the root of what actually leads to the poor lifestyle choices. And participation in these programs is typically less than 24 percent. We realized that the way of measuring success—cost avoidance—was flawed. You have some companies paying millions of dollars for these programs and are showing zero impact on anything. That led us to the insight that we needed to flip the paradigm on wellness and wellbeing programs.

"The real problem is that workers operate in conditions and cultural environments that don't allow us to fully achieve wellness, which stems from the organizational cultures. While there's nothing wrong with treadmills and broccoli—we should all eat more broccoli and be on the treadmill more—those things aren't going to happen until we first meet basic human needs. There is a fallacy that people don't want to be healthy, that they want to feel like shit every day. But that's not true.

"To flip this paradigm, you have to go from the traditional health-and-wellness approach focused solely on offering flu vaccinations, lunch and learns, and biometric screenings to thinking about organizational environments, cultures, and creating caring and passionate organizations that make sure the people are connected with purpose and meaning. In one study, researchers found that there was less turnover, higher morale, and better productivity when employees talked more favorably about the employer. And there are brand implications that come with it too, because there's so much transparency today with how businesses treat employees. If a worker doesn't feel their employer cares about them, the first thing they are going to do is 'go social media' on them. Companies have to guard their brand, because once you lose it, you are left with rebranding and hoping that no one recalls who you were originally.

"There's also a body of work that looks at how caring for employees affects the brand's customers. One study looked at caregivers. Typically, they are more stressed out and have more turnover than in a lot of other types of work. The researchers found that when the organization focused on creating a caring environment for their employees, it actually went through to the people the employees were taking care of, who reported a higher quality of life and had better outcomes than expected. I think you can extrapolate those findings to your customers as well. A lot of leaders who get it say that if you take care of your employees, it will spill over to your customers. Likewise, if you treat your employees like crap, chances are your employees are going to treat your customers that way as well. So, there is a kind of downstream domino effect with it.

"Whereas wellness was once a nice to have, it is now a business responsibility to take care of their people beyond just offering flu shots, which we should continue to do. We have to care about employment conditions, starting with the basics of preventing assault and harassment, but, eventually, we need to create conditions that are *not* going to create mental instability or depression. People in countries like China and Japan call it Karoshi and are starting to track death by overwork, including suicide. And families are now getting benefits if they can show or prove to the courts that their family member died as a result of working conditions and not as an accident.

"Even from the community perspective, we are seeing small communities around the country using it as an economic viability strategy. St Cloud in Minnesota is losing businesses and young people to the Twin Cities, so companies there are leading with wellbeing as a way to attract the talent back into their community, which is really more about economics and responsibility and less about health. And this gets back to the insight that started WELCOA. We were founded in 1986 in Omaha Nebraska by a prominent insurance executive from the area, Bill Kizer, who happened to be best buds with Warren Buffett. He assembled Warren and a few other executives to start the organization based on the insight that wellness was the key to creating strong communities and strong organizations.

"What are the benefits of caring? For those old-school business folks who look like Mr. Bogart, you can look at your turnover rates relative to your location or competitors. People won't stick with the organizations that don't address them as a person. We're seeing this more and more, especially with millennials. They want more meaning in their work; to feel like they are cared for; to have more work-life balance. So, if you don't create caring environments for your employees, you're not going to be as competitive because you're going to lose your top talent, even in hard economic times. And ultimately it's going to impact your bottom line. CEOs intuitively get this, and the CFO is often the naysayer who says, 'Look, we need to cut costs; we're going to cut non-revenue-generating programs; I can't see a straight line; and you know we're not here to be nice people; we're here to run a business.'

"Lowering health-care costs is critical, but establishing a strategy built just on that metric alone is where people get in trouble. We've seen organizations that have lowered health-care costs by focusing on caring, which makes sense. If you're not stressed, you're not going to be sick as much. There is certainly a correlation between the two. But it is a long term-investment. It needs to be part of the organization's mission and vision, and it should be explicitly stated. Then caring needs to be built into the organizational systems—the norms, policies, rules, and traditions that inform the day-to-day life of the organization.

"Here are some examples. A construction company implemented a wellness strategy to lower on-the-job injuries and reduce their worker's comp claims. That was their focus. And they successfully reduced it by 6 percent. What they did was put pictures of family and loved ones on their job site hardhats, creating greater compassion and caring for each other. It also served as a reminder on why I'm going to work every day. Look at Costco versus Sam's Club and Walmart: Costco is known for providing better benefits, better pay, and a better working culture for their employees, and Costco is outperforming Sam's Club by a pretty large margin. Finally, Southwest Airlines is typically one of the top airlines. They're known for their quirky culture. My brother-in-law is a pilot for Southwest, and my sister has been dealing with cancer for a couple of years now. Not only did they fly my sister to the Mayo Clinic for treatment; they sent flowers and care packages after chemo and some of her operations. It's pretty exceptional to also take care of your employee's family. I've probably told that story to a hundred thousand people at all the conferences where I've spoken, which elevates the brand.

WELCOA'S Seven Benchmarks

THE NEW SEVEN BENCHMARKS SPEAK TO THE FUTURE OF THE WORKPLACE

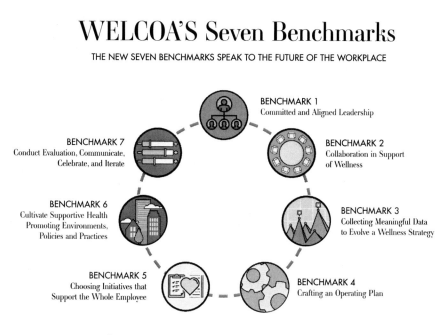

BENCHMARK 1
Committed and Aligned Leadership

BENCHMARK 7
Conduct Evaluation, Communicate, Celebrate, and Iterate

BENCHMARK 2
Collaboration in Support of Wellness

BENCHMARK 6
Cultivate Supportive Health Promoting Environments, Policies and Practices

BENCHMARK 3
Collecting Meaningful Data to Evolve a Wellness Strategy

BENCHMARK 5
Choosing Initiatives that Support the Whole Employee

BENCHMARK 4
Crafting an Operating Plan

WELCOA's seven benchmarks for creating a truly caring and compassionate organization.

"As a not-for-profit organization that helps our members create caring and compassionate organizations, we have a process that's called the seven benchmarks. We started with a definition of wellness which has seven components to it, and that became the foundation for the seven benchmarks. The idea behind the benchmarks is that they become an iterative sort of cycle. They are less about creating extrinsic rewards and motivations for doing these things and more about creating the conditions where people intrinsically can pursue wellness. The seven benchmarks are:

1. **Committed and Aligned Leadership**: Wellness and wellbe-ing cannot be owned by a person. All levels of the organization from the CEO down to frontline workers need to have a shared

understanding and shared commitment to the health and wellness of all employees. It's not a department. It's not a committee. It really has to be a shared responsibility across the organization. As businesses become decentralized, everybody has to have a seat at the table, be committed to wellness, and agree with what that looks like.

2. **Collaborating in Support of Wellness**: Creating collaborative teams dedicated to building and sustaining a successful worksite wellness initiative is an important key to success. These could be formal or informal, but they need to engage the stakeholders at all levels, and they need to help ensure a cooperative approach to the organization's worksite wellness initiatives.

3. **Collecting Meaningful Data to Evolve a Wellness Strategy**: Organizations oftentimes don't even know the right metrics to collect, which probably goes back to looking for cost savings as the outcome. Rather, the data collection should measure what matters most to both the organization and its employers and should be based on understanding your unique employee population and what matters to them through confidential and secure data collection. Remember, what a caring culture looks like in an organization is as unique as the organization. Understanding the specifics of your organization and what data elements you can collect to make sure that you know if you're winning or losing is key.

4. **Crafting an Operating Plan**: You need to put together a multiyear plan for wellness like the other initiatives you're implementing. Just like implementing a software solution, a wellness strategy needs to have money, people, goals, timelines, milestones, and all the other things that go into a plan to make sure that you have the support and resources you need to ensure

success and serve as a roadmap to achieving it. In crafting it, be sure that it reflects the vision, values, and purposes of your organization.

5. **Choosing Initiatives That Support the Whole Employee**: You need to identify the interventions that truly support the whole employee and what they really need. You wouldn't run a smoking-cessation program in an organization where no one smoked. Rather, the programs might address caregiving issues, a sick child, financial stress, getting married, retiring, even the unmentionables such as sexual health—everything that keeps us up at night. It all needs to be thought through and based on data, so your organization can offer the programs that actually support your employees and enable them to lead healthy and thriving lives.

6. **Cultivating Supportive, Health-Promoting Environments, Policies, and Practices**: We spend 80 to 90 percent of our time indoors, so our work and home environment has an impact on our health. You need to evaluate your environment, policies, practices, and overall culture—and understand the impact of all these dimensions on your employees—to ensure that you're able to support a successful wellness initiative. Of course, your wellness program should also be grounded in the core vision and purpose of the organization, so you need to align the wellness culture throughout your organization and ensure there is a consistency of resources, interventions, and the experience at work.

7. **Conduct Evaluation, Communicate, Celebrate, and Iterate**: Finally, you need to look back and evaluate the results, communicate them to employees as well as celebrate them, and then iterate to adjust course to improve even more.

"I've seen caring in environments where there's very low unemployment and super high unemployment. In Jamaica, for instance, their unemployment rate is about 40 percent. I was in a rural part of Jamaica—not a lot of tourists—and I asked a doctor there, 'Why do you think worksite wellness is the answer?' His response was that it's the only way to bring a developing nation onto the world stage. And it's the right thing to do. I don't know how anyone can argue with it. Companies that have a history of taking care of their employees will just continue to do better. I don't think there's any question about it."

Section Two:

SELLING THE PLAN

Chapter 5:

PREPARING THE PITCH

We all know the famous quote, often misattributed to either Albert Einstein or Mark Twain, "The definition of insanity is doing the same thing over and over again and expecting a different outcome." And while we don't know the actual origins of the quotation, we do know what the "same thing" is as it relates to organizational caring; focusing on reducing health-care costs rather than creating an environment that facilitates holistic wellbeing to support employees. While we now know the serious costs to business of not caring, and what needs to be done to improve the situation, the reality is that knowing is not enough. You need buy in from the top down. To affect any lasting cultural change, you will first need to sell-in your vision for a better future—this is true even if you are the CEO. However, if you do not hold the top spot but rather occupy another C-level position, or work in HR, marketing, sales, or engineering, you will need to have the ear of the CEO. There's a caveat, however: as we shall see, the CEO must be persuadable. If not, get out—without CEO support you will be doomed to failure. As for the rest of the leadership team, we will cover strategies to win them over in this chapter.

Before, you can sell the vision up, down, and around, you must first figure out how to sell it. That's what we will cover in this chapter. Think of it as creating your marketing plan. And like a marketing plan, it's not the final formal plan that actually matters, but it's understanding the issues and opportunities, the process of figuring out the details, and then executing and adjusting in real time, which we'll discuss in the next chapter, that is important. So, what do you need to understand? We have already explored the need to understand your employee base as well as your organizational objectives, but the first step is to fully understand your business goals and issues as well as any barriers. What do you hope to see in terms of performance through the transformed culture? Ryan Picarella, whom we heard from in the previous chapter, told me to look for the long-term financial struggles, adding, "Is it a sales issue, an employee turnover issue, an innovation issue, or some other issue? You need to clearly tie taking care of employees back to solving chronic business problems." Creating this connection will help you overcome the objection of the individual most likely to have one: the CFO. One caveat: Ryan warns against promising unrealistic results. In the meantime, you also want the CFO to think, quoting Ryan, "If I don't do this, I'm harming the company." It's going to be that fine balancing act to craft the message that encapsulates the two.

The next step for your transformation plan is to identify the influencers and the decision makers at your organization and understand their priorities and their pain points. When we think of influencers, we might think of those on social media, promoting T-shirts, makeup, and other items as much as they promote themselves. But that's not what I mean. Virtually everyone is an influencer at some point. Who becomes one is determined by the situation. Think of it this way: an entry-level worker who is interested in cars and rebuilds them on the weekend might be more of an influencer to a coworker buying a car than a top manager who prefers biking to work and claims that his or her cousins prefer a certain car brand. My point is that you need to identify the employees who will be the most effective influencers for this situation—and it might not be who first comes to mind. As John P. Kotter wrote in his book, *Power and Influence*, "Important changes that are shaping the nature of work in today's complex organizations demand that we become more sophisticated with respect to issues of leadership, power and influence."[124] In other words, as he recommended, look beyond the mere titles.[125] As for the decision makers for a cultural shift at your organization, they're easier to spot. If you're the CEO, you need to get buy-in from two levels: your board and your management team. If you are lower in your organization, you might have multiple levels up in which you will need to sell your vision. And, again, these people need to be persuadable—particularly the CEO—and you need to be close enough in rank to have the ear of this individuals. And among these influencers and decision makers, you need to identify those you feel will never be swayed to your vision of a more caring corporate culture. In other words, you want to find the detractors, so you: 1) won't waste your time on them, and 2) they won't work against you as you try to sell-in your vision. It's not that I am advocating you hide your vision from them. Instead, you simply need to figure out how to work around them as well as anticipate their objections and craft the arguments for overcoming them.

For larger companies, you might even want to segment influencers and decision makers by personality traits as well as behaviors before creating any messaging to answer their concerns and move their opinions and actions to a point where they embrace and advocate for a more caring environment. One powerful way to make a composite is through the creation of personas. When creating them, go beyond job titles and simple demographics such as age and income. Rather, look at their personalities, interests, and behaviors. Be sure to personalize each one with the brands they use, the people they follow, the performers they enjoy, the platforms they use, and more. And, of course, capture their motivations, priorities, and goals as well as the types of stories they want the world to know about themselves. You also want to identify their pain points. One more thing for decision makers: you also want to understand and capture how they make decisions, the criteria they use, and their trusted information sources. Do they ask questions of others and solicit lots of opinions, do their own research online, or just "go with their gut"? When creating a persona, you could also grab images and logos of their favorite brands, performers, hobbies, and more to give you a fuller picture of the individuals, further humanizing the descriptions. Finally, you should be sure to point out cultural differences, particularly for multinational companies. Be rich with your language and imagery, as you can always edit and cut back after you've identified all the important traits. The bottom line is that you want the descriptions to help you personalize the messaging.

Think about "nudging" them along the decision journey

Once you understand your influencers and decision makers, you will need to identify the steps that will "influence the influencers" and incrementally move the decision makers toward your vision. This won't happen overnight. When one makes a decision for cultural shift, it's unlikely that the decision makers will go from idea to complete implementation in one step. Rather, you'll probably need to take smaller steps along the way. As a result, in your plan, you'll need to break down the decision steps, which in marketing is called the path-to-purchase or the consumer journey. Let us call ours the path-to-decision or decision journey.

The best place to start when creating a journey map is at the end[126] with what you want your influencers and decision makers to think, feel, and do. Rory Sutherland, the vice chair of Ogilvy UK, likes to think of it like a traffic planner; they start at the destination and map backward to eliminate roadblocks.[127] Then you should refer back your personas to identify their current beliefs, feelings, and actions. Next, comes the hard part: identify all of the multiple, often nonlinear routes from today to your goal of where you want your influencers and decision makers to end up. If you start at the end, however, you can guess the most likely views and behaviors one would have right before it. Think of all of the options. You will probably be able to eliminate some once you have mapped the possible journeys. Repeat this approach at each point until you "map back" to the current perspectives and actions.

Then you need to think in terms of small steps and the choices you provide at each one to eventually get them to the decision to embrace a caring environment as well as the actions to advocate for one. Often called "nudge theory" from behavioral economics,[128] the idea is to make the desired choice the easier one, a strategy that can and should also be employed when designing your wellness programs. A common example is to think of dessert at a cafeteria. Right now, the pies and puddings are placed at eye level and are easier to reach (because of the higher profits they often produce for the establishment). But if you wanted to facilitate healthier eating, your designer would put the fresh fruit at eye level and make it easier to grab than the pies and puddings. After all, more people will grab the item that requires less work. Another common example is that people in the aggregate save more when they have to opt out of their employer's retirement plan then if they have to opt in.[129] You need to employ this approach to your goal of swaying influencers and decision makers. How can you make it easier to decide on advocating for a more caring culture than not advocating for one?

The secret is in the behavior. Remember, as I said in the previous chapter, we need to inspire our people to action. Driving behavior is important when you want to "nudge" people in a certain direction, because you will more likely change their belief systems in the process. That's because, as the trained clinical psychologist Adam Ferrier pointed out in his book *The Advertising Effect*, "action changes attitude faster than attitude changes actions."[130] Here's why, according to Ferrier: "The reason it works is through psychological principles including cognitive dissonance—we like our thoughts, feelings, and actions to be aligned. When you involve people in your mission through action, they adapt their thoughts and feelings to make sense of the action." This is key because as Ferrier points out, your actions are public while your thoughts and feelings are private. As a result, it's easier to change our thoughts and feelings to be in alignment with our actions, since our thoughts and feelings are not observable by the outside world. On the other hand, because our actions are public, they are harder to deny. What is your relationship with each individual? If you have a strong one, how can you expand it—a good idea no matter your goal—and who else has a good one with them and can advocate for your vision? In many ways, we do this intuitively, but in this instance, it might even make sense to be explicit about it. And finally, what kind of time investment would you need to make?

You have to be ruthless to end up caring

By completing the map, you can then identify your message and "activation" points, the places where you can nudge the influencers and decision makers. But you need one more thing: to review your organization's mission or purpose, vision, values, and even personality. I know we've talked about the importance of living the mission, brand purpose, and values for all of your employees, so you may need to adjust them as you transition to a caring culture. But now is the time you need to take another look at them for another reason: your brand foundation can either help you sway your influencers and decision makers or give them reasons to ignore your efforts. By reviewing them now, you can identify the ones that can help your cause.

Just as Amazon founder Jeff Bezos once purportedly said, "Your brand is what they say about you when you're not in the room."[131] Your culture is how your employees perform when you are not there as well. And your internal culture is based on your lived values—not on your stated ones found in your posters, handbooks, and website. Just look at the "values" of Enron. As I noted earlier, here's one they claimed to have embraced: "INTEGRITY: We work with customers and prospects openly, honestly and sincerely."[132] Clearly, with the collapse of the company and its outside accounting firm due to fraud,[133] as well as jail sentences for fraud of many of the leadership team,[134] they did not truly live it. So, a good place to start is to assess the values your leaders and employees are actually demonstrating. You can then compare them to the values your organization claims to embrace. What are the gaps? And which ones are more important?

ENRON'S COMPANY VALUES 2000

Communication

Respect

Integrity

Excellence

Enron's stated values, which they clearly did not live.

Then list the purpose and values you want the organization to embrace. If you're in the leadership position, you are in a position to change, tweak, replace, and even delete values. You must be truly ruthless. As William Falkner once advised, "In writing, you must kill all your darlings."[135] The same goes for corporate values. While you might not need to kill all of them, you can't be sentimental or hesitant because it sounds good. Rather, they need to be authentic to the organization—and actually "livable." I bring this up now because you should base your argument for the cultural transformation on your mission or brand purpose, vision, and values. At this stage, you need to identify the ones that can sway the influencers and decision makers to embrace your vision and help you achieve it. Keep in mind, at this stage, it's an organic process, so you can go back to deemphasize and reemphasize various selected influencers and decision makers; change your goals; and tweak your mission, vision, or values, until everything aligns.

Then, when building the story, be sure to make it personal by sharing the pertinent parts of your own life story. Explain how caring for a sick parent or child affected your work. Oftentimes, leaders hide big life events from their employees and peers, as they don't want colleagues to assume the personal event will take away from work performance. This not only creates a barrier that inhibits the building of close connections, but also stops you from socially modeling the appropriate performance in such situations. On the other hand, sharing your story can create powerful movements. Just think back to my friend Juliet de Baubigny and the nonprofit Beyond Type 1, which I mentioned in the previous chapter. The same kind of results and public victory can happen internally at your firm as well. And it's not just your stories but also the stories you collect of your coworkers, industry colleagues, and even those beyond your professional sphere. They will not only help you dramatize the points you're going make; they will also help you add emotionality to the process, which is key because most if not all decisions (it depends on the researchers you ask) are based on it.[136]

While the emotion of human stories is key, we also need the facts and figures, because once people decide, they then look for support to rationalize their decisions. Many of these figures are easy to obtain. We know, for instance, that the chance to get better workplace benefits is one of the three top reasons why millennials change jobs,[137] and a whopping 61 percent of employees are willing to accept a lower salary if the new company offers greater benefits.[138] What's more, in another study, 66 percent agreed that a strong benefits and perks package is the largest determining factor when considering job offers.[139] Meanwhile, 55 percent report that they have left jobs in the past because they found better perks or benefits elsewhere,[140] and 42 percent say they are considering leaving their current jobs because benefits are inadequate.[141] And, according to the human resource consulting firm Robert Half International, 73 percent of professionals they surveyed are seeking better health-and-wellness offerings from their employers.[142] On the other hand, companies with high investment in an internal culture of health experienced a 115 percent increase in their stock value, while the companies with a low investment in these areas grew by only 43 percent,[143] and at companies where managers showed sincere interest in millennials as people, the organization saw an 8x improvement in agility and a 7x increase in innovation.[144] You get the picture—actually two pictures:

1) that data to support your case is easy to find, and 2) that data just conveyed as a list without the context of emotional stories just becomes a sea of numbers that can either make your eyes gloss over or your brain tune out.

Your internal newsletter is not the answer

Once you understand the network of influencers and you have your stories and supporting figures in hand, now is the point to assess your communication and activation channels, craft your key message, and develop the initiatives that will sway and eventually convince the key players in your organization. While your internal newsletter is the vehicle to celebrate the successes after your cultural transformation, it's not the right place to start in garnering support for one. Rather, one of the best places I've found for you to start is with direct conversations, engaging those you'd identified as influencers, asking the hard questions, and using the Socratic method to draw them toward your vision. It's a give and take through the answers they give and follow-up questions you ask. The goal is to indirectly guide them to the conclusion, rather than directly aiming for a "close." In other words, you should be laying down the dots, so they can easily connect them. Or, in the words of advertising legend Alex Gossage, "When you build a mousetrap, be sure to leave room for the mouse."[145] Of course, their responses can help you refine your messages, and it might even inspire you to change or refine your vision. The point is to be open and authentic and to embrace the process. Then if your influencers come on board with your vision (or you are on board with their take on it), you can ask them to help with the cause. You can ask them to talk to the influencers and decision makers in their networks. Along the same vein, another opportunity is to engage your employees and peers in the effort by inviting them to tell their stories. You can either retell them anonymously or encourage them to speak up. Be sure to give them some ownership as well. And if you don't sway them, move on. You can't be successful with everyone. And some of them might help later in the process.

The vehicles for initiating your campaign are unique to each organization. In addition, a key channel for you to sway minds is conferences, both virtual and live. Encourage your influencers to attend conferences that cover workforce wellness and corporate cultures. There's nothing more powerful than outside experts making the same points that you are making. And, of course, you can use outside reports and studies. (By the way, the first part of this book can also serve as a powerful tool as well.) Just think of these documents as your internal form of content marketing. You can then share these reports, studies, and data on social media, particularly on LinkedIn, and particularly if you have a large number of internal contacts. Based on research into what is being called "social selling," an emerging technique for business-to-business sales,[146] this technique is a very powerful way to build relationships, get in early on discussions, and show that you are a thought leader. Best yet, it can provide what Robert Cialdini calls "social proof"[147]—a powerful form of influence where people change their behaviors and, thus, their beliefs—by seeing how others are performing or behaving in similar situations. Comments from friends and even thoughtful comments online (i.e., internal word-of-mouth marketing), celebrity endorsements, expert recommendations, and even the influencer marketing we talked about earlier, are just four of the many types of social proof you can use to help you add credibility to your approach.

Once you get the ball rolling, you might then need to prepare and deliver your formal pitch, whether to your board of directors or advisors if you are the CEO, or to the C-suite if you're a level or two below them. We'll talk more about it in the next chapter. In the meantime, you need to have the formal pitch in mind, because through the "nudging," you're leading up to it, so your key messages should be consistent. Aim to keep it simple—and as short as possible. For instance, Airbnb's initial VC Pitch deck was reported to be only about fourteen slides long.[148]

In your presentation deck, start with the problem, or if the problem is clear to your audience, with the promise of a solution through your vision of the future. You should address assumptions and common practices that cost money and morale without actually generating any of the promised savings. And you should lay out the proposed steps and projected costs to move your organization to the "promised land." Whenever possible, use visuals—charts, graphs, and images.

Some final thoughts: don't oversell. When people show that they are in agreement with you, confidently acknowledge it and start talking about the next steps. I've seen too many people ruin the "sell," no matter the topic, because they have continued with their points after they have received signs of agreement, which results in the listeners starting to question your points. They become unsure. No matter the value of your goals and the validity of your points, the listeners start to wonder about them. They might even begin to think that you are hiding something. Remember, as I stated earlier, people decide emotionally and then look for the rational support. And overselling can override the emotional decision, which no amount of rational support can overcome. As you're making your points, be sure to ask lots of questions. Not only can it help people see your answer; it can serve as a feedback loop to let you know they're in agreement. After all, your goal should be to get people in agreement as soon as possible. But what makes a great question? And how do you get your prospects into agreement? Well, that's the topic for the next chapter. Stay tuned and join me again in a few pages. In the meantime, be sure to study the following guest perspective. I think it will help in your quest for creating a more caring organizational culture.

♥ ♥ ♥

Six Dimensions of Wellbeing and How Aetna Transformed Its Culture into One of Caring

A Guest Perspective by Kay Mooney, Former Vice President, WellBeing, Aetna, a CVS Health Company

Now let's hear from someone who has driven a transformation, Kay Mooney, who retired in 2019 as vice president of wellbeing, at Aetna, a

CVS Health company. At Aetna, she led a team responsible for integrating a holistic approach to wellbeing into their culture. Developed through a research partnership with Harvard T.H. Chan School of Public Health, they implemented a groundbreaking approach that looked beyond physical, emotional and financial health to include such determinants of wellbeing as social connectedness, purpose, and character strengths. With the data identified through the partnership with Harvard combined with internal studies, Aetna built solutions that reflected their holistic approach and helped employees, consumers, and communities achieve their best health. Before she starts, I'd like to point out that in her twenty-five-plus years with Aetna, Kay served in many leadership roles, including serving as chief of staff for the office of the chairman & CEO. Beyond CVS Health, Kay serves in many leadership positions, including on the board of directors for Pet Partners, the nation's largest organization committed to connecting people with the health benefits of animal-assisted intervention. She holds a bachelor's degree in mathematics from Penn State and is a fellow of the Society of Actuaries as well as a member of the American Academy of Actuaries. Here's what she has to say:

"When building the case for a wellbeing transformation, there are two main arguments that I've seen be fairly effective over time. Some companies and senior executives will gravitate to one or the other, and a growing number will embrace both. The first argument is focused on the war for talent. Millennials and Gen Zers are seeking out employers that will support all aspects of their wellbeing, and they are spurring employers to wake up and join that movement. Even today, it's a competition for talent both from an attraction and retention perspective. Employers are having to compensate with signing bonuses or higher compensation for the fact that they may not be a strong employer of choice. The second argument—one that definitely resonated at Aetna and many other employers that I've spoken to along the way—is focused on employee engagement and productivity. When employees are healthy and happy, they're more engaged, they are more productive, and they have lower turnover and lower health care costs. Think about it—if your employees are struggling with any of the dimensions of wellbeing, they're likely distracted. If employees are worried about how they are going to pay their bills at the end of the month, they are going to be distracted. If they are battling chronic conditions, depression, or loneliness, they are probably going to be distracted too. The personal issues that they're dealing with will take them away from focusing on your customers. They aren't bringing their full selves to work. You are not getting the full value of your investment in them. Your payroll is one of your largest line items. If you're not maximizing the value of that investment, you're hurting your bottom line.

"To embark on this type of transformation, ideally you get buy-in from the very top right away. If your CEO gets it, that's the most effective path to success. If she or he is not a believer, then it's certainly harder but it's not impossible. In that case, I recommend finding one to two key influencers that truly get it and also have the trust of the CEO. While data works in some business contexts—we all like to believe we're data driven—there will just be some senior executives that don't intuitively believe it and will discount the data, even if you have the most compelling facts and business case. You will hear it and I have heard it from people that say you can have data that can prove anything. So, it's absolutely critical that you also have the key influencers that can help sway the CEO. They tend to trust people over data. So, if they have a trusted adviser who gets it, the advisor can help the CEO understand why it is important. These trusted advisors could be internal or external. If you don't have internal influencers that buy in, encourage your CEO to talk to CEOs of companies who do embrace and understand this strategy, and ask them to share why it is working for their companies. They need to state what their company looked like before they adopted it and what it looks like now.

Aetna's six dimensions of wellbeing.

"Next, you need to define your wellbeing model to focus your efforts on the areas you believe will drive the greatest impact. For Aetna's transformation, we identified six dimensions of wellbeing, a model that we developed in partnership with faculty at the Harvard T.H. Chan School of Public Health based on their extensive research and also what we had been seeing in the work we were doing:

1. **Physical health:** I think this one is fairly straightforward: Are you getting enough movement in your day? Are you eating right and exercising? Are you sleeping enough?

2. **Emotional health:** Again, pretty straightforward and certainly an area where more and more companies are waking up to the importance of focusing on the emotional health of their workforce.

3. **Financial security:** Do you have the financial means to meet your life goals? Are you overly worried about your financial position? It's not about having an absolute net worth or income, because we all know that someone can make seventy-five thousand dollars a year and be entirely comfortable

and happy, and another person can make two hundred thousand dollars a year and be totally overextended and very worried about how they're going to meet their financial obligations.

4. **Social connectedness:** Do you have sufficient meaningful relationships in your life? When times are tough, do you have close friends or family members you can turn to? And when it's time to celebrate, do you have people that you can share in those great times? It's not measured by how many Facebook friends you have. It's about having a sufficient (defined by you) number of close relationships, which is very personal. This dimension is gaining more and more interest these days, not only in the senior population but also in the younger population. Even though technology allows us to be more connected than ever before, we are actually less connected and more lonely than ever before.

5. **Purpose:** Also gaining a lot of traction and interest is having a purpose that brings meaning to your life. Your purpose could be being a parent, having a meaningful career, practicing spirituality, etc. However you define it, it is what gets you out of bed every day and brings meaning and purpose to your life.

6. **Character strengths:** This last one is something that not many people are talking about, but our partners at Harvard said no wellbeing model is complete without it—and that is a focus on character strengths. It dates back to the Plato and Aristotle days. We defined this dimension as "having consistent thoughts and actions that contribute to the good of oneself and others." This is actually the only dimension that not only impacts your own personal wellbeing but also impacts the wellbeing of those around you.

"Here's a simple way to think about this dimension. If you spend your time doing what you are good at and what you enjoy, you will actually be happier, be more productive, and ultimately be more successful. Think about the year-end performance management process. Too often, managers spend the majority of the review talking about how to correct performance and skill gaps. I'm not suggesting that we shouldn't be improving gap areas, but I believe we should shift our focus to finding new ways to leverage employees' strengths. Not only will your employees be more successful, your company will be more successful as well.

"After getting buy-in from the top and defining your model, the next step that's really important in a transformation is laying the foundation around a culture of wellbeing. At Aetna, we laid the cultural foundation over a very long time. You can offer the greatest wellbeing programs and digital tools, but if you don't have the culture supporting it and its in alignment with your company values, employees are going to say it's not authentic to who you are as a company.

"To help drive the cultural proliferation, we leveraged local wellbeing committees and champions, people who are passionate about wellbeing and about cultural change, to take our enterprise strategy and make that relevant at a local level. We created toolkits that those committees and champions could leverage. We gave them best practices, talking points, and local data about what their employee population looked like and the struggles they were experiencing (without violating any privacy requirements), such as the percentage of employees getting flu shots, levels of obesity, and the percentage of employees contributing less than the company 401k match. In addition to the local data, we provided them with guardrails, so that they understood how far they could go, making it as easy as possible for them to implement the strategies locally. We knew if we attempted to implement the enterprise-level strategies exactly the same way in every location, it wouldn't be successful. And we had no shortage of people who wanted to help. It was exciting. We were up to thirty-five different locations (and growing) around the company with a full committee and an executive leader supporting, and well over 400 champions within a few years. In addition, we also identified wellbeing executive sponsors by business line; these people were one level below the people who reported to the CEO. And in really large businesses, they could be even one more level down. For instance, our CFO identified an executive in his organization who served as finance's wellbeing executive sponsor and who incorporated wellbeing strategies and goals into their three-to-five-year strategic goals. We did this for all of the major business lines and functions within the company. We were driving cultural change at an enterprise level, at a local level, and within a business unit level. The messages were consistent at an overarching level yet tailored by geography and business unit in order to maximize excitement and adoption.

"Our results were compelling. We found having a culture of caring and wellbeing fosters trust in an organization and leads employees to take more risks, be more innovative, and give more. We saw that when our employees are healthy and happy, they're more engaged, more productive, have lower health care costs, and have lower turnover. And we found that this cultural transformation led to our becoming an employer of choice which improved our talent attraction and retention efforts. Bottom line, I strongly believe that prioritizing the wellbeing of your workforce and instilling a culture of caring isn't just the right thing to do for your employees, it's the right thing to do for your business. Employers can do good and do well at the same time. These are not mutually exclusive. The companies and CEOs that really embrace this philosophy are going to be the ones that succeed going forward. And the others that don't are going to be trying to catch up.

Chapter 6:

MAKING THE PITCH

While there are myriad marketing books, multiday seminars, and well-respected executive MBA classes on making the perfect pitch and selling it in at multiple levels, there is one simple, tried-and-true approach that has never let me down. I developed what I call the 10-Step Mini-Deck Approach over the course of my twenty-plus years leading teams in nascent markets and industries where I had to convince the most sought-after talent and investors to join me on various journeys into the unknown. Whether attempting to attract my very first hire prior to launching eBay Canada way back in the first dot-com boom cycle before anyone had heard of it and when they assumed it was just a garage sale, or raising venture capital financing for Grokker fifteen years later when the pundits were still declaring that no one would pay for premium fitness, mindfulness, or nutrition video content, this blueprint has helped me lay out my vision in a compelling and concise manner.

Being concise is a relatively straightforward concept, but as famously expressed in Mark Twain's requoting of French mathematician and philosopher Blaise Pascal, "If I had more time, I would have written a shorter letter," it is far more difficult than it sounds. But being concise is of utmost importance when it comes to selling to executives at multiple levels as well as reaching frontline employees. While you may have thirty minutes to present your material, you'll actually have just approximately five minutes[149] at the very start to captivate your audience if presenting in person, and six seconds if presenting online,[150] which is one second shorter than the attention span of a goldfish.[151] The key to brevity in this context is to reverse engineer the telling of your story. You start with the punchline and your key takeaway, their emotional reaction, and their intellectual pay off. Then you can home in on the core of your message and create your story brick by brick, stripping away all the extraneous variables to carefully craft it until only the most important information remains.

Once you've gotten the pitch down to the essentials and are confident the length can hold the audience's innately short attention span, you then have the far greater challenge of making it interesting. While you're passionate about the subject matter, your listeners will have competing priorities, perhaps even a bias against investments in culture or employee experience that you may need to overcome. I recall a New York City meeting in 2002 when I was about to pitch the eBay platform to the CEO of one of the largest high-end Fifth Avenue retailers. The CEO told me flat out before the meeting even really began that he had been in the fashion business for twenty-five years and that in spite of my enthusiasm, e-commerce would never be a significant factor in retail and that his customers were far too sophisticated to shop on an erstwhile flea market–type website. He shared two preexisting biases: 1) e-commerce was not worth his time because it would not be a revenue driver, and 2) eBay was a down-market site that would never attract his existing high-end customers. Fortunately, he was not my first retail CEO pitch, and these were now well-known biases to me. Having anticipated this, I cracked a joke about how we should place a wager on the ten-year future of e-commerce. I went on to say that my rationale for his company listing on eBay was not about increasing current top-line revenue or reaching existing customers but rather about dropping millions of dollars to their bottom line by reducing excess inventory through selling marked-down goods on eBay to less affluent customers who would never step foot in his stores in the first place nor pay full price for in-season merchandise. But these customers would gladly pay ten times more than the wholesale liquidators from which they currently bought their end-of-season goods. It was a win-win. He could keep his biases and still decide to partner with eBay. It would have been a futile exercise to try to convince him that he was wrong, and frankly, most people don't like being shown they are wrong, so if you can figure out the bias and work around it, well, that is the highest percentage winning strategy.

For a presentation to be interesting to a wide variety of audiences, it needs to connect with each individual irrespective of their preexisting conceptions. It should provide an experience that feels inviting to all and not be preachy or patronizing. Your goal is to win people over, not tire them out or force them to submit. This requires patience and a healthy dose of confidence. It also requires unconditional positive regard for your audience, and that means you have to come at it from an assumption that their intentions are pure and even noble. A few traps to watch out for: be careful to minimize the use of acronyms and avoid insider industry-speak that may alienate your listeners or undermine your message. It should be drop-dead easy to follow your presentation. Don't make your audience work to keep up, and everything should flow naturally. It should convey positive energy and illustrate that something exciting and inherently good is underfoot. It must also be emotionally resonant and click at a deeper level with your audience.

This is why the most compelling presenters infuse their presentations with stories as well as statistics, graphics, charts, arresting imagery, and all manner of visuals beyond plain old copy. As Dr. Murray Nossel, a member of the teaching faculty at Columbia University, wrote in his book *Powered by Storytelling: Excavate, Craft, and Present Stories to Transform Business Communication*, "Anyone can break down barriers and spark a culture of connection and collaboration with a communication method rarely seen in the office—storytelling."[152] Nossel's research and numerous other studies show that storytelling creates interpersonal connections that are more profound, enduring, and resonant. The author of a 2014 *Harvard Business Review* article entitled "The Irresistible Power of Storytelling as a Strategic Business Tool"[153] carefully explains how strategic storytelling is "enlisted to change attitudes and behaviors," and goes on to illustrate how "the most successful storytellers often focus listeners' minds on a single important idea and they take no longer than a 30-second Superbowl spot to forge an emotional connection." Connecting, resonating emotionally with your audience is the goal, and given that you have precious little time in which to do that, your pitch will in fact need to tell a story, be succinct, and be memorable. This is not nearly as daunting as it may appear at first blush. As long as your core message is authentic and you are passionate about the objective, all you need to do to create compelling, persuasive business cases for any audience is follow my 10-Step Mini-Deck Approach™:

Step 1. Start big

Knowledge is best retained when structured into larger ideas. These larger ideas are then emphasized as the focal points from which further learning is derived. Rather than creating a list of relevant facts and piecing them together, research on the effective transmission of knowledge reveals that the most effective strategy for the conveyance of knowledge is to organize around core concepts, a.k.a. Big Ideas. By framing your pitch around the most important and impactful concepts, you can delve into more powerful potential outcomes and arguments than you could if simply sharing a laundry list of facts and figures. So, start BIG. What is the Big Idea, and why should your audience care? What is the backdrop/context for your Big Idea in your industry, what is on the precipice of change, and how big is the impact going to be? Use whatever credible data you can get your hands on to substantiate your claims, including industry reports, competitors' public filings, analyst presentations, government data, and more. This becomes your big reveal—your "ta-da" moment—when you show that you can secure your company's reputation as a great place to work and increase productivity while simultaneously reducing employee stress and helping them improve their holistic wellbeing.

Step 2. State the inarguable

Now that you have painted an awe-inspiring picture of a powerful future state, it's time to pave the access road with a smooth surface. You can do this by setting out what everyone can agree upon. Since people are most comfortable with what they already know as well as with the common and accepted point of view in their industry, simply lay out the incontrovertible facts to build your case. This provides welcome aircover and a safe route. Then, once you have established the facts that everyone agrees upon and have underscored how this is either negatively impacting your company or presenting a unique opportunity for you to act upon, you can introduce your solution. But how do you make your audience feel safe when you are introducing new ideas and concepts? You use an approach employed by many successful advertisers. Think about how many breakfast cereals are sold on Saturday-morning cartoon commercial breaks. Everyone can agree that the whole fruit, glass of milk, and wheat toast are indeed in keeping with the Food and Drug Administration guidelines, but how is the bowl of sugar-laden breakfast cereal qualifying? The answer is in the technical legal language, "part of this complete breakfast." The cereal doesn't add anything other than calories to the meal, but it is certainly part of the complete breakfast meal—approved by the trusted FDA, no less—and hence gives parents the comfort that the cereal is a safe food to feed their children. By stating the inarguable, the FDA sets out guidelines for nutrition and is a trusted source of information and has established what a complete breakfast can be. Our sugary breakfast cereal is part of this complete breakfast, so you can trust that it is safe, period. It is this same simple technique that can also be used for good to put people at ease and bring them along with less resistance. Using some data we referenced earlier, here is a sample argument (Note: the bolded items can be the points on your PowerPoint slides):

Voluntary turnover, the $1 trillion problem.[154] And the most astounding part is that most of this damage is self-inflicted. According to the Bureau of Labor Statistics, average annual employee turnover is 26.3 percent overall, and the cost to replace an employee is estimated at anywhere from 33 percent to as much as two times the annual salary of an employee when the costs of lost productivity, plus costs to fill the vacant position, onboarding and orientation costs, and productivity ramp-up costs are all taken into account.[155] In a five-hundred-person company like ours with a $45,000 average salary, the annual cost of turnover can add up to over $5 million per year.

Turnover costs are more than financial. Losing our highest performers isn't just an inconvenience, it is a threat to the future of our entire organization. Left unaddressed, the brain drain of the regrettable turnover can permanently damage a company's reputation, as we witnessed happen to (name a company), and leave us vulnerable to poaching from competitors like (name a company), who are recruiting heavily in the area.

Turnover is preventable. The good news is that over half of employees who leave voluntarily report that their company or manager could have prevented them from leaving by addressing their concerns prior to their departure. Otherwise said, it isn't too late until it is. In fact, half of those who leave their jobs voluntarily say that no one asked them at any point in the ninety days prior to their resignation whether they were satisfied with their jobs or their future prospects. It's hardly surprising if no one is speaking to you about your present or your future that you might be interested in looking elsewhere to secure both.

Okay, so this was the inarguable part. Nothing controversial and everyone is buying in and everyone is nodding in agreement. You can sum it up by saying: "As you can see, turnover is ridiculously expensive in both financial costs and organizational impact. Of course, it is also largely preventable, and we can have a fair degree of control over it. We are not powerless. It is terrible to not even speak to employees about their careers and just let top performers walk. We can all agree."

Then you follow the glide path to introduce your simple yet effective idea that will ensure you don't fall prey to this problem or that you take full advantage of this opportunity. For instance, you can say: "This is why it is absolutely critical for managers to have easy-to-implement development plans put in place for all employees and to carry out simple and effective quarterly discussions with all employees. We just can't afford to risk the future of the business when such a simple solution is at our fingertips."

Step 3. Unique vision, approach, solution—what is defensible?

After you've shared your Big Idea and gotten buy-in regarding the obvious challenges facing your company by stating the inarguable, it is time to set out your unique vision and approach to solving it. You'll want to focus on what makes your solution different, more effective, and ultimately defensible. You are seeking to convey the particular edge that your approach brings to the opportunity and separates it from the lesser alternatives.

Your vision must be personally authentic to your motivation, consistent with your corporate values, and easy to grasp. Back when I was developing the business case for Grokker, there was no such thing as an expert-led video wellbeing solution providing employees with programs tailored to their interests, abilities, and goals, but I could articulate my vision of enabling physical, spiritual, and emotional wellbeing globally, and then delve into my unique approach of combining 1) patented premium video, 2) experts in a variety of wellbeing topics ranging from fitness to sleep to nutrition to financial, and 3) a robust community at the core to help people of all ages, skills, and abilities move more, eat better, reduce stress, sleep better, and holistically take care of themselves whether they had five or fifty-five minutes. Which would be on any device, any time, any place. This mattered deeply to me as I had been struggling with managing my own personal wellbeing as the busy mom of three children. Similarly, you will have to pare your vision and approach down to what you know to be the most compelling drivers of the change you are proposing.

In the case of Grokker, we explained that you cannot copy our videos because they are patented, and it would take someone years—if ever—to figure out how to try to mimic our quality at our low-cost base; that our approach is 100 percent future-focused, delivering anytime, anywhere, any device including devices you haven't heard of yet, but we know about; and that our experts will drive engagement and create a healthy self-reinforcing cycle of interaction with our viewers. We remind them that we built Grokker with community at our core to encourage support and dynamism and that our three pillars of Content, Community, and Experts set us apart, delighted the end user, and will be defensible over time. You can apply this same approach to the solution you're trying to get adopted, simply adapting it to your vision, approach, solution, and defensibility.

Step 4. Competitive landscape

You'll be making the case for why this is a "need to have" rather than a "nice to have" in your competitive environment. You are setting the scene for why it is far riskier to not offer this to your teams than to go ahead and add it. You need to motivate with fear here. It is very important to lay out what your competitors are doing and make sure you emphasize the importance of staying a step ahead or not being left behind. The point you need to get across is that the train is leaving the station, and you're going to ensure that your company doesn't miss out altogether You can use examples from other industries that have been earlier adopters or examples of similar phenomena to make your point. For example, if you were advocating for telehealth benefits, you might start by showing how video interview software was initially adopted in the early 2010s in your industry. You could then share statistics on the adoption of the telehealth benefits you are advocating for among your top competitors as well as survey data from employees and industry sources backing up the importance of this particular benefit to employees as well as why. Data doesn't lie.

Step 5. The dream team

Beyond having the Big Idea, inarguable logic, a compelling vision, and competitive intelligence that makes it clear you must act quickly, you will also need to convince your audience about why it is that you will succeed and who has the expertise internally to make it happen. This is where you elevate the power of the people in your company and let them shine. We seldom take the time to sing the praises and remind our superiors of the resumes and impressive accomplishments of those with whom we work. This is the time in the presentation where you break out the roles-and-re-sponsibilities chart mapped to faces with mini bullet pointed skill sets that will fill your audience with confidence and pride in the team you have assembled at all levels to implement the plan. These are people that man-age, report to, and work alongside the audience you're presenting to, so they are already largely trusted and known. You are merely refreshing their memories and underscoring why this project is going to succeed.

This is also where any words of support or encouragement from the C-suite should be skillfully dropped into your presentation in quotations with proper attribution to convey support for your idea. This need not be a direct endorsement but can be a general quote regarding an underlying principle taken from an earnings call or company meeting. The key is to convey support for the core principle and by association the team you have amassed to execute the vision.

With confidence in the team that will be tasked with implementing the plan, you'll find it much easier to gain approval and green light your project from the powers that be. If you curate your team with a variety of well-established, well-liked, and well-respected individuals, you will find that their very involvement will elevate your pitch. Much like any political campaign, if you want people to join your movement, you need influenc-ers that your constituents know and trust to be stumping for your candi-date. So, stack the deck in your favor with the influencers in your company that will lend credibility and curry favor with decision makers. After all, everyone wants to be part of a winning team. All you need to do is amass the team of known winners and invite your audience to be your sponsors.

10-Step Mini Deck Approach™

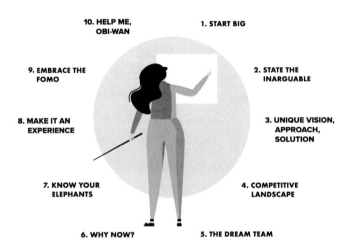

If you paint the future that prospects want and help them visualize the ambitious outcome, they'll be able to see it and feel a part of it, and they'll ultimately want to help create it.

Step 6. Why now?

One of the most important questions to answer in any business presentation is, "Why now? Why is it imperative that action be taken at this moment as compared to any prior time?" If you can show why your project needs to be seized upon with a sense of urgency, you're well on your way to gaining approval. Perhaps there have been recent shifts in the employee landscape that research shows will have significant impact on your ability to attract and retain top talent if you fail to proactively address the opportunity. Maybe your competitors have already begun to consider similar innovations, or you are seeing them in an adjacent industry and have a limited window to lead the trend in your market. As the great hockey player Wayne Gretsky said when asked about his secret to winning, "Skate to where the puck is going to be."[156] As an innovator, your role is to foretell the change that is already in motion before others can see it. While I often say that being early and being wrong can feel exactly the same, your task is to help your audience see the future and how your plan prepares and protects the company and your employees for it, but they must act now, or the opportunity will be lost. Of course, this is when the second famous Gretzky success quote comes into play: "You miss 100 percent of the shots you don't take." In other words, it isn't enough to see the future, you must act quickly and decisively. It is that simple.

When I was launching Grokker back in 2012, what was clear to me was that with the proliferation of smartphones, tablets, and connected TVs, the appetite for premium video was going to increase materially and that consumers who had been trained to pay for scripted content on Netflix and HBO would willingly pay for valuable lifestyle content to help with their physical and emotional wellbeing, as would employers who needed highly engaged and productive workers. At the same time, the trend of fitness as an industry and the massive increase in reported stress and anxiety among workers of all ages portended a future where video that addressed holistic wellbeing and was available on demand, anytime, anywhere on any device would be of great interest and need on a global scale. The convergence of these two trends—1) mobile device penetration, and 2) the insatiable appetite for video with the willingness to pay for premium content—presented a sense of urgency for me to launch Grokker and master both the reengineering of video production and the creation of a new holistic wellbeing solution designed for the enterprise. There was a clear answer to "Why now?" and I had the perfect vantage point to see into the future, which I then painted for investors as well as to employees I recruited and the experts I approached as we began shooting our first fitness, yoga, nutrition, sleep, financial wellness, and mindfulness programs.

Brian Chesky, cofounder and CEO of Airbnb, tells a story about the critical importance of timing to the success of his company launching on a national scale.[157] "In the summer of 2008, all anyone was talking about was Barack Obama. And the Democratic National Convention was coming up, and they had moved him from the twenty-thousand-seat Pepsi Center to the eighty-thousand-seat football stadium where the Denver Broncos play. Suddenly, all these mainstream media outlets are saying, 'Where are we going to stay?' And we're like, lightbulb goes off: 'They're going to stay at Airbnb! Obama supporters can host other Obama supporters all over the world.' " Brian then decided to try to attract attention for his Airbnb service by creating a collectible breakfast cereal which he called Obama O's, The Breakfast of Change[158] and hand-built thousands of cereal boxes with a hot glue gun that he then sold online for forty dollars per box. The cereal boxes sold like wildfire during the Democratic National Convention and helped keep the fledgling start-up afloat at a time when Brian and his cofounder had each run up tens of thousands of dollars in credit card debt. By anticipating an unmet need, Airbnb was able to take advantage of knowing where to be at the right time in order to offer the right product to the right people and delight them. But if you can't answer "Why now?" ask yourself: what harm would it do to the company and our employees if I wait? Then list all the good it would do, all the benefits that would inure to the business if you acted now as opposed to later. It is the opportunity cost of waiting that you need to capture and capitalize on.

Step 7. Know your elephants

A big lesson I have learned in business is that I have far more to learn from those who disagree with me than from those who concur. However, most people are conflict averse and don't want to tell you they dislike your ideas or point out where you are wrong, so this can be tricky. For instance, some investors, analysts, and industry experts agreed with my vision, which was fortunate for me and for them as it turned out, but others did not. One expert investor told me back in 2012 that he didn't believe that consumers or employers would ever pay for premium lifestyle video when they could just get it for free on YouTube and that quality didn't matter on the internet because it wasn't like TV. He believed that TV would continue to be dominated by traditional studios generating scripted shows supported by brand advertising, not subscriptions, and that internet content would be relegated to indie vloggers shooting cheap torso and tail content on their phones with a smattering of higher-quality video that no one would end up paying for. He didn't buy into the future vision I was seeing. Rather than wasting energy trying to convince him, I decided to get curious and use the meeting to fully hear his objections, draw out his criticism, and learn from them to be better prepared for future meetings. I've found the best way to encourage someone who disagrees with you to share their rationale fully and productively is to drop your defenses and approach them as an unbiased investigative reporter who is merely seeking to understand their perspective. I have learned to employ a number of phrases that invite feedback in a constructive fashion and use them liberally in conversations when I am trying to assess weaknesses in my argument and uncover the objections:

- "Tell me more about that."
- "Hmmm, I hadn't considered that fully, is there more?"
- "What else am I missing?"
- "Why might someone feel this is risky?"
- "What are examples of similar attempts that have failed?"
- "What would you need to believe to be compelled?"
- "What part of this did you find the weakest?"
- "Where is my logic flawed?"
- "What will smart people think but not want to say to my face?"
- "How could I improve upon this?"
- "Who else do you recommend I speak to in order to learn more about this?"

Once you have uncovered the objections and rationale, you can prepare your responses. In fact, what I recommend is by anticipating objections, you weave into your pitch the countervailing arguments that neutralize the objections before they ever come up. Consider those early objections I uncovered that no one would pay for premium fitness, mindfulness, nutrition or sleep videos. Rather than just wait for the objection to be made, I made sure that early in my investor deck I shared a side-by-side screencast of a premium Grokker video experience, including the search, filter, and playback and the experience of a similar search, filter, and playback on YouTube. I also shared data on the explosive growth of the global wellbeing market, the paid consumer video market, consumer attitudes toward this importance of premium video quality, their willingness to pay for video, and select industry report statistics. Essentially, I made the case that premium quality matters to the consumers, that Grokker produces mass amounts of premium video across a wide variety of wellbeing categories at unprecedented low cost, that we held patents we could enforce to do so at scale globally, and that this was a key to the future success of what would become a mass market category that had yet to emerge. Eventually the objection just stopped coming up at all because it was prehandled in the pitch.

Anticipate the most likely objections to your proposal, research them well, and be prepared to respond thoughtfully but not defensively to neutralize them.

Of course, not all objections can be successfully dealt with in this fashion. This is why you need to know what they are and be prepared to address them. The best advice I ever received on objection handling came from a dear friend and mentor in the early days at eBay, known to all as Uncle Griff. Griff was an early community manager, and he taught me how to anticipate and respond to the predictable and often aggressively posed questions journalists would always ask me in on-camera interviews about fraud on eBay. As you can imagine, fraud was the big fear consumers had about trying eBay in the early days. Not only was e-commerce brand new as a concept, but buying used goods and collectibles from strangers, sight unseen, on a virtual garage sale was a daring and, for many, a scary proposition. Gaining consumer trust was mission critical to eBay's success. I dreaded getting the "gotcha" tone of the fraud question, and I would reply defensively, refuting that fraud was a significant issue at all (in truth, it was not at all as the eBay community was very successful at self-policing, but the issue was greatly overblown by the media) until Griff pulled me aside and took me to objection-handling finishing school. He taught me to start off by thanking the journalist for raising this important issue as trust and safety was critical to the success of eBay and to the livelihood of the hundreds of thousands of small businesses owners who operated stores on eBay, so we took the issue very seriously. Then he coached me to continue like this: "In fact, eBay is extremely proud that 99.9 percent of all transactions are successfully carried out on the platform without incident, and that is not a coincidence. The feedback system that allows every buyer to rate every seller they transact with and leave comments on the interaction for all other community members to read ensures absolute transparency and encourages positive behavior. Sellers with high feedback ratings garner higher prices for their goods and this in turn has a very positive impact on everything from sellers' response times to questions from buyers to the inclusion of handwritten thank-you cards in packages when goods are shipped. This is all part of what makes the eBay community so special and safe. We have even had couples fall in love and get married after meeting through a sale on eBay." Griff taught me to expect the question and to embrace it as a strength of eBay's so that anyone concerned about fraud would hear the answer and dismiss it as a reason not to give it a try.

Step 8. Make it an experience

My seven-year-old nephew knows how to create a PowerPoint presentation. He can add numbered bullets and colored font for emphasis. An accomplished Roblox player and naturally adept software user, he also figured out how to add sound clips, high-res images, and video snippets he found online. Best of all, he decided to create an avatar of himself and bring a book report to life by narrating each slide of it through the eyes of this character. He learned this in first grade when mastering how to write book reports during a COVID-19 statewide school closure. I dare say his presentation skills are superior to many of my former colleagues, whose ho-hum, copy-heavy decks I've had to sit through with the aid of various caffeinated beverages during the course of my career as an executive. Take a cue from a first grader and make it a shared experience.

As part of making it an experience, you need to enable your audience to visualize the outcome of your proposal. Alan H. Monroe created a model for organizing highly persuasive speech, in which the penultimate step is to help the audience visualize a better future where the problem has been solved.[159] "In essence, the visualization stage is where a speaker can show the audience why accepting a specific attitude, value, belief, or behavior can positively affect the future."[160] Of course, you must be sure to demonstrate how this future benefits your intended audience, for without the nexus to them directly and personally, there is no persuasive punch. Visualization can be effectively employed in two different ways: 1) depicting a uniformly positive outcome or 2) a disquietingly negative one.

When using the positive method of visualization, you will want to show exactly how adopting your proposal will lead to a better future for your company and your audience; for example: "If we offer preventive on-demand video mental health benefits, we'll have healthier, happier, more productive, and resilient employees who love working for us. Our employees trust that we have their backs and that we value their mental health. They do not feel there is a stigma at our company around mental health and feel that they can safely speak to their managers if they need help. Our employees work through their struggles and bounce back more quickly because they feel supported and understood. They work harder and feel greater loyalty. They refer their friends and are brand advocates for the company. And they value us as an employer because they feel valued as whole people in return. This virtuous cycle enables our employees to be more creative and innovative and to care passionately for our customers, which helps make us more competitive even in difficult economic times. Therefore, by providing preventive video mental health benefits, we are a more resilient and profitable company whose managers are respected and admired by their teams for being compassionate."

Conversely, the negative method of visualization is where a speaker shows how not adopting the proposal will lead to a worse future: "If we don't provide preventive on-demand video mental health benefits, our employees will suffer in silence, be less productive, struggle to meet the demands of their lives, and be dissatisfied with their work and with us as their employer. They will hide their mental health struggles from us for fear of how this will impact them in the eyes of their managers, who count their missed days as evidence that they lack commitment. Our employees fear retaliation and water cooler gossip by their colleagues. They feel hopeless in the face of overwhelming emotional turmoil, which they attempt to suppress in vain, not knowing where to turn for help or treatment. They are unable to complete their work even when they clock in, as their inability to focus increases week to week, and adds to our already exorbitant costs of presenteeism while they hide behind blank, expressionless faces, pretending to be all right. They visit the ER as panic attacks begin to overwhelm them and are prescribed anxiety medication and three weeks of bed rest to recover with no counseling or long-term plan. Months of this back and forth from medical leave will ensue, with employees never sharing what is actually going on and their managers now pitted in an adversarial position against their subordinates, and the whole while, the company never knowing how they might have been able to help prevent this downward and costly spiral."

Finally, your visualization can also include a combination of both the positive and the negative in order to offer your audience both possible outcomes and let them decide which one they would rather have. Whatever you choose, your goal is to end with your audience thinking, "Yes, I can see it. I am at the vanguard of this seismic shift, and I will take action to secure the positive future outcome that benefits me and my company."

Step 9. Embrace the FOMO

Now that you have laid out your Big Idea with the inarguable rationale, your unique vision, defensible capabilities, urgency of timing, and competitive landscape, while anticipating the likely objections and helping your audience visualize a better future as a result of supporting your plan, it is time to make it crystal clear that this is their only opportunity to join your noble movement because it is already in motion. The term FOMO, or Fear of Missing Out, was first coined in a 2004 Harvard Business School magazine op-ed[161] that cleverly poked fun at the social life of a Harvard MBA student constantly juggling the opposing forces of FOMO against FOBO, or Fear of a Better Option, coming along. This may sound trite, but applying the psychological pressure of FOMO is an effective technique and one that is often essential to ultimately garner support for your proposal. It is the social pressure that results from an exclusive and time-limited opportunity to be part of a positive collective experience. Fear of missing out on the proverbial train leaving the station, combined with the desire to be part of the in-crowd already on board can drive decision-making in your favor.

Start by showing who has already bought into your proposal. Name drop and list quotes from a few key influencers about why they love the idea—the more influential and senior the better. Not only will others want to be part of this impressive crowd, but this kind of social proof will help persuade your audience that failure to back your idea may be a mistake they live to regret.

Next, create scarcity and share the credit. Another effective technique is to create a limited number of high-profile, low-effort leadership roles to enlist your internal advocates to help you spread the word. Think of these individuals as goodwill ambassadors who share a passion for your mission. With a small time investment, they will excite and enlist others around the cause. The key here is there can only be a small number of people included in this exclusive group, and there must be a recognition of some sort, be it a public acknowledgment at a companywide meeting, attending a major presentation with C-suite executives, or adding their names as a steering committee to a slide in your now visually compelling deck. By creating an opportunity for a subset of the team to serve the greater good in a visible yet low-effort leadership capacity, you can generate a lot of support with a modicum of effort.

Step 10. Help me, Obi-Wan Kenobi

Psychological, emotional, and social factors impact decision-making so strongly that Nobel Prizes have been awarded to economists whose works have established the "predictably irrational"[162] manner in which human judgment operates when influenced by stress, positive reinforcement, loss aversion, and a variety of other factors.[163,164] In other words, decision-making is radically influenced by the emotional, and the existence of emotional stimulus can override the normal, logical process of evaluation. So, when faced with decisions under stressful circumstances, such as time pressure, a person will narrow their attentional focus and naturally seek quick, decisive information to gain confidence so they can make a decision and move on. Rather than undertake a study of behavioral economics, I'll give you an effective shortcut to triggering the emotional response that will be most important to seeding support for your cause.

Tell your audience that you need their help and that without their support you cannot succeed in achieving your bold vision for the company and for your employees. They hold the keys; they have the power. There is no time to waste; they must act quickly and decisively. This is exciting, and this is the right strategy at the right time. Together you will secure this ambitious outcome. "Help me, Obi Wan Kenobi. You're my only hope."[165]

Getting People to Enlist in Your Vision: A Few Words That Can Deeply Impact Your Creation of a Caring Corporate Environment

A Guest Perspective by Geraldine Laybourne,
Inductee, Television Hall of Fame

A lot of people know how to create a vision but are unable to share it with the C-suite or the board and sell in the vision. Geraldine Laybourne is not one of those people. Gerry is a cable programming pioneer and visionary who knows how to enlist people to make her vision a success, which shows in her history of accomplishments: First, she led the team that created Nickelodeon and Nick at Nite. Then Gerry served as the president of Disney/ABC Cable Networks. Next, she cofounded Oxygen Media, which was eventually sold to NBC Universal. Her current focus is on the city of Poughkeepsie, where she is cofounder of DAY ONE Early Learning Community, which aims to create a model for early-learning opportunities. She is also working with MASS Design Group on community-oriented revitalization projects and is on the executive committee of the Poughkeepsie Children's Cabinet. Gerry currently serves on the board of directors of 9 Story, Common Sense Growth, Katapult Studios, and Betaworks; is on the board of Vassar College; and is vice chairman of the board of Vital Voices. She previously served on the board of directors at JCPenney, Electronic Arts, Symantec, Move.com, and Kindercare. In 2020, she was inducted into the Television Hall of Fame. Here's what she has to say about getting people to enlist in your vision and then getting people to follow it:

"When I started in business, I was given a test of many personal variables. I was off-the-charts high in empathy and listening and off-the-charts low in ego drive. I had very little promise as a salesperson. I was told I was in the lowest 10 percent. If I was ever going to 'sell' anything, I was going to have to do it through listening.

"I was at Nickelodeon for three years before they let me lead it. And during that time, I'd observed a lot of things and taken notes on my philosophy. I reported to a standard command-and-control alpha dude who felt like he had to have all the answers and didn't want any of us to know what other people were doing, so there were no group meetings. Okay, I am a nerdy, no-fault person, and I kept a notebook of what I would do differently when I got a chance to lead. I looked to build a team of people who wanted to work together to do something great for kids and were aligned in our mission. It had to do with trusting employees and getting out of their way. I also knew I had to get rid of the ones who did not play well with others and had to cancel out a third of our employees. I had some preconceived notions (like involving kids and trusting independent creators), but I didn't really know how we were going to succeed. I did know that if I shared the problem from the very beginning, however, I would have a better shot of succeeding. I'm not a top-down manager, but I'm a particularly good amalgamator. I'm good at listening to what everybody is saying and making sure people were heard and then be enthusiastic how ideas combine. I never had to sell a business plan to my team because we created it together.

"There were very few expectations with Nickelodeon. It was created to be a throwaway service to make cable operators popular in their communities. My company didn't think that it was ever going to make any money. My previous boss thought that the most that we'd ever make is five million dollars a year with advertising. Because we received very little financial support from corporate, there wasn't very much supervision of Nickelodeon. We were on our own, and they were tickled that we outperformed expectations, became a juggernaut and proof point that a kid's business was a really good business to be in.

"We grew quite quickly. I'd asked everyone who came to interview what they were like as a child. By asking it, I could really get lots of information about the person. It also helped them understand that I really cared about kids and that we're not going to sell kids out, we were going to do things that were fun and popular with kids. I had my supporters—Sumner Redstone, Tom Freston, and Frank Biondi, among them—and they all got a kick out of Nickelodeon. Once Frank Biondi dressed down an auditor for auditing a Nickelodeon show. It costs twelve thousand dollars to produce and it made well over a million dollars on each episode. He told the auditor that if she ever audited anything else on Nickelodeon again, he'd ask for a rebate of her salary!

"Oxygen was a different picture. It was 1998. We had to come up with a business that could attract investors. At the time everybody was excited about the internet and what it was going to do to change the landscape. We worked off of the idea of combining TV with the internet. Unfortunately, it was still a dial-up world where we were way ahead of our time, but we were able to attract investors like Paul Allen, Oprah Winfrey, Carsey Werner, and others. We built our internet business as fast as we could, but when the bubble broke in 2000, we had to pull back on the internet, which was terribly hard, because we had about five hundred employees, and we had to take apart the whole functioning team. That was heartbreaking. But we'd raised enough money to become a successful television network. I would say part of the reason why we were able to raise that amount of money was because Nickelodeon was incredibly popular with the cable operators. We made them look good. I also happened to like the cable operators—they're a very interesting, entrepreneurial group of people—and I spent time with them. They knew how much I liked them and how much I liked the industry. So, when we went for distribution, we got to be the last fully distributed analog television network. By the way, it's really a lot better to be the first of its kind in a category than the last. For Nickelodeon, we were the first kids' channel. There was no model of what a kids' channel should be. With Oxygen, we wanted to be the first convergence network, but we ended up being the last analog one. It sounds quaint now with the new order in the world, but your channel position was more important than programs in terms of ratings. Oxygen was able to get on a good channel position in New York City, and ratings were ten times higher in that market compared to others where we did not have a good channel position.

"Over my career, I tried different things. At Nickelodeon, executives could bring up topics they wanted to discuss that week and we'd vote on them, which was good in itself because it ranked what our priorities would be. We often spent more time talking about what we should talk about. We also had 'show-and-tell,' where people got to show off what they were doing. And at Oxygen, when we were failing and weren't getting any ratings, I knew that we were going to get slammed. I turned to my assistant Ed and asked, 'What do people want to know at our town hall?' He said, 'They want to know what to do when they go to a cocktail party and people say you're about to lose your job.' So, Ed and I did a skit for about three different town halls where I was the nasty neighbor saying horrible things about Oxygen, and Ed would have to defend it. It was very funny, and it showed that I was empathetic with our employees; I knew what was coming; I didn't have my head in the sand; and it wasn't a perfect launch. But nothing works all the time. There was a time where everybody at Nickelodeon wanted to be in every meeting. We'd grown from just twenty people to four hundred people. Everybody was in meetings all the time. I decided we should have recess every day at three o'clock. During recess, people were not allowed to be in meetings. Rather, they had to be in the hall.

"In terms of learning how to sell, I could think laterally and see opportunity, connecting things, and listen hard to what somebody else needed. Together with Sara Levinson (then head of new business for MTV Networks), we got Universal Studios Florida, which was just starting out, to build two soundstages, which cost close to twenty million dollars. Nickelodeon was not yet the juggernaut it became. We listened hard to the marketing challenges facing Universal in Disney's back yard; we suggested that we would hold audition and produce shows and market USF.

We promised, 'if you build it, kids will come and bring their parents!' It was a win-win.

One of my favorite bosses, Bob Pitman, would either like something right away or hate it. And when he would hate it, I would get him to tell me all the reasons he hated it, and then I'd leave his office. I'd never argue with him, because he would always win. He was faster. He was smarter. So, I'd go away with his list of why he didn't like something, and a week later or even two days later, I'd come back and say, 'I heard you on this, this, and this, but here are five reasons why I think we should go ahead.' Most of the time, he'd say, 'fine, do it, you listened to me.'

"I believe a big part of success is having fixed goals and a regular reporting system. I believe in that type of discipline and in everybody knowing what everybody else is working on, so they could all get a comprehensive picture. I also believe that a good culture is where everybody is looking out for each other and making sure that each other gets As and where the executive teams don't just see themselves as a department chair or a division president, but as CEOs in training, thinking about the business in total and making decisions based on it, not based on headcount or how many windows they have. Finally, over the years, I've come to believe in starting with a joint agreement on values before creating the goals. How did we want to operate? How did we want to treat people? How did we want to compete? What did we care about? I found that the conversations about the values they wanted to operate behind was as important as anything else.

"In many ways I'm disappointed with the fact that when women came into the corporate workforce, we didn't do a better job changing culture. Often, we tried to fit in more than try a different way to manage. It is curious now that most theories about effective management are expressed in 'female' terms (collaborative, nurturing, empathetic, customer-centric). People who feel that they're appreciated and celebrated do a much better job than people who are in fear that they're going to lose their job.

With one corporate board I was on, I really was troubled by the relationship it had with management. When I approached the chairman of the board about leaving the board, he said, 'You think the same way we do, You are just kinder.' And I said, 'I guess you can say I'm ruthlessly kind. I'm kind because it works. I'm kind because that helps people take risks and try things.'

Section Three:

CREATING THE CULTURE

Chapter 7:

MAKE CARING OKAY

Your board is on board. The senior management team has given their nod, a few perhaps hesitantly. But you'll take them. Now what? In chapter 4, we talked about how to care. As you recall, we explored the need to be authentic, inspire action, create a safe space for employees, make it personal, and give permission for them to take care of themselves. Now let us talk about how to inculcate wellbeing into your corporate culture, so your employees actually believe the organization is a truly caring one. How will you prove to your rank and file that your company cares about them and actively encourages their personal pursuit of physical and emotional health, as well as a sense of purpose, belonging, and balance? While it may seem like you have surpassed some huge hurdles with the previous steps, this one is probably your highest and hardest hurdle to overcome. Words alone won't do it. People today are simply too cynical, as most of us have likely been burned by empty promises as workers. As a result, you will need to show it, model it, and reinforce it.

The need for employees to feel empowered to take care of themselves became even more apparent to me during the COVID-19 pandemic when I read news articles about organizations putting pressure on employees to show up at work even when they were ill,[166] other reports on how many COVID-infected health-care workers lacking sick pay benefits were feeling pressure to return to work,[167] and a UK research study revealing that one half of employees feel pressure from their boss to go to work when sick, with one in fourteen saying they would go to work in spite of COVID-19 irrespective of the severity of the symptoms.[168] In fact, some large U.S. manufacturers, retailers, and health-care facilities were being sued "for gross negligence or wrongful death since the coronavirus pandemic began unfolding," according to the *Wall Street Journal*, as a result of their failure "to protect workers from the deadly virus."[169]

As an enlightened employer, you surely recognized the dangers of exposing your healthy workforce to the potentially deadly virus by an infected coworker. I am equally sure that you saw the inhumanity of compelling sick employees to come to work and the folly of failing to provide appropriate personal protective equipment and take steps to screen for and combat the virus. It shook me profoundly to learn that some sick workers were showing up to their workplaces out of fear of losing their jobs if they took a sick day. Like every other armchair epidemiologist, I even took a stab at calculating how many fewer people would have been infected in the United States if they had just stayed home. If employees inherently felt that they had the ability to take care of themselves, employers would not have had to explicitly state the expectation that COVID-19 symptomatic workers stay away from the workplace. Now, as a glass-half-full kind of optimist, my observation is that the need to make caring okay in the corporate setting became part of the collective consciousness during this scary and unpredictable time. Employers realized that their corporate survival was in fact reliant upon the holistic health of their workforce and the positive perception of them as a caring and trustworthy employer of choice by their workers. This put the worker and the employer on the same side of the wellbeing equation for the very first time, and I believe bodes very well for the future.

At the same time I do wonder how many higher-risk workers decided not to take advantage of the temporary accommodations afforded through the Americans with Disabilities Act[170] during the pandemic because they were afraid that it would hurt them later with their employer—even if these accommodations were low cost and easy to implement. In other words, I bet there were many, particularly among older workers who were taught to "suck it up," who put themselves at risk for a longer recovery period, complications, or even death because they perceived they'd put their job at risk.

This speaks to another issue that we explored earlier: a lack of trust among workers. Again, telling employees that they are going to be okay if they do something is not enough, because they have already been burned; rather, they need to inherently feel that they will be okay. In other words, it's not "giving permission" in some old-fashioned, paternalistic way of the benevolent boss. (I bet you can see him in a blue button-down shirt patting his obviously under-the-weather subordinate on the back and telling him to go ahead and take the afternoon off to rest.) Rather, it is having a true culture of wellness, so employees have the confidence to do what is right and healthy for themselves without explicitly needing to ask. And it's having the track record, so your employees will know that you'll stand behind your promise. If you want lower rates of absenteeism and presenteeism and, ultimately, improved bottom-line results, then you need a culture of wellbeing that makes it safe for employees to care for themselves and their families. This is the permission to which I am referring. This requires a feeling of honesty, security, and trust among employees. And this takes work, I admit, and might be beyond the current ability in organizations that experience a high or even an average rate of turnover in the C-suite, since the tenure tends to be so short. In fact, the average tenure in the C-suite, according to organizational consulting and search firm Korn Ferry, is 4.9 years,[171] so you might not have a lot of time to build your track record.

So, what are we to do to set the culture on the right path? It doesn't "just happen." It's not a happy accident, as I've found many believe. You must actively develop and nurture it. As you have surely gathered from previous chapters, it starts at the top. Likewise, both situations I just described can be fixed at the top. I like the ancient saying that a fish stinks from the top down[172] and, for organizations, I believe that this is surely true—any failure within a business can be traced to a failure at the top. Success also starts at the top too, because the leadership sets the culture. Without the proper culture, we're doomed. As the famous Peter Drucker line goes, "Culture eats strategy for breakfast."[173] I agree. We spend an amazing amount of time searching for the right strategies, and then refining them, socializing them, and operationalizing them. But if you don't have the right culture, even the best product, service, and go-to-market strategy won't save your business. The best way to inculcate culture is to take a cue from Anton Chekhov, the famous Russian playwright, who said, "Don't tell me the moon is shining. Show me the glint of light on broken glass."[174] In other words, "Show, don't tell." This seminal storytelling rule is just as important when you want to create the culture you desire. The mandate is to lead with action rather than exposition.

When "showing," you should start with your physical space. As Geraldine Laybourne, cofounder of Oxygen Media (and who we had just met in the previous chapter) pointed out to me, the office is the first key to the corporate culture. It all begins with the grand gesture of the lobby—first impressions, even for potential employees, matter—but it extends all the way down to the little things such as the touchless washroom sink faucets that work just as well with darker skin tones as they do with the lighter tones,[175] so everyone feels truly included and recognized. Think of all the various cultural messages your office setting conveys. Take your reception area: What does it say to your guests and employees as they enter? Does it make all people feel comfortable? How about your conference rooms? Are they tucked into private corners near where the executives sit and hidden behind floor-to-ceiling smoked glass promoting total secrecy, or are they more of an open-concept fishbowl in the middle of the floor where everyone walks by and can see the CEO taking customer meetings or whiteboarding new ideas? Are your workstations comprised of low cubicles where you can easily call out to colleagues or high dividers that provide maximum privacy? And what are all the physical accessibility features that you've designed into them? (Hint: Adaptive technology can actually help everyone.) What choices have been made with respect to color, lighting, and aesthetics? Are there spaces set up that encourage small or large groups to interact or gather socially? All of these things—and more—convey what you value.

Some businesses don't have a cue

In the marketing world, what I just described are called cues. Cues are a simple concept. They are unstated signs that a behavior has taken place, or that a brand promise has been, or is being, fulfilled. My favorite example of a generic cue is one that we have all encountered at hotels. How do you know that your room was cleaned? The answer: that cleverly folded sheet of toilet paper that some origami-trained housekeeper left in your bathroom. Another example: Instead of saying that their drive-thru is fast, McDonald's aims to have their crew hold the take-away bag out of the pick-up window as the customer drives up to it. This fast-food chain has even used this imagery in their television commercials and, as I understand it, are so committed to it that they made some of their drive-thru lanes longer so that they could better fulfill on the promise.

Cues can also be used to help distract people from anxiety-producing situations, actions that take longer than comfortable, and other forms of uncertainty, so that people can focus on their ultimate goal instead of the inconvenience of the immediate situation at hand. Anyone who's traveled through the United Airlines Terminal 2 at O'Hare Airport in Chicago has experienced the seemingly endless walk through the long tunnel over from Terminal 1. If you have had the pleasure, as I had regularly while living in Chicago and traveling frequently for work, you might recall the music and faintly disco-evocative moving light show along the walls and ceiling, all designed to distract you from the tunnel's length. On a grander scale, if you've ever visited Disney World, you may have enjoyed countless hours being entertained by the immersive cues that set the stage for many of the rides. Before making your way to the best roller coaster, Expedition Everest, which speeds you through the Forbidden Mountain and into an encounter with a mythical Yeti, you will trek through the regional tourism office, local shrines to the Yeti, and well-documented photo sightings, footprints, and newspaper clippings of the terrifying creature, all the while queuing for the ride but without even realizing that the cue is merely an exceptionally well-designed waiting room.

Use behavioral and physical cues, such as the light show United Airlines employs in the walkway between Terminal 1 and Terminal 2, to define your employees' experience.

You can develop cues for your organization to build and reinforce your culture by focusing your employees on the important details and distracting them from situations that might create uncertainty or undo stress. The place to start is your employee brand promise. What do you want your team to feel and authentically believe? Once you have clarity around the attributes of your brand promise, then you need to identify the signs that these promises have been fulfilled. Creating physical manifestations of those signs are your cues. If part of your brand promise conveys a sense of creativity and you want your team to feel and believe they are creative, how might you establish cues in the physical office space that reflect and reinforce this? Perhaps providing butcher paper and crayons on cafeteria tables, an on-site woodshop or pottery studio, free memberships to museums, subsidized art classes for all employees, a guest lecture series with visiting artists/writers/poets, open house nights where employees showcase their visual art projects, or any number of other ideas both low and high budget, local and international in scale, can be implemented as cues.

Of course, the most important cues are beyond the physical. Rather, they are the behaviors you and your leadership team express to your employees. The example set by the routine manner in which senior leadership conducts themselves is what truly sets the cultural tone. This in turn results in the behaviors and beliefs you accept and reward among your employees, and it informs the behaviors that your team expresses to your clients and customers. I believe it is these leadership behaviors during the execution of their day-to-day mundane duties that actually have the most influence in shaping and reinforcing the culture you want to achieve.

By observing how your leadership team conducts themselves in their daily work lives, you will see the behaviors and beliefs they are patterning, the cues they are establishing for your company. If you don't like what you see, you will need to make some big changes because when difficult challenges arise, you need to trust that the inculcated culture will ensure that leadership behaves in the manner you expect. Remember, culture is what happens when you aren't in the room.

Sharing is caring

During the pandemic, I found myself taking deep breaths throughout the day to help me keep focused on the myriad things I needed to do to manage my company and take care of my employees. I felt the pressure, fear, and strange isolation of sudden confinement at home, away from my colleagues and clients. One of the most effective things that I did to help my team cultivate and sustain a sense of community full of support, understanding, and togetherness, was to share my personal experiences as they unfolded, being honest about how much I missed our usual in-person camaraderie, and inviting them to join me in making the best of things. How did I do this? Well, like most teams, we were living on video conferences, so I asked my team to start each video conference meeting with about ten minutes of free-form personal chat to check in, talk about how we were doing, and have some laughs before delving into our fifty-minute business session. This ritual was much like the way we'd congregate at the coffee machine prepandemic or walk around the office to say hello on a normal day. I knew that it was these small, personal moments of interaction without an agenda that we were going to miss the most during the weeks of remote working. We had plenty of time to "get down to business," and we even enjoyed it more when we spent some time connecting as people, remembering what it felt like to be in touch with our humanity and not simply transacting as colleagues.

In addition, when none of us could escape the resulting stress and anxiety caused by the pandemic (even if one could escape from contracting the actual virus), I also scheduled a daily five-minute stretch break every afternoon, where I invited my team to hop on a video meeting to chat a little about the day. Some would have pets or kids in the room, which was really nice as it felt like we were sharing personal glimpses into our lives. Some would change their backgrounds daily, which became a topic of great excitement. Once we caught up, I led the team in a group stretch. Sitting on the floor or in my chair, I would do some much-needed back, hip, or shoulder stretches, in which everyone joined me. Or I played a short Grokker stretch video by sharing my screen, so we could literally unwind together. There was also a touch of smack talking (we're a competitive bunch) and a lot of encouragement (lots of coaching behaviors in our corporate culture) but most of all, we simply connected. The time we spent together was a true break, and we all felt a little bit better. At Grokker, we have long understood the connection between managing stress—whether physical, emotional, or financial—and maintaining a healthy immune system. It's why, at the start of the pandemic, we took immediate steps to provide support to individuals, nonprofits, and corporations by taking down our paywall when millions of people found themselves sheltering in place at home and struggling to balance family demands while working remotely for the first time and facing unprecedented global uncertainty. It's why we created a free three-part COVID-19 Coronavirus Preparedness program based on published recommendations from the Centers for Disease Control to make sure everyone had access to dependable information on containment and basic health practices, as well as managing stress and wellbeing. And it is why every team member then took turns leading the daily stretch break sessions I had started, which expanded to include everything from trivia and Pictionary-like games to stress relief and sleep enhancement. In essence, the whole team participated in the sharing of cues that reassured everyone that we were still connected and cared for in spite of our physical distance during the outbreak.

Parenting loudly (again)

In chapter 4, we talked about "parenting loudly." Let us spend some more time with it, because the concept of it is a key to setting the culture. I believe that employees need to see the struggles of the executives up your organization's chain of command—not just the struggles of their peers—and see that we're also imperfect human beings grappling with similar second-shift challenges. Encourage your senior leadership team, and even the midlevel, to share their stories, because it will help set the groundwork for making the workplace a safe place for everyone to share stories about home life as well as to swap ideas about caretaking. By having senior team members initiate the conversations around the realities of their own complicated lives, they will normalize the discussion for others and make room for real sharing without fear of judgement.

Keep in mind, it is not always easy to get executive buy-in for any change, particularly in the softer areas, even if your new approach is practically guaranteed to significantly improve the employee experience and the bottom line. That's okay, because at first, all you will need is just one executive "hero" to champion your new wellbeing culture initiatives. This key individual can positively influence other leaders and help get the entire management team on board. In fact, many companies, like eBay, link their cultural goals to each manager's MBOs[176], creating accountability while driving measurable results tied to employee engagement, retention, attendance, and productivity metrics. The former CEO of eBay, Devin Wenig, informally adopted the title of chief culture officer for the organization, the perfect example of a leader who walked the talk. Devin believes incredible companies have great cultures. Since day one as CEO, not only did he demonstrate the company's values through his leadership style, but he also held his management teams accountable for supporting cultural goals and for defining eBay from the inside out, earning him a slot as one of the most innovative leaders, according to Forbes.[177] Wenig's example shows that when managers are given the tools and incentives to promote wellbeing among their employees, the net result is a workforce that builds connections around wellbeing. This is where the "rubber meets the road" and employees become ambassadors for wellbeing and keep the culture infused with the fuel it needs to thrive.

But incentivizing and training managers is not enough. You'll then need to cascade the behaviors down from the top to everyone else in your organization. While conventional wisdom contends that effective leadership helps create the organizational results we seek and that nothing can take the place of C-suite sponsorship and, as we have explored, their active participation, when it comes to shaping an amazing culture, there is a danger that these behaviors stay at the top if your team only sees the senior management team taking advantage of the perks. To fully give "permission" for employees to care for themselves and inculcate the behavior into your organization, you will still need to have all employees showing their struggles and solutions and embracing self-care. In other words, you need to create "social proof" that your organization truly embraces wellness in all of its forms. As compliance guru Robert Cialdini wrote in *Pre-Suasion: A Revolutionary Way to Influence and Persuade*, "The great strength of social-proof information is that it destroys the problem of uncertain achievability."[178]

Like the management team, you can start with as few as one employee. It shouldn't be hard to find someone to showcase how she is embracing her self-care, and to inspire others to take up the charge. Remember, today's employees are asking for more than a paycheck but may need help figuring out how to make it work at your company, so go ahead and show them. Better yet, showcase employees doing all kinds of different self-care variations and being supported by their managers, or even with their managers. Since employees expect a partnership that's truly built on the way the world works today—both inside and outside of the office—I am sure you can find an employee and manager willing to be the example for others. The pandemic has shown that employees can be just as productive working remotely. And employees, particularly working parents, don't necessarily want to work in a traditional office setting or from nine to five. Find someone who embraces that attitude and let them show the others in your organization the results. Our head of product felt he wanted to spend more time with his family a few years ago but didn't want to stop working at Grokker, so we decided to promote one of his direct reports to take on greater responsibilities, and he reduced his schedule to three days a week. We got to keep his vast knowledge and killer sense of humor, and he got the flexibility he had been craving while retaining a professional challenge at a company he feels passionately about. Where are these opportunities in your company? They are the win-win situations that build world-class cultures and deliver enviable results. Because the structure of your business must answer the demands of life today, once you set the example, I am sure the rest of your team will begin to feel comfortable with taking advantage of "the permission" as well.

The benefits of growing your benefits

A big part of my strategy is to listen and evolve with my team's needs. When our millennial employees started having babies, we asked the new parents what our benefits package lacked—even though our parental leave is consistent with the top quartile of Silicon Valley start-ups. As an outcome of my asking, we transformed a conference room into a mother's room and tacked an additional month of transition time to our parental leave policies to help parents adjust more comfortably to the back-to-work process. There are more benefits I'd like to offer, and as we grow, I hope to delight employees with more opportunities to support their life balance. Change is indeed a work in progress, but at Grokker, we're working hard to keep improving the work and life experience for our employees and their families. A big part of that is continuing to support all the women—and men—who give their very best to carry out our mission, every day.

Once you connect with employees and understand what they want, you can better define your true mission and link your culture to your shared purpose. Employees need to feel that they intuitively understand the connection between your company's culture and mission, and their role in carrying it out. Think about how you can get your "insides" and "outsides" to match—how can employees start walking the talk? Maybe there are ways to insert company culture into your daily workflows or special events. One-on-one meetings can be taken to the walking path, or happy hour can turn into a volunteer opportunity. If you link your company's mission to what your employees value, you'll provide that sense of purpose they're looking for.

As a leader, I'm sure you too recognize that a company culture is constantly evolving and always has room to grow. I think of my company as a living, breathing entity, comprised of people whose ideas, feelings, and actions enable me to achieve my organization's vision, mission, and values. Therefore, making room for wellbeing in my organization is as natural as providing tea and coffee. It requires some thoughtful messaging to get your teams excited, as well as access to basic tools, and as with anything else, you will get out of your culture what you put in. Change may happen slowly, but give it just a little bit of time, and wellbeing will find its place.

Measuring what matters

When determining the value of your workforce wellbeing program, what metrics matter? Your answer depends on what you're measuring, of course. As the workforce wellbeing landscape has evolved, we have seen an expanding definition of success, and the concept of wellness has found a more comfortable place as the more all-encompassing "wellbeing." You might be targeting a constellation of goals ranging from lowering your major medical costs to higher employee retention rates. But what about the increasingly essential—yet difficult to measure—components of your employee experience that actually keep your employees happy? As Susan Schuman advises, "Before trying to solve the problem, you need to work on defining the problem." And she is right. It is asking the right questions, spending time with it, and making sure that everything you do is busines-driven and gets you to the best solution. If your wellbeing program design centers around offering incentivized biometric screenings, you could force decent program participation, but the results they produce are not holistic and, as we explored earlier, they are not something that is actively and enthusiastically embraced by your employees. That is why, when assessing your workforce wellbeing program, you should ask the following three questions:

1. Are you paying attention to the common comorbidities associated with the leading causes of absenteeism and presenteeism?
2. Are employees feeling connected and supported by you as a result of your wellness program design?
3. Are employees changing their risky health behaviors and pursuing a broad range of whole-person wellbeing goals that enable them to truly bring their best selves to work?

If not, your program is probably missing something that can transform your approach to measuring—and realizing—its success. Let's take a closer look.

The trouble with traditional wellness ROI

If you define wellbeing program success by direct cost savings alone, you could be in for a disappointment—as evidenced by research published by *The Journal of the American Medical Association (JAMA)*. This study examined the short-term health-care cost savings delivered by a narrowly focused wellness program to over thirty thousand BJ's Wholesale Club employees, which consisted of a health assessment, biometric screening, and eight in-person program modules. The findings, as reported by a variety of major media outlets, featured discouraging headlines like "It's Time to Believe the Research: Wellness Isn't Working,"[179] and "Much Touted Workplace Wellness Programs Don't Live Up to Hype."[180] The study cast a dim light on the work so many of us are doing to help our employees feel and be at their best.[181] But upon even a cursory examination, it turns out, unsurprisingly, that the study itself was flawed in its design and in fact proved that even poorly designed programs can stimulate positive lifestyle behavior change in employees.

When creating a wellbeing program, be sure to include all of the critical design elements.

The study took a very narrow approach by only targeting one lifestyle risk, nutrition and weight loss, as opposed to providing a holistic approach to wellness. Even worse, the study relied upon webinars and basic analog support to communicate to employees as opposed to modern digital means and covered a meager eighteen-month timeline, which predictably failed to produce the kind of utilization, let alone significant savings or improved employee health outcomes, that we all know can be achieved through better wellness program design. Like many well-intentioned corporate wellness programs, the program in the study lacked critical design elements that have been shown to result in better engagement and outcomes. Here is where you need to pay attention and take notes. For starters, participants didn't have 1) on-demand access to 2) holistic (or whole-person) content and weren't given 3) community support to explore with or be motivated by, which are known keys to success. Plus, the program in the study did not include 4) personalization or 5) gamification, two powerful concepts for encouraging wellbeing (which we'll explore in the next chapter), thereby ignoring key requirements to ensure relevance and encouragement.

In spite of these five critical design flaws, there is a very encouraging takeaway from the study: BJ's Wholesale Club's wellness program managed to move the needle on behavior change. Let me repeat that: despite the fact that the program lacked five of the most important elements in a properly designed wellbeing program, it still succeeded in positively impacting behavior change. The *JAMA* study shows that employees who participated in their programs reported exercising more often and eating more healthfully, adopting the types of healthy behaviors that lead to a happier, more engaged, and more productive workforce. But behavior change wasn't what *JAMA* was measuring, and that's why it didn't make the news headlines.

To be fair, the holes in BJ's Wholesale Club's wellness program are not uncommon. With the very best intentions—and using metrics as their coat of armor when defending their budgets to management—benefits administrators continue to compel and incentivize employees at great expense to take health risk assessments and sit through biometric screenings year in and year out, and then pray that upon receiving the results, the employees will magically change their unhealthy ways. But where's the motivation to change? There's little chance of achieving the kind of results you're hoping for when the follow-up content and social support you provide to your employees is sparse, limited, and frankly, not much fun. The first lesson to be learned is that if you are looking for cost savings, you won't find them at the end of a stethoscope. Assessments and screenings provide a metric— not savings. Likewise, if you want sustained behavior change, you won't find the means for ongoing engagement buried in a series of webinars. Information, even if it's provided by a friendly expert, is just information— not the behavioral change you need for health and wellbeing. It's time to embrace a more expansive view of how wellbeing programs can benefit your company and learn what it takes to deliver real value and returns that are meaningful to your employees—and your bottom line. And this is where it comes back, full circle to culture and genuinely caring about your employees.

Leading employers are implementing a different kind of wellbeing program

Today, the most successful workforce wellbeing initiatives serve more than cost needs. They're aimed at delivering an exceptional employee experience, which includes the competitive benefits that top talent has now come to expect. There has been a shift in emphasis in what companies offer. They are supporting holistic health with evidence-based programs that accommodate a wide variety of individual needs and goals across the interconnected lifestyle factors of nutrition, exercise, sleep, financial wellbeing, and mental health. When employees are empowered to "choose their own wellbeing adventure," they are free to work concurrently on whatever goals are most pressing and address the lifestyle issues most impacting their life (and their work productivity) at that moment. In doing so, they will be helping you tackle the underlying risk factors directly tied to absenteeism, presenteeism, and lower productivity, which should also help you boost retention and profitability.

So, how do we capture the type of unequivocal proof we—or at the very least your board of directors—need to invest in programs that will help you reverse the nearly $2,000 per person, per year on average productivity loss caused by poor health? One step for implementing an evidence-based approach is by conducting an employee survey at least once per year, but better is twice a year or even quarterly, so you can identify perceptual and behavioral trends and address them in near real time. To identify the trends, you should keep many of the questions the same, but you can retire some along the way and integrate new questions into your survey. In the survey questions, you should explore the perceptions of your company's mission, vision, ethical behavior, communication style, strengths and weaknesses, and culture as well as explore how your employees feel supported by the company and their manager in their growth, workload, and ability to achieve their immediate and long-term career plans, among other topics. You can even ask if they have recently interviewed for a job at another company. Be careful to avoid all questions in your survey, however, that can expose personal information, enabling the reviewers to identify a respondent, because, for truthful answers, anonymity should be your goal.

Another simple way to take the pulse of your workforce is to capture your Employee Net Promoter Score, which you can also have in your longer survey as well. For those of you unfamiliar with this metric, it is a simple one: You just ask, "Would you recommend your employer to a colleague, friend, other?" For a very simple metric, you can settle for a yes/ no answer. Once you get the results, you subtract the nos (the detractors) from the yeses (the promoters) to determine your score. This helps you determine how many "promoters" you have on a percentage basis which indicates the level of satisfaction and even enthusiasm for your organization. But, as Andy Polaine, Lavrans Lovlie, and Ben Reason write in their book *Service Design: From Insight to Implementation*, "the disadvantage with the method is that it does not tell you much about what you need to get better."[182] However, it can serve as an "early-warning system," so you can react quickly should your scores drop.

Whatever approach you select, you have to be very careful to ensure that your team gives you accurate and honest answers. If employees think that they will be "punished" for their honest answers by reduced opportunities, raises, or training, they will tell you what they think you want to hear. And if employees think that their responses won't lead to positive change, they might not even respond to the survey request. In fact, according to Rachel Hill, a research analyst for Horizons Workforce Consulting (of Bright Horizons Education & College Advising), situations where employees feel their input or ideas for workplace improvement will fall on deaf ears and be futile, are "1.8 times more likely to lead people to opt out of a survey,"[183] according to a Cornell National Social Survey.

Of course, ultimately, you should judge the success of your wellbeing programs on how well they help you overcome your specific business challenges as well as achieve your business goals, from higher productivity and profitability to reduced employee turnover and number of sick days. In many ways, when caring for oneself becomes okay, you will know. Your research among employees should be just to keep you on the path. Long term, your goal should be that your organization becomes and then stays the employee brand of choice in your category. That way you can attract your optimal workforce, ensure optimal focus and productivity even when times are tough, and retain key employees during times when the job market is hot. But you should also recognize that employees today are not going to stay with you for fifty years—or even four years. A strong culture of wellbeing, however, can help influence how former employees talk about your organization, making them, in essence, loyal recruiters for it. You can also determine your Employee Net Promoter Score for departing and former employees to get a sense of why they opted for other opportunities. Often, it's for growth, which means you can bring them back to your organization for new opportunities in the future. I believe that these "boomerangs" will happen even more often, as leaving a position is not seen as a form of disloyalty. To create this type of goodwill, you need to offer the benefits they want when they want and need them as well as encourage success with them. These points will be explored in the next two chapters.

♥ ♥ ♥

From Allyship to Accomplice—Five Steps for Creating a Truly Diverse, Equitable, Inclusive Culture

A Guest Perspective by Dr. Akilah Cadet,
Founder and CEO, Change Cadet

Ensuring a diverse, equitable, inclusive workforce is often much more involved than employers originally think, but a business can't have a truly caring environment without achieving these goals. So how do you achieve these goals and set an organization up for success? To explore additional strategies, I talked to Dr. Akilah Cadet, founder and CEO of Change Cadet, a consulting firm that offers a broad array of antiracism and diversity services including strategic planning, crisis rebuilding, advising, executive coaching and facilitation. It's interesting that Cadet (her last name) is a French term that means soldier, because it's often an uphill battle for Black, Indigenous, and People of Color (BIPOC), women, and other underrepresented communities achieve success and equity in the workplace. Through Change Cadet, Akilah helps prepares soldiers of change to overcome these continuous battles so individuals and companies can thrive. Akilah has more than fifteen years of experience working in various organizations, with both private and public sector companies. She literally has all the degrees; lives in Oakland, California; has a rare heart condition; and is a proud Beyoncé advocate.

"A truly caring, inclusive environment is the result of leadership. Leaders are the ones who set the culture, and often fail to build a caring foundation but do not revisit it until they are forced to. In my work, I usually don't come into caring environments. Rather, I am called into big brands that need help course correcting after messing up somewhere along the way. The problem may reveal itself in how the CEO and exec team talk to staff, or in who is being promoted, and who is not. But by the time I am invited in, leadership already knows that they need to be better, and do better. I look at those in leadership positions, as well everything from the recruitment process, to exit interviews, and examine the frequency and content of employee surveys, and how company policies and procedures are succeeding in creating a place of belonging, as well as where they are falling short on making people feel like they're valued and appreciated. I look at where they are and what they've been doing, and then help paint a picture of where they want to go, which often results in a strategic plan, a roadmap, coaching, advisory sessions, facilitated discussions, and other actions. I also provide the critically important nomenclature of inclusion and bias for the leaders so that they feel confident in naming and calling out the behaviors that need to be either rooted out or instilled in order to create a caring environment.

"We know that ego is a big part of being a leader. If leaders lack confidence and do not feel they are experts in a topic, they can feel like they're not in control or losing power. And, given that leadership tends not to naturally want to hold themselves accountable for passing over women, Black people, and others, it is important to start with language mastery over the subject matter. This entails explaining what a microaggression is, and how to counter unconscious bias, or call out white privilege. Over time, if we get the policies in place and we have the language and behaviors we're role modeling, then we can get to a place of belonging where all people are being held to the same standard and regard and they don't have any exceptions to the rule. Instead, there is transparency, communication, responsibility, and feedback. The result of which, is that people will feel valued and appreciated as employees. They'll know that if something's not okay, management will take action. And they know if something is great, that it will be celebrated and perpetuated. That is how leaders get to the happy place. So, when you want to get to that happy, caring place and set up an organization for success, there are some concepts that I teach in work environments that can help your organization get there:

Step one: Make your leaders accountable

"If your leaders are not held accountable for their actions, you're not going to be successful in creating a truly caring environment. The first step for leaders is often admitting that they don't know what they're doing To address it, you can hire an expert to help you understand what you need to learn. Next, you need to be transparent about inclusion and the consequences of failing to provide it. That's why policies and values are really important, starting with recruitment. The best practice is to share what you stand for and what you enforce up front in the interview process and onboarding packet. In straightforward language you state that you are an anti-racist organization and have a zero-tolerance policy. If you get employees to sign your policy saying that they agree to it, then give them the resources in the event of a misstep to help them up the learning curve to get them the right position, and they still choose to be racist, well then you have everything you need to exit that person.

"If someone is choosing to *not* unlearn a problematic behavior, and the same microaggression is happening over and over again without improvement, even after training and coaching, that person should be removed. If the person is not removed, the organization is choosing to not be anti-racist and is in fact setting itself up for being in a position where they are going to have a culture problem. When everyone's held with the same positive regard, and to the same standards, it is simple. Others will see that that person who was removed did not fit the values of the company and that H.R. did all of the things it could. This is the time for your leadership to shine, and to clearly communicate that the individual removed didn't meet our anti-racism policy. You don't have to go into detail about what it was, who it was with, or what happened, but the message is that there's a zero tolerance for racism in our workplace. The words and actions match. If those individuals are not removed, however, you will have toxicity and an unsafe workplace. You will have people who will check out. Some might magically go on medical leave. And, more importantly you will lose the Black person, BIPOC person, or woman to another company because they didn't feel supported.

Step two: Offer help and role model behaviors

"Typically, what happens, especially in larger companies, is that they hold a 'catch all' management training—if they do one at all. It's not specific to the different departments or company roles, in spite of the reality that Distribution is different from Fulfillment which is different from Finance which is different from Engineering. The better approach is to take the time to customize training and workshops. You also can't assume that managers know how to lead, coach, mentor, communicate, give feedback, de-escalate, resolve conflicts, manage people, or have courageous and crucial conversations. On the contrary, most managers need to be taught how, and leadership needs to learn how to perfect people management, which is completely different from traditional HR compliance activities. If a manager does not do well receiving feedback, they will not do well giving it. So, they need to learn how to structure meetings to involve their team, and they need to be taught how to be creative with their annual evaluations, and even how to praise people.

"Management training should not just be part of your onboarding experience. It should be a thirty- sixty-, ninety-day, and beyond-type of thing. There will probably be mistakes along the way, but if trained ongoing and from the outset, those mistakes might come with an apology. And that can make all the difference. When remorse is shown, you can offer coaching to the perpetrator and therapy for the team or the person attacked and acknowledge that they went through something instead of sweeping it under the rug. You can then check in on them, or maybe reassign the victim while the aggressor is learning. Your EAP may come into play but it's all with patience and within reason. Most importantly you are opening up the lines of communication and are able to be real with your team about what's going on.

"The other key thing for setting your company up for success is having your leaders role model the behaviors which every team member should have. Your people will then follow the desired behaviors. These behaviors could be something as simple as how to greet people or as complex as how to address a communication issue or a microaggression. Eventually through role modeling of the desired behaviors, organizational and cultural change will come. You don't need to have all the answers, you just need to be honest. If your leaders don't yet have all the right behaviors instilled, they should be transparent about what they are learning and unlearning. We've all learned things that are not fully accurate, we are human and products of our environments. But we all have the capacity to grow and change if we want to. For instance, elementary and high school textbooks imply that Susan B. Anthony was a really great person, leaving out the part that she was racist.[184] Unlearning is realizing that what you thought was learning—your image, for instance, of Susan B. Anthony—is in fact not 100 percent true. Admitting what you are working on as a leader shows enormous strength.

Step three: Become an accomplice

"Allyship is just the beginning of understanding privilege and is building the muscle for advocacy. When looking at the allyship between white people and Black people, between nondisabled and disabled, between heterosexual and the LGBTQ+ community, you have different lived experiences. When you want to understand how your privilege impacts that dynamic and relationship, you can immerse yourself in the community you'd like to know about. You should read, check out movies, listen to podcasts, and take the time to get the complete story. As a result, you'll be listening to people who are more versed, experienced, and knowledgeable in the area. And you'll be building the muscle of advocacy as you learn to speak up when no one's watching for the least represented in the group.

"But allyship is just the start of the journey of becoming an accomplice. An accomplice is someone who understands their privilege and how its added to systemic and institutional racism and oppression. We all know a lot about calling out and calling in, but accomplices do it internally to themselves. They might ask, for instance, why am I feeling like she "talks white"? What microaggression is happening right now? Is it because I'm looking at her as a Black person rather than as someone who introduced themselves as a doctor? In other words, you're checking yourself. And, even more importantly, you're able to advocate confidently for those who don't look like you.

"Becoming an accomplice is something that takes time, because unlearning takes time. Lots of people get stuck in allyship, because they've read all the books and they have listened to all the podcasts. Allies may wake up in the middle of the night and question something they did years ago and get stuck not knowing what to do to move forward. An accomplice understands all of that. They're no longer letting past mistakes make them feel stuck or held back. Rather, they're just going to take action and keep moving forward by continuously doing the work, knowing that it's a triathlon and not a sprint. It's never ending to be an accomplice. Until we have true equality for all BIPOC people, white people as well as white passing people—those who look white—have to continually figure out how they can become accomplices and do the work.

"If a person says an offensive, racist joke or expresses a microaggression towards a Black person, either that Black person has to feel safe enough to say that it was offensive and explain the microaggression—or through allyship, an accomplice might use their privilege to pull the aggressor aside to explain it or shut it down. Privilege is a really important part of allyship and being an accomplice, because we have power from our privilege.

"A common pitfall is performative allyship, which is where the organization will broadcast some external statement, (insert good cause here that definitely deserves money) and may throw in a "BLM." Some may even claim to fully commit to Black Lives Matter and say they want to be held accountable, and then feel and act like they can check the anti-racist box. Everyone knows, however, whether the company leaders have actually done anything meaningful for the staff to combat racism. If all that was done was the hosting of a lunch and learn by a Black speaker who may also be a mom and queer (to capture all aspects of diversity), well no one is going to be fooled. Internally, you must back up what you say with action and update employees, because combatting racism and creating inclusive environments is a long-term, involved process. If you can't have a whole strategic plan completed in three months like promised, you must say something and demonstrate that leadership is holding itself accountable. Otherwise, you cannot succeed in making organizational change.

Step four: Apologize (and watch your words)

"Choose to be human and apologize. This will free you to change your process and improve the system to make things better. It will also make all of your people feel valued and appreciated which is another way to set them up for success. Studies show that when doctors apologize for an error, malpractice lawsuits go down. When apologizing, leaders need to recognize that language is important because in general, people don't realize the power of words. One company I worked with said, 'We have these allegations of black people saying…women saying…queer people saying…' In these statements, by characterizing the articulation by employees as "allegations", the employer used a word that implied they didn't believe the complaints. If you put people immediately on the defensive, that's a problem. Instead, they could have said that they had received feedback in which we needed to review and improve our systems and culture.

"It's actually very hard for women to say they've been sexually harassed, because we already know that they're going to be treated differently. Similarly, a Black person saying, 'I'm being discriminated against' is hard to do too, because Black people already know that they get passed over for promotion; don't get paid the same; and have to think about what they say all of the time. So, when a BIPOC person says they've been harmed in the workplace, you have to listen to them. If you go with the skeptical investigator approach and find things aren't 100% what they have reported, you still must figure out why things got to the point where you were notified. There's still a problem somewhere in the system or culture. So, pay attention to the content of what is being said, and be curious as well as caring.

Step five: Do the work

"It is not quick or easy, but you must rinse and repeat these steps I have outlined above: accountability, role modeling behaviors, and apologizing. As I said, it's the triathlon, not the sprint. Leaders need to realize that people change, and that change is constant. Some people are only on day one of their journey and have an enormous amount to learn, while others are far down the path to becoming advocates, and so it requires patience. Patience is just crucial because, if people aren't patient with themselves, that's where they make mistakes and get stuck. It's ironic because getting stuck is a privilege in itself. I can't do that as a Black person. I can't be stuck. I don't have that luxury, which is why I'm doing all this work. Once I go outside, I'm constantly disproving stereotypes and bias and making sure I'm safe. It probably won't be my generation, but I hope the generation after me can just go outside and not have their blood pressure go up when a cop is near even though they did nothing wrong. That they can be confident in knowing that an advocate will come to their aide every time.

"More importantly, it's not so much about someone being ignorant. People don't know what they don't know. While mistakes will continue, being committed to learning and unlearning is what's important. Don't go into that place of gaslighting or white centering, saying, 'that is not what I meant' or 'you blew it out of proportion.' Just like the use of the word 'allegations,' you can't tell the person you harmed that you didn't harm them. It's impossible. The only thing you can do is apologize. That's when people need to be patient with themselves and be patient with the other people around them.

"When I talk about being an accomplice, it is a lifelong journey, just as it is a lifelong journey just for me to be Black and safe in America—to not be harmed verbally or physically. We're going to work on humanity and equality for me. You're going to work on being anti-racist. We're going to work together, which is how we get humanity and equality. For your organization to be inclusive, you need to make it okay to make mistakes and make it okay to call people out in order to help them correct those very mistakes. It is not about shaming but about accepting the existence of ignorance and working toward enlightenment. The goal is to teach your people to say, 'I'm sorry. That was not okay. I was unaware, but I am going to learn more. What resources do we have as a company for me to learn more? Can I talk to our diversity consultant?' The goal should be to learn from the mistake, do better, and move forward.

Celebrate the little wins

"Celebrating little wins is incredibly helpful. Leaders are always looking for big moments—new deals, clients, hires—but they really have to celebrate the little things. The guy who had racist behavior made it through his thirty days and he's working well with the team. The guy who didn't realize he had discriminatory behavior figured it out. Or we finally had our first diversity committee meeting. Celebrating that is important because we have more little things to celebrate than big things.

The future is here

"Finally, there's one more thing to keep in mind: Organizations have a unique workforce right now, because we have Baby Boomers, Gen X-ers, millennials, and zennials. There are different ways of learning, different ways of activism, and different ways of allyship. Millennials and Gen Z may feel awful when they aren't promoted after being in a company for six months, and Baby Boomers and Gen Xers may feel that the millennial or Gen Z employees are not doing their jobs because they have headphones on and are constantly checking their phones, but they have to learn to value and respect one another despite their perceived difference. With so many different views and values in the workplace, we have to work to understand one another and to find common ground. When Mike Brown or Ahmaud Arbery died, a lot of white people didn't care. When the pandemic hit white people cared about Breonna Taylor and George Floyd. But brutality against Black people always affects Black people, and we bring it into the workplace. We are at a moment in time where more people are questioning their own feelings—am I racist, am I not racist? That's why it's really important to figure out our common language, our resources, and our approach to learn and unlearn, advocate, and support each other. The time to start is now."

Chapter 8:

BENEFITS ON DEMAND

Shortly after I moved my family out to Silicon Valley in 2002 for my new role at eBay, my husband and I were invited over to a colleague's house for Sunday brunch with our then seven-, five-, and two-year-old children. In order to give the grown-ups time to talk in relative peace after we ate, our host offered to let the kids watch cartoons along with his three-year-old daughter. As we settled the children into the family room in front of the TV, the three-year-old told her father that she wanted to watch *Blue's Clues*. Unfortunately, their DVR was on the fritz, and recorded shows could not be accessed. The dad told his daughter that she couldn't watch *Blue's Clues* and suggested a bunch of other shows that were airing on cable in real time. The three-year-old was confused. She again asked for *Blue's Clues* and became extremely upset when neither Joe nor her favorite animated blue dog appeared on the screen. She welled up in tears, cry-shouting, "I want *Blue's Clues*! Start *Blue's Clues*, Daddy!" She could not understand why her father was refusing to play the show she had always been able to watch when asked for. She walked up to the TV and began slapping the screen with her angry little hand, "*Blue's Clues*, play *Blue's Clues* now." To her, all programming lived in the TV and could be summoned to the screen whenever she wanted it on demand.

My children did not have a DVR at home yet. In 2002 only 1.8 million homes in the world had DVRs, and so my kids tried to console the three-year-old and explain to her that they could watch something else that was "on." The concept of "on" was meaningless to her as she insisted

Blue's Clues was always on. Needless to say, the brunch ended early as a result of the ensuing temper tantrum. As we drove home, I recall discussing the phenomenon with my husband. It was gobsmacking to see how a preschooler was so accustomed to watching what she wanted, when she wanted, that she had no concept of the fact that her favorite cartoon did not live in a state of perpetual accessibility, merely waiting for her father to press Play when directed. This was so different from our life experience growing up with just the three major networks (ABC, CBS, NBC) and public television, and even from our children's experience with dozens of channels thanks to the expansion of cable networks, and the introduction of VHS, which allowed us to record shows and rent movies on video tape from Blockbuster.

Growing up, if I was unable to tune in for an ABC Afterschool Special or an episode of *The Love Boat*, I didn't get to see it, period. I would ask friends at school to fill me in on what I had missed and would feel embarrassed when I could not contribute to the animated discussion about whether Captain Stubing knew the truth about the mystery guest all along. I learned early on that TV was ephemeral: you had to watch what was on or miss out. In fact, NBC created the slogan "Must See TV"[185] to promote their Thursday-night prime-time lineup and used the term in advertisements that encouraged the audience to stay home for "Must See TV Thursday."[186] Consumers in the twentieth century were trained to watch what was available when it was available, and this made for a dynamic where programmers held the balance of power, and consumers shifted their social calendars in order to be able to watch what was scheduled. In the '70s, Saturday early mornings were for children's cartoons, Saturday evenings were for variety shows like *Donny & Marie* and *The Carol Burnett Show*, and Sunday evenings were for wholesome family TV shows like *The Wonderful World of Disney* and *Animal Kingdom*. Gen X-ers and boomers entered the workforce understanding that just like entertainment, which was available when and how studio execs decided, employers called the shots, period. No one asked you for your opinion on what to work on or whether you would prefer a standing desk or sitting. And no one offered to make expected workday hours flexible to suit your scheduling preferences. Gen X-ers and boomers essentially did as they were told, brought their own brown-bag lunches, and felt largely grateful to be employed at a solid company with upward mobility and, perhaps, a bit of a retirement plan.

But millennials and Gen Z-ers had a different life experience. With the advent of on-demand streaming video, the tables have been turned; now it is the consumer who dictates what they watch and when. As a result, video viewing has skyrocketed, and people have been trained to ignore that which is not personalized or convenient, in favor of all that is tailored to their wants, needs, and tastes. Let's face it, up until twenty years ago, the only restaurants that delivered food to your door outside of New York City were pizza joints. You couldn't conjure up dinner or a rideshare on demand with the press of a button. The world began to revolve around the consumer, and naturally, they loved it.

Employees now behave like consumers who expect on-demand access to what they want, when they want it, and how they want it.

This same egocentric trend, initially rooted in new-media consumption, now extends to your workforce expectations. In fact, it applies to how you need to approach everything, from the benefits you offer to your internal communications. To have any chance at relevancy with millennials and Gen Z-ers, you must radically change your old-school ways of designing the employee experience to be in favor of video and on-demand tools that can be accessed when and how employees want to view them, and truly treat your people like the consumers that they are. Digital transformation has occurred at an unprecedented speed and has irrevocably altered human behavior by turning us into cyborgs whose "physical abilities are extended beyond normal human limitations by mechanical elements built into the body."[187] Whether we like it or not, the form factor changes catalyzed by the smartphone demand a corporate revamping of how we share information with employees if we hope to be heard.

Smart phones and tablets and connected TVs—oh my!

The explosive growth in on-demand video can be traced back to the proliferation of mobile devices in the early 2010s. From 2010 to 2019, smartphone penetration in the U.S. skyrocketed from 20.2 percent to 81.9 percent.[188] In May of 2011 35 percent of Americans owned a smartphone, and that increased by 11 percentage points in just 8 months to 46 percent by March of 2012.[189] Experts began forecasting the death of TV as a natural consequence of the rise in smartphones. They were partially right, in that the viewing of programmed broadcast network TV (along with the commercial ads that paid for the production), would decline and in fact be dwarfed by over-the-top video services and apps that delivered a personalized experience to consumers with highly curated on-demand video. In 2012, Netflix had 33.3 million total paying subscribers worldwide,[190] and Hulu had 3 million.[191] By 2020, Netflix had 167 million subscribers and was adding nearly 26 million viewers every six months,[192] and Hulu had over 35 million total subscribers.[193] Video consumption also grew 133 percent from 2012 to 2013,[194] as the shift to smartphones was clearly in full swing and driving the appetite for more video. TV wasn't dying; it was just moving to the small screen in consumers' back pockets. Mobile video plays only accounted for 7.5 percent of total plays in 2012, but by the first half of 2020, video views on smartphones accounted for a whopping 52 percent of all views globally.[195]

There were more than 220 over-the-top video services available to consumers in 2018, more than double the number available in 2013 in North America, and that number is dwarfed by the number of services available in the rest of the world, especially in emerging markets where it is far less expensive to light up or expand a mobile network than it is to expand a wired one. Not surprisingly connected TV is now the emerging trend driving the explosion in streaming networks aimed at satisfying the insatiable consumer appetite for new and better-targeted content. This explains how Disney+ topped 56 million subscribers in the first half of 2020.[196]

The broadcasters and media companies who recognized the consumer shift to smartphones early on adopted aggressive mobile video strategies that would prove to be critical to their survival. As one analyst warned in a 2013 report with respect to the trend in consumer preference for watching video on smartphones: "For broadcasters, operators, media companies and TV networks, these insights are critical for maximizing both engagement and revenue. Companies taking a one-size-fits all approach to programming and advertising across all devices will soon find themselves well behind the competition."[197] This warning is as relevant for employers today as it was to media companies back then. If you don't adopt a personalized and digital approach to your employee experience and the benefits you offer, you will soon find yourself well behind the competition.

Whole person wellbeing

As mentioned earlier in chapter 1, the mid-twentieth-century tactic of biometric screenings did not achieve its objectives, and the bloom has come off the rose on this "check-the-box benefit." The modern and more strategic approach engages employees in whole-person wellbeing inviting rather than ignoring the full examination of the interconnection between sleep, stress, nutrition, physical activity, financial health, family, and social connection. Beyond understanding the importance of holistically addressing all of these aspects in order to positively influence our employees' overall wellbeing, it is imperative to make the tools digital and on-demand. It is also critical that they are woven together like a tapestry rather than kludged in as a bunch of stand-alone solutions. In the 2000s and early 2010s days of corporate wellbeing and culture initiatives, there was an emphasis placed on the launch of engagement platforms to track incentives and measure employee activity. What was learned from those legacy platforms was that measuring engagement doesn't create it. While employees could be incentivized to log onto an engagement portal daily to collect points that equated to dollars deposited in their paychecks, those incentives did little to create ongoing healthy behaviors.[198] Much like the iconic Wendy's hamburger ad, the encasing platform bun was delivered, but where was the beef? And, in fact, it was much like the results of biometric screenings, producing revenue for suppliers and negligible results for achieving its intended health-improvement and cost-saving goals.

"Platform fatigue" was the term used to describe the disenchantment with these benefits and their suppliers. So, an entire world of corporate point solutions replete with entertaining content and gamified triggers to encourage repeat usage was born to address individual aspects of wellbeing: apps for workouts, apps for meditation, apps for sleep, etc. These were digital and on-demand and enjoyed higher participation than static, analog resources. However, they were disparate niche apps that failed to weave wellbeing together into a reinforced fabric of support and required the employee to use half a dozen different apps, each targeted at an isolated aspect of wellbeing. This made the employee work far too hard, tended to appeal only to the small fraction of employees already committed to the aspect of health addressed by the app, and resulted in employees' growing frustration at the lack of connection between apps. No one wants to have a separate fitness app, yoga app, and stress reduction app because all three of these areas work together and influence one's health. Forcing me to silo myself into a mindfulness app that doesn't take into account my physical fitness or my nutrition felt tone deaf for the vast majority of employees who wanted to be seen and heard as whole people. At the same time, this army of apps became difficult to manage by employers while proving ineffective at addressing employees' full scope of needs. This hub-and-spoke approach just wasn't working.

And, so, the benefits pendulum swung back, and employers began searching for engaging resources across multiple dimensions of wellbeing, with content that could be delivered digitally and on demand that would appeal to all of their employees' interests, abilities, tastes, and needs. In other words, the time had come for truly holistic, integrated health at the corporate level, and this would be accelerated exponentially by the global COVID-19 pandemic, launching us into the 2020s and the era of whole-person wellbeing.

Customizable and personalized

Customizable, personalized to my specific needs, offering a wide variety of options to choose from, intuitive, digital, and available to all: this is how employees want their benefits today. After two decades of e-commerce perfecting the online shopping experience, consumers now expect what they want, when they want it, at their fingertips—in the form of premium video, of course, because no one likes to read when they can watch instead. The newer approach demands that we start with personalization so that the user feels the experience was designed with them in mind and has the confidence to believe that investing their time in it is worth it. In web design there is a famous three-second rule, which says that you have three seconds to form a positive impression and capture visitors' attention when they land on your site. If you fail in those first precious seconds to earn their interest, you lose the opportunity to convert them into a user. If you want employees to click deeper to explore your benefits, you must make it relevant to them as well as easy.

A forty-five-year old diabetic long-haul truck driver who spends his weekdays transporting goods out of state is unlikely to have a strong interest in spin classes or a step challenge. But alleviating lower back pain is probably high on his list of health priorities. So, rather than promoting what you have traditionally offered at your headquarters (in person and in the past), you need to refocus on connecting with what each employee is interested in at that moment, making it easy to access, and offering motivating encouragement as soon as it is humanly possible. And if I am a first-time expectant mother, I want prenatal fitness and nutrition advice, not weight-loss programs, so don't promote them to me, or I will quickly form the opinion that you do not offer what I need and tune you out. Instead of pushing for biometric screenings and heavily incentivizing your employees to take them at great financial cost to your company, what if you shifted your thinking toward supporting employees in wellbeing engagement in the ways that speak to them and actually achieve their goals for better health? Fortunately, it doesn't require a Herculean effort to provide the opportunities for employees to take care of themselves, how they want to, and when they want to. It just takes a little creativity and a willingness to listen.

Global access and inspiration

Too frequently I hear from senior executives that while they have historically offered enviable in-person programs at their headquarters, they have not found great options for their international and satellite offices. In an analog world, that was understandable, but the world has changed. The good news is that it is relatively easy to give all employees access to the same digital wellbeing resources. Whether your teams are in Nebraska or Nairobi, nowadays no one needs to be left out. Five years ago when we were first working with eBay to design a program to help provide on-demand wellbeing benefits for their global workforce, the head of benefits made it absolutely clear that her top priority was the international workforce and ensuring the employees in the more than thirty-five countries outside of the U.S. would feel like first-class citizens. As part of the prelaunch strategy, Grokker's Customer Success team hosted calls with eBay's international country managers to introduce them to us and solicit feedback on their particular needs and desires, which we then fed back into the launch and communications plan. The country managers were delighted to be proactively engaged before decisions had been made, and they proved to be among the strongest advocates for our wellbeing engagement solution, resulting in strong over-indexation in international adoption and usage.

Of course, giving employees the permission to take care of themselves and fostering a culture of wellbeing can be trickier when dealing with international populations whose customs may vary. Even so, leaders like the eBay country managers can make wellbeing more inclusive by visibly walking the talk and inspiring their teams by creating opportunities for participation. Pinterest does this particularly well. Pinterest's company mission is to help people discover the things they love and inspire them to go do those things in their daily lives. That's why, as I mentioned earlier, the company hosts "Knit Con," an annual two-day event in which employees teach each other cool skills that they know, from hula dancing to wine tasting to coding. It's a highly engaging, inexpensive, and really fun way to connect employees back to their company's purpose.

Torpedoes away

While we cannot blow up the antiquated systems already in place and magically substitute in new ones, it's a truly exciting time to shift your thinking from "How can I get biometric measurements?" to "How can I leverage wellbeing strategically to support employee engagement?" By reallocating budget and focus from "check-the-box benefits" to solutions that improve employee happiness and job satisfaction, you can strengthen your connection with your workforce as well as drive productivity. As the workforce becomes increasingly diverse and dispersed, it's only going to become more critical to offer benefits that are truly inclusive, are easy to implement, and lead to desired outcomes—and that employees genuinely enjoy. Plus, with the increased focus on the importance of wellbeing benefits in attracting and retaining top talent,[199] digital content and personalization tools are a necessity. Employees expect access on their terms and want the benefits that fit into their lives, making their wellbeing journeys more fun, successful, and rewarding.

When it comes to employee health-and-wellness programs, the very definition of "wellness" has changed dramatically over the years—and employee expectations have changed along with it. In fact, the trend away from the word "wellness" in favor of the modern term "wellbeing" more accurately describes the all-encompassing approach to multidimensional health people are now aiming to achieve. The new, enlightened approach also acknowledges that the various dimensions of wellbeing affect one another and must therefore be considered as a system. If an employee is suffering from stress-induced insomnia, she is also more likely to be increasing her intake of sugary and high-fat foods,[200] which in turn may lead to weight gain, metabolic syndrome, or diabetes. Sleep deprivation reduces the amount of leptin your body produces; leptin is a hormone that works as a natural appetite suppressant. Lack of sleep also increases the production of ghrelin, a hormone that triggers feelings of hunger. So, a lack of sleep literally makes you hungrier and less able to feel satiated when you do eat. If the employer focuses solely on encouraging weight loss with screenings and incentives, because that is easiest to uncover and track, an employee with insomnia will not only be unlikely to succeed in achieving the weight loss results sought, but more importantly and sadly, she will continue to suffer in silence without anyone pausing to dig in deeper and figure out the root cause of the issue.

So how do you stop this well-intentioned misapplication of corporate resources? Your first step is to acknowledge the complexity of wellbeing and admit that there is no silver bullet. Your employees are diverse, and their struggles are multifaceted, so as tempting as it is, you cannot apply a one-size-fits-all approach and expect it to work across the board. Instead, by accepting the complexity and identifying the interrelationships between physical and emotional health factors, you can refocus on the actual targets—plural—and launch new torpedoes.

The best way to promote and reinforce workforce wellbeing and engagement—to really bring it to life—is through a formal digital-first benefits program. As we've discussed, today's top talent considers wellbeing benefits as more than "perks," especially when they know their programs are designed to make their lives better as opposed to being used as tracking or surveillance tools for the employer or as a way for the employer to save money. Wellbeing programs, as we discussed in chapter 2, are an essential part of bringing purpose, belonging, and balance into the employee experience. And practically nothing proclaims "we care for our workforce" more clearly than offering employee-centric wellbeing resources and activities that are customized for your diverse and dispersed employee base. This means offering holistic, on-demand programs that incorporate all aspects of an employee's health: exercise, mental health, sleep, nutrition, and social and financial wellbeing.

Provide programs that help employees feel seen and understood

Multiple interactive wellbeing events, activities, and "challenges" should be offered concurrently, so every employee can find something that interests them. Instead of hosting an annual step challenge where everyone is limited to the same solitary experience of walking to Rome, offer a walking option, but also offer a Carb Reset nutrition option as well as a Stress Buster resilience option at the exact same time with the same incentives. This will appeal to a much broader set of your workforce, and participation will be higher. What's more, your employees will feel seen and heard by your inclusive approach. As part of their corporate wellbeing program, one of the world's largest media and entertainment companies offers each of their 160,000+ employees the opportunity to participate in one of four companywide wellbeing journeys: yoga, mindfulness, nutrition, or exercise. This way, everyone can decide for themselves what's most important and enjoyable for them, whether they're learning how to cook healthier meals or practicing advanced yoga poses. Your mantra: what they want, when they want it, and how they want it. Just like in the consumer world. Try it, and I'm sure your outcomes will improve.

Encourage success through gamification, not punitive actions

Professor Rima Touré-Tillery and Ayelet Fishbach of Northwestern University's Kellogg School have identified three forms of motivation: intrinsic, extrinsic, and self-signaling.[201] Keeping employees engaged in a wellbeing program (in any benefits program, for that matter) requires some degree of fun (intrinsic motivation)—or they won't stick with it. Employees also need to want to participate and see results (extrinsic motivation) that motivate employees to come back for more. Finally, enabling them to set up personal goals and then rewarding them with some material item—some company swag, a gift card, or even a donation to a favorite charity, preferably accompanied with a printed or digital certificate, for each wellness milestone reached—can provide the self-signaling motivation that fuels and sustains itself. Just think about the number of employees you have who are trying to simply "muscle through it"—and force themselves to adopt new and healthier habits. Without rewards and recognition that stroke the ego and stoke the commitment to carry on, employees are less than half as likely to stick with it. This is not the same thing as reliance upon one-off or gimmicky incentives that can trigger an isolated action but fail to inculcate systemic changes. Applying the best practices from the world of gaming is an essential ingredient when encouraging sustainable behavior change, and this too is best delivered digitally. Let's explore this practically so you can see how easy it is to apply.

Gamification: From Russia with love

Gamification is simply the use of game elements in nongame contexts. There is nothing new about the application of gamification in behavior change; in fact, it's been around for almost one hundred years, and its application in the work setting has a surprising origin story. The Soviet Union began using gamification techniques in the mid-1900s when the Communist regime needed a distinctly anticapitalist and non-monetary-rewards-based approach to increasing worker productivity.[202] "The Soviet approach focused on games to increase productivity, via experiments ranging from purely competitive games directly tied to productivity, to attempts at morale-building via team games and workplace self-expression."[203] Rather than paying workers bonuses for greater output, Soviet factories and their laborers were incentivized with point systems to out-perform one another. This way, everyone could still be paid the same wage under Communist rule, but workers would willingly compete against each other for points, with increased productivity as the overarching desired outcome. Gamification would later be adopted and, in fact, mastered by U.S. business leaders who appropriated and then augmented the concepts by adding monetary and social incentives to motivate employee behavior.[204] Today Western organizations have embedded this evolved form of gamification into the work environment and widely recognize its effectiveness.[205] But for our purposes, the question to examine is how do you use it to be a force for good?

Game mechanics and game dynamics

A paper on the MDA framework (Mechanics, Dynamics, and Aesthetics) in game design[206] explains that the rules of a game are the Mechanics, and the systems, such as time pressure or the ability to earn tokens, are the Dynamics. While the video game system is fully designed and the rules are literally hardcoded when a game is released, neither the moves an individual player will make nor the results of their gameplay are known. What's more, the player's decisions trigger results in the game, and the game results, in turn, trigger the player's future actions. Games train their players and each player's actions determine how they will be taught. By rewarding and punishing decisions through the application of rules (i.e., Mechanics), and the run-time effect of the mechanics in response to player inputs (i.e., Dynamics), players learn how to play the game. These are interdependent systems where the rules affect the player, and the player's reactions affect progression through the game. As Hunicke, LeBlanc, and Zubek wrote, "Thinking about games as designed artifacts helps frame them as systems that build behavior via interaction."[207]

In designing benefits programs at work, where certain outcomes are highly desirable, it is important to examine the Mechanics introduced, to ensure that they are supporting the desired Dynamics. What rules, rewards, and systems would you institute if your goal was to encourage consistency in physical activity versus weight loss? Time pressure might be a useful Dynamic, reinforced by the Mechanic of earning a reward of daily points for a minimum unit of activity with a cutoff at 10:00 p.m. Positive peer pressure might be another useful Dynamic reinforced by creating the Mechanic of teams with shared physical activity goals wherein points are only earned if all team members complete their daily activity.

You can be infinitely creative in your decisions about what to offer, but the starting principle must be clear: you are optimizing for a well-understood, desired outcome. If you want consistent physical activity, you're probably wasting your money on a stand-alone annual biometric screening with a $200 cash incentive, because the Mechanic does not support the desired outcome. While you can get employees to do the screening before the end of the year because $200 is a lot of money, they will not be trained to do anything other than wait to collect their $200 every year and then go back to their regular sedentary behaviors. Rather, the goals, behaviors, and incentives you offer must be focused on ongoing physical activity.

If you don't apply these gamification lessons as an employer, not only will your programs be less effective, but you will be missing out on the opportunity to make your employees feel seen and heard because the benefits you offer will be tone deaf to their actual needs. But rather than kill all your darlings and start from scratch, you can simply begin by adding a requirement that all future programs or solutions be digital and on-demand. This simple enhancement of your criteria will ensure that when you evaluate solutions to increase employee engagement or enhance community and connection, you review the options through this new and necessary filter in addition to your existing filters. If your company seeks to add emergency childcare as a benefit, instead of merely looking at cost, proximity, and safety, you would also seek to ensure that the back-up care is accessible and usable purely through one's smartphone without requiring a phone call, that all forms may be completed on the mobile device, and that the childcare is available on-demand when and how the working parent needs it.

Applying gamification to your benefits program

When the objective is to boost engagement and increase motivation, you must also seek to remove any unnecessary friction in the programs you offer. If you have an excellent employee assistance program but it is not accessible 24-7, or a great medical plan but it doesn't offer telemedicine, you are erecting roadblocks to stop your employees from using the resources you prefer and are encouraging them to use alternatives. If fifty-two-year old Barbara, whom we met in chapter 1, cannot reach the EAP line at midnight when she is feeling hopeless and scared, she'll self-medicate with another two glasses of chardonnay to numb the pain and be less likely to ask for help in the future. If thirty-six-year old Laura doesn't have access to an ob-gyn digitally on Sunday morning when she isn't feeling movement in her belly, she is going to drive to her nearest ER for an urgent-care visit. Not only will that prove financially costly for the company, it will fail to help Laura quickly feel calmer by coaching her through having a glass of milk and lying down on her back to feel the resumption of fluttering kicks in response.

In addition, if you want people to use what you provide, you must also require that your program enhancements be intuitive for employees to use and do not make them work to figure it out. No one is going to read an instruction manual or suffer through a lengthy tutorial, so if you can't figure it out instantly without assistance, don't even consider it. Vendors may try to convince you that their tools are the best, and most comprehensive, but if the tap test on your phone doesn't make it obvious that anyone, anywhere can learn the ins and outs in a matter of minutes without using up a lifeline or phoning a friend, stay away. Similarly, it has to sell itself to your target audience. If the solution doesn't interest them or draw them in deeper within a matter of seconds, your employees are not going to give it a chance. Without a personal "aha" moment, you won't garner mass appeal or usage. So, take the time to check how the people you are solving for might like it. As we discussed in chapter 7, there are many ways to listen to your employees and find out what they want. You can conduct a short survey or a focus group or add a few questions to your annual employee review where you actually solicit feedback from your workforce about how they'd like to be better supported. Make sure these are digital, of course, and easy to complete in just a few seconds. Or you can dig in much deeper and explore the specific service you are contemplating to take out all of the guesswork.

Back in 2016 during a comprehensive and lengthy RFP with Aetna, the stakeholders requested a penultimate step, a thirty-day large group trial of Grokker by actual Aetna employees. We were to invite five hundred volunteer testers who'd opted in to provide their feedback and report on their usage at the end of the month-long trial. Most companies don't have a built-in panel of five hundred employees on a wellbeing team to do such a trial, but the opportunity was a big one for us and for them, and we of course agreed. I know that most companies would find such a test terrifying, but we relished the opportunity and put the trialers through our regular onboarding process, complete with personalization and multiple concurrent welcome challenges. This allowed the company to kick the tires and get valuable feedback from the target audience, not just about our proprietary workout and yoga videos, but also about Grokker's nutrition and sleep programs, our mindfulness and resilience training, the community features, the communications and reporting functionality, and our incentives and rewards capabilities. Happily for everyone, the trial was a huge success, and the stakeholders were able to offer the new wellbeing solution as a benefit with great confidence. We have been working together ever since and now also serve the entire population of CVS Health, which acquired Aetna in 2019. No surprise that it all went well because by taking the time to check, Aetna knew they were giving their people what they wanted.

A little neon never hurts

We all notice the blinking neon lights of the vacancy sign on the motel as we drive past. It grabs our attention and compels us to look at it. It may be kitschy and garish, but it's remarkably effective, because a little neon never hurts. You must make what you are offering known by your target audience and use the medium most likely to capture their attention to do so. Digital video is what you want because it's what they want. Downloadable video is another requirement, so that employees can watch even when connectivity is slow to avoid the dreaded buffering spiral. A recent study of the top health and fitness apps finds that apps that offer video are installed 65 percent more than those without video. What's more, those apps with video capture 38.5 percent more daily active users (DAU).[208] These same user preferences apply to the benefits you offer and are even more important, because your employees are conditioned to expect a poor consumer experience from corporate benefits. To overcome this negative bias and entice employees to try what you have, you must lure them with the blinking neon and then provide an experience that will delight them. Yes, delight.

Your employees expect a lot, and you have the ability to satisfy those expectations without breaking the bank, thanks to our technology-enabled world. The trick is to understand what they want (digital benefits that support them as a whole person and are both entertaining and video-centric), how they want to interact with the content you provide (on smartphones, tablets, and connected TVs), and then making it available. If they were raised to expect *Blue's Clues* to play when they want it, then you would be wise to give it to them and watch them thrive.

Integrity, Passion, and Caring: The Secret Sauce for Selling a Vision

A Guest Perspective by Susan Lyne,
Mass Media Legend and Managing Partner, BBG Ventures

Creating your vision is one thing. Getting those to whom you report to accept it is another. To gain insights into how to get others to accept your vision, I talked with Susan Lyne. She is the founder and president of BBG Ventures, an early-stage investment fund focused on mobile and internet start-ups with at least one female founder. Prior to BBG, Susan served as CEO of AOL Brand Group, Gilt Groupe, and Martha Stewart Living Omnimedia. Earlier in her career she was president of ABC Entertainment, where she developed shows such as *Desperate Housewives* and *Grey's Anatomy*. Susan started her career in print media, where she served as managing editor at *The Village Voice* and founding editor-in-chief of *Premiere* magazine. Here's what she had to say:

"When I started working back in the '70s, I really wanted to have a career. I started in magazines because, at the time, if you wanted to impact the way people thought about politics, culture, or society, magazines were where you did it. Back then, the editor-in-chief was almost always a man, even at the women's magazines, so I didn't go into magazines thinking I'd become the top editor—I was just thrilled to be invited to the party. It turned out that while I had male bosses who I reported to, my day-to-day experiences were with the people who I had hired and brought together. It was always a very varied group, particularly gender—lots of women and guys. And in that day-to-day work, I owned the decision; I didn't have to ask permission. I was lucky in that sense, and it was probably different for a lot of women who were in law firms or corporations where every waking hour was spent within the hierarchy.

"In 1987, I started a magazine called *Premiere* for NewsCorp, and I had a great time with them. I actually enjoyed working with Rupert

Murdoch. He was a straight shooter. He told me exactly what he was going give me and exactly how it was going to work. He said, 'I will give you two test issues. We're not going to spend any money on marketing, but it will get great newsstand play, and we'll see if people want to pick it up.' It seemed fair, and I was game. He gave me the ability to create a magazine, build my own team, and never told us what to write. I was given the ability to make something that I thought was good without his people looking over my shoulder. I would call him when we were going to publish something that I thought could be problematic for him. He was nothing but a straight shooter about that stuff too. He would just ask me whether it was true.

"When I started working at ABC, I still had no role models. That's a weird thing to say, but there just weren't people I could look at who were female and who ran big entertainment companies, were directing movies, or whatever. They just didn't exist. Ultimately, I lost my job at ABC because a group of guys didn't want to report to me. Truthfully, I should have played it differently, but that's a whole different story. It's all to say that I certainly had my fair share of challenges, but I never gave a moment's thought to why the world was like that because I didn't have any other examples.

"My next step was the Martha Stewart company, where I served as CEO for four years. I left in 2008 to join what was then a very small start-up that was reinventing shopping: Gilt. It brought together two things I knew and loved: e-commerce and entertainment. We claimed a time period and programmed the daily sales in a way that made it fun, even addictive. Gilt was founded by five people, including two women—and it was there that I started meeting a lot of female founders. If you look back to the eight or ten years before its founding, the cost of starting a company had come down dramatically, which opened the door to a very different kind of founder than the traditional Silicon Valley tech bro. In New York, that included a lot of women. New York is a heterogeneous economy with dozens of different sectors that that call it home—so you had women coming out of B schools or out of companies where they had sector expertise who were convinced they could solve a consumer problem that was driving millions of people crazy. Companies like Rent the Runway, Birchbox, Learnvest, and scores of others. And the founders all had similar stories about raising money.

"The VC world at the time was incredibly homogeneous: very male, very white, very concentrated in the schools they attended. So, these women would go into a room filled with guys, start their pitch, and realize they had to explain how women think about X or Y before they could get into the business they were building. It was clearly a problem, but it also struck me as a massive opportunity. I had spent my entire career focused on what we call the dominant consumer. Woman are responsible for 80 percent of consumer purchases. Look at any category, even categories that were once considered male, like where the family banks and what house they buy; women own those decisions.

"I thought that if you could identify great founders who intuitively understood that end user—knew what she needed and what was going to appeal to her—it would be a no-brainer and would give us a competitive advantage. That is why we started BBG Ventures. We put a stake in the ground and said we were going to back companies that had at least one female founder. We were among the first funds to focus on women, so we had a lot of deal flow from day one.

"When we started BBG Ventures in 2014, I heard over and over again from male friends who were VCs that it was a really nice idea, but there just weren't enough women starting companies to build a strong portfolio. But we've seen over seven thousand companies since we started, all with a female founder. I think the key issue is that venture capital has always operated the same way—and it's true even today. It's about the "warm introduction." If your network is people who look like you, they're going to send you founders who look like the other founders you've backed before. And you start to develop pattern recognition. This kind of founder started this kind of company, and it was successful, so, therefore, we should be looking for founders like that.

"I look for an idea that, in success, could be adopted or bought by millions and millions of people. Increasingly, we look for companies that open up access to underserved consumers, or that increase consumers' control over key aspects of their lives. Small really doesn't work. But whatever the idea, I'm actually spending the majority of my time trying to figure out whether I want to be in business with this human being for the next ten years. Do I believe that they can actually execute on this and ride that rollercoaster? It doesn't matter how great your idea is, you're going to have days where you feel like this could completely blow up or that someone else is coming out with X Y Z, and that's going to change the game significantly. You need a founder who is resilient and passionate, and who knows how to identify talent, recruit people, take care of them, and keep them close. There are so many things about that founder job that are intrinsic to you as a human being. Pitching can be learned. The question is whether you have the grit and resilience to be able to take something from an idea to a big, lasting company. That's what I'm looking for.

"When you're building your core team, you have to know the difference between good and great. One good question when you're "diligencing" a founder is asking who they have hired in the past. Have they launched stars? And do those people have great things to say about them? I often ask people if they'd work for that founder again. Was it a positive enough relationship that you'd say to someone who was thinking about going to work for that founder, 'Do it. It's going to be a life-changing experience.'

"The most important skill for a founder is the ability to identify the best talent and recruit them—make them want to work for you. It comes from the ability to paint a picture of what you are building and why you're excited about this journey. It's not that they're 'nice' people, although I think that the best founders are people who take care of their talent even to the point where, when that person is ready to go off to do their own thing, they lift them over the curb and tell them they're going to back them. You need to believe that this leader is going to teach you and is going to have your best interests at heart along the way. It's both the right thing and the smart thing to do.

"Even with what might seem like a small idea, I go back to who the person is who's pitching it. Everybody thinks they have a great idea. At the end of the day, this is the key question: 'Is this someone who I believe can take whatever idea they've just pitched and actually turn it into something that has depth, color, and surprises. There is no idea that works outside of the person who's going to execute it. There just isn't. And I don't care whether it's a start-up idea, a business transformation, or an idea for a show."

Chapter 9:

ENCOURAGE SUCCESS

When my first child was born, I read a lot of parenting books. Not much stuck with me over the years from these dense tomes, or perhaps I just didn't follow the well-intentioned psychologists' advice. But one line from one book has always stayed with me. In essence, the line explained that if you are trying to change a behavior in a child, the best way to do so is by "catching them in the act of being good." In other words, to help permanently rewire the brain, one requires positive feedback (and plenty of it) while engaging in the new behavior, so that the association is made between the new pattern and the pleasure stimulus in the brain that is activated by the parental praise. Do the new thing, get praise, feel great. Do the new thing, get praise, feel great. Rinse, repeat. Do the new thing enough times, and your brain learns to always do the new thing because your brain quite literally becomes encoded to expect the positive feelings, and so the new behavior becomes the norm. The same is true for adults, except adult brains are harder and take more time to rewire. Making matters even tricker when it comes to grown-ups is the challenge of finding opportunities to employ this strategy in the work environment, where managers often have ten to twenty direct reports, have competing deadlines, and may not have the same innate desire to help their subordinates' personal growth.

In truth, many of the strategies used in raising children and educating them can be applied to work situations. As CEO and president of Kaplan Thaler Productions, best-selling author, and inductee into the Advertising Hall of Fame Linda Kaplan Thaler said:

I think having children and teaching school was a fabulous—no pun intended—breeding ground for learning how to manage a company and managing clients. We are, in fact, all children. We all need to be complimented, and we all need to be heard and validated. A child struggling through a challenging book report assignment may say, "Mom, this book is stupid and sooo old. Who cares about how Huck's character is commenting on society? How am I supposed to get this dumb report done when I have math and Spanish homework due tomorrow, and baseball practice in an hour? My teacher is so mean, and I don't care about English anyway, I'm just turning this in, and she'll give me a C." If you say, "Stop complaining, apply yourself, and just finish your report or no practice for you," you haven't validated his or her feelings, and the child will shut down and feel pushed into a corner. You may get some talking back with yelling and screaming which will make you escalate and use your power to force the immediate action you want. "That's it, no practice today and if you don't finish your homework properly, there will be no practice for the rest of the week." You can extract acquiescence in this manner, but nothing to help the child in future or in life.

If on the other hand, you view the interaction as a "teachable moment" you may learn to say something like, "I love your passion for baseball, and I am excited for your game this weekend. *Huckleberry Finn* is old indeed, but it's actually one of the most important books written and studied because it teaches us a lot about the world we used to live in and sadly in many ways we still do. You are really smart and capable, and I know how hard you work to be great at the things you love like baseball. But if your coach doesn't know how to explain things to you, you get frustrated. This is exactly the same. I don't care about the grade you get, but I do care that you try your best and get the help you need to understand what is being asked of you. Why don't you tell me what is confusing about the assignment and I can try to explain it better, so you can take another swing at it. I'd love to help you and then get a chance to read the book report. I read *Huck Finn* when I was in Middle School too believe it or not." This way, you have validated your child's feelings, and their ability. You have encouraged perseverance with positivity. And you have also steered them in a direction that is safer, better and more likely to result in success. Most women learn this instinctively when they become mothers. And you need to learn to do the same, without condescension, with employees, co-workers, and clients.[209]

I bring this up not to infantilize your employees, but to emphasize the universality of the strategies for encouraging success. As the manager and executive, you need to keep your focus on what matters long term, but for your employees, you need to break it down into smaller components they can grok and complete. When they hit a snag, let your employees take little steps, make it easy for them, and then concentrate on the small wins so they feel successful. You want your people to want your help, not hide their problems or undermine the objective. But for them to want your help, they need to feel safe and confident that in asking for help, they will not be embarrassed in front of you or their peers, look dumb, or be punished. Like I mentioned in the introduction about my experience at HP, asking for help was actively encouraged and rewarded as part of the corporate culture, as was providing guidance to others. This made it incredibly safe to speak up, ask questions, and seek advice, which made individuals as junior as I was at the time ask questions to do their jobs better, and this in turn made the company more successful. The "open-door" policy was a brilliant part of the culture, designed to encourage success by making each person's success a group responsibility. You were never alone in facing adversity.

At your company, if you already provide programs that help employees feel seen and understood, you know exactly what I am talking about. It's not just elevating those who invest in others but crafting an approach to people that sees them as individuals and makes them feel accepted. It's doing away with one-size-fits-all thinking and being prepared to go deeper as a matter of practice. This applies to one-on-one interactions and reporting relationships, but it also extends more broadly to the kinds of programs and benefits you offer. A personalized approach to wellbeing offers a broad variety of events, activities, and "challenges," so the widest group of employees can participate and are motivated to do so because they can actually find something that interests them. By covering this broad spectrum of opportunities from fitness and mental health to sleep, nutrition, and financial wellbeing, a much larger swath of the population can have their needs met. This way, everyone can decide for themselves which area of interest appeals to them, whether they are motivated to learn how to cook healthier family meals in under thirty minutes or practicing advanced yoga poses to lower their blood pressure.

To make people successful at caring for themselves and safeguarding your culture, you need to take into account the different kinds of motivation and what combination works for the individuals at your company. As I mentioned in the previous chapter, there are three types of motivation: extrinsic, intrinsic, and self-signaling. What does that mean? External factors that influence me, like praise or awards, are what generate extrinsic motivation. To tap into extrinsic motivation, you break down goals into smaller chunks, so employees feel that they are making progress and being rewarded for each step. In this way, employees feel their actions are resulting in success as evidenced by the praise or reward and are driven to come back for more. After all, feeling great fuels and sustains itself. Internal motivators, like pleasure or a desire to be healthier, are what create intrinsic motivation. Keeping employees engaged in a corporate wellbeing program, for instance, requires some degree of fun—the intrinsic motivator—or your employees simply won't stick with it. Just think: as Professor Rima Touré-Tillery points out, "People work hard at what they enjoy."[210] So, apart from infusing fun into the experience, you want be careful to not add friction into the process. Friction can come in the form of hard-to-understand rules or unnecessary extra steps; so, rather than introducing a barrier, like forcing employees to fill out forms or only making things available at work, you want to make everything accessible on a smartphone and available 24-7, whenever your employees want to engage. Add to that small, achievable steps that are easy to perform and a sense of playfulness through your tone, program design, and execution, and you are headed in the winning direction.

"Motivation increases with the expectation that actions will enhance or protect the self-concept."[211] The idea here is that people will act more when the action reinforces a self-belief that they find important. This is called self-signaling. It could be that they want to think of themselves as smart, skilled, and dedicated, or friendly, supportive, and a team player. Whatever the attribute they aspire to, if an action results in making people feel like they are achieving this positive attribute, they will engage in the action and feel validated because they are signaling to themselves that their desired self-view is indeed a reality. So now ask yourself: what signaling does your current wellness program generate? Are they attributes your employees want to embrace? Standalone biometric screenings, the way they are practiced today, tell people that they're not in shape in some way. And since their results are generally the same year after year, it conveys that they are hopeless and stuck, and if penalties for poor results are employed, they are even made to feel like a corporate line item expense because of the higher insurance they pay, or that they are a cog in the uncaring benefits design of the company. Yes, having this information can be helpful and serve as a benchmark, but it must be conveyed in a form that conveys an achievable, realistic way to a better outcome—something that tells a better story about themselves and a way to achieve it in small steps.

Ultimately, you want your employees to say, "I'm reaching my goals and I'm having fun doing it; this program just proves that I'm (name the attribute)." Achieving this outcome is tricky but powerful, because it is based on their own self-image. Yes, you want your employees to reach their goals and have fun doing it, but seeing oneself in a new, better light will radiate out to encourage them to attack additional goals and accomplishment. You need to make them feel good about who they are and where they are in their journey, every step of the way. I bet your *Biggest Loser* weight-loss challenges, biometric screening, and 1950s top-down management structures can't do that!

Let's get physical

Another way to ensure success that actually reflects your corporate values—and the self-image of the employees who buy into it—is in the design of your physical work environment. You want it to reflect who you are from your reception area as well as your employee entrance. Physical environments, in fact, greatly influence perceptions and performance. Geraldine (Gerry) Laybourne, whom we met in chapter 6, told me a story about when she visited a building designed by Norman Foster. Gerry was rifling through her stuff looking for her ID to present at reception, and the woman at the security desk with a big smile on her face said, "Just take your time. We are not in a hurry. Just take your time." Gerry told me that she was shocked and delighted at the words of caring, and she recounts responding in this way: "'Oh my God, you're the first security person who has ever smiled at me.' And then I went upstairs and had exact same experience. Everything was kind and great. During the conversation my host told me that he believes that the bright, thoughtful, people-loving, community-building architecture of the building helped to build a kind and welcoming culture." And Gerry agrees: "I think architecture is a very important tool of companies as well."[212]

What does your environment say about your culture? How does it speak to your values, attitudes, and the experience you want employees and visitors to encounter? The right environments will help set a positive, caring tone, while the wrong ones will just get in the way. Walk through your environments and make sure each place tells the story you want. If your reception area is bright and welcoming, but your employee break room is drab and uncomfortable, you are essentially saying the guests are important, but employees are not. How do you want your people to feel, and does the workspace they occupy encourage those feelings? At Amazon, Jeff Bezos built his first desk out of a door purchased from the Home Depot across the street from the then start-up's offices. Bezos couldn't afford much, and doors were considerably less expensive than proper desks, so he added some legs, and the makeshift desk was constructed. For a long time, door desks were the norm by necessity at the struggling company. But even after the company's fortunes turned around, they persisted. As employee number 5, Nick Lovejoy, explains, "As Amazon grew, a decision was made to keep using door desks as a symbol of one of the company's core values, frugality. Today, a version of the desk has even become a makeshift trophy. Amazon recognizes well-built ideas that help deliver low prices to customers with a Door Desk Award." For Lovejoy, it also represents "ingenuity, creativity and peculiarity, and the willingness to go your own path."[213] So, what are you saying with your furniture and décor choices? How are your employees taking in the physical plant, and is it what you intend? If not, it's probably time to figure that out.

Make sure there are no ghosts in the machine

Ghosting is now such an unfortunate part of culture. Due to our technological world where millennials and Gen Z-ers/zennials are more used to connecting over their devices rather than in face-to-face conversations, ghosting has become a way of breaking up—one party just vanishes and stops returning texts and more. It's easy for the one who is doing the ghosting, because he or she doesn't have to face the other, but painful for the recipient, whose expectations as well as hopes are dashed. Recruits have even taken to ghosting employers. We all know of the individual who doesn't respond to a job offer but, rather, just vanishes. The same can be said for employers, whose recruiting arms often lose their grip and leave candidates hanging with no reply for weeks on end. My brother told me a typical story that happened to him about eight years ago. He was interviewing for a new role and in fact had multiple competing offers. The senior-most investor in one of the companies told him that they absolutely wanted him and asked my brother to promise that he wouldn't take another offer without at least calling this person to give him a chance to counter. Several months later my brother was comfortably ensconced in his new company and had never heard from that investor again. My brother was ghosted in broad daylight.

But the most painful form of ghosting in corporate America comes from the C-suite after a new initiative is announced with great enthusiasm and well-orchestrated fanfare, only to be followed by radio silence. There's a big splashy launch celebration with executive speeches about the importance of personal wellbeing followed by a fun run and participation T-shirts and water bottles, and maybe even some kind of healthy values mascot, but sadly, no follow-through or follow-up.

Following through on the program doesn't need to take as much of your time as you may think. In fact, much of your program can be automated. A big piece of the wellbeing puzzle, inside and outside of the workplace, is having access to both experts and a peer community to inspire and support your efforts. In other words, for your wellbeing program to be effective—and to really take root as a driver of company culture—you need to provide the right tools and information at the right time and place. The right time and place are simply when your employees need and desire them. Think of it as the *Blue's Clues* of wellbeing access (and if you don't get what I mean, you clearly skipped a chapter).

In this day and age, the easiest way to empower your employees with personal wellbeing is digitally. And, thanks to 24-7, easy-to-access, on-demand, app- and web-based content and tools, your employees can be in touch with their wellbeing advocates—nutritionists, personal trainers, financial wellness experts, coworkers who share their goals, and others—when and where they need it. Employees are already connected, using smartphones and other devices to stay in touch with their friends, family, and coworkers over mobile apps, email, text, and social media. And they're consuming more and more multimedia content, such as video, for information and entertainment. Consider the impact on their engagement, too. Without these digital tools, your employees simply wouldn't be able to connect with other individuals or groups on a daily basis, and they may not receive enough of the all-important positive feedback and inspiration to make their wellbeing journeys successful in the first place.

As the workforce increasingly becomes diverse and dispersed, it's only going to become increasingly critical to offer the benefits that are truly inclusive, easy to implement and adopt, lead to sustainable change, and that employees genuinely enjoy. Plus, with the increased focus on the importance of wellbeing benefits in attracting and retaining top talent, personalization through digital content and tools are a necessity. Employees expect access on their terms and want benefits that fit into their lives, making their wellbeing journeys more fun, successful, and rewarding. You can even enable employees to pick the types of incentives they want to incorporate into their wellbeing program, giving them more ownership over the success of it. It's also important to note that when it comes to employee health-and-wellness programs, the definition of "wellness" has changed dramatically over the years from the old-school "absence of physical disease" to the modern holistic meaning. In fact, today, the term "wellbeing" more accurately describes a true, all-encompassing approach to multidimensional health that people are now aiming to achieve, covering—as I listed earlier—physical health, mental health, sleep, nutrition, social health, and even financial wellbeing.

Remember, it's not about creating work-life balance, which was derived from a work-first mentality and was centered more to answer the organization's needs, despite the overwhelming stress placed on their employees. Rather, your values and wellbeing program should enable a bottoms-up approach, one that is focused on creating an embraceable employee experience. People naturally want to do a good job. So, don't force their lives into artificial "work" and "life" silos. Rather, give them the tools they need to support their whole lives, and set them free to thrive.

What would your managers do?

Once you follow through (and, of course, stick with your support of it), the success of your wellness program, as well as the inculcation of your more caring culture then depends on your managers. Their behaviors can matter as much as yours. To help ensure that they are on the right track, I compiled a list of fourteen questions that identify the ideal leadership behaviors. Can you answer with a convincing yes to all of the following? If so, you're indeed moving in the right direction:

1. **Do managers openly recognize extraordinary effort or only the desired outcome?** In today's world of 24-7 innovation, not every effort succeeds. In fact, the entire discipline of design thinking is built around the idea of continuous iterations of prototypes and testing until one iteration actually works. Another way to think about it: Without extraordinary effort, nothing will succeed. But if you keep rewarding effort, your employees will keep trying.

2. **Is helping out teammates rewarded?** In the old GE world of eliminating employees performing in the bottom 10 percent on an annual basis, the better-performing employees might be understandably reluctant to help others out, because it would raise the average performance of their competitor colleagues. But isn't that the point—making everyone better! Half of your employees are below average by the very nature of how averages work. In other words, during the top-down, eliminate-defects era, helping could jeopardize one's ranking, because the other would rise. In the new, enlightened world, everyone rises when we help each other, because you're raising the bar of where the average falls.

3. **Are setbacks proactively raised and examined by leadership as learning opportunities?** By embracing and learning from our stumbling blocks and failures, we can more easily find success. It's that simple. Careers are akin to a long-distance steeplechase, not a short, flat sprint. People who take a more realistic view of

the difficulty and endurance required still set their standards and sights as high as they can but are the ones who become more valuable.[214] The same philosophy can be said of organizations. If you think of your operations as a race with hurdles or obstacles, you begin to anticipate them, examine them, and more efficiently overcome them.

4. **Are successes shared and celebrated broadly?** Celebrate even the little wins. Everyone wants to know they are on a winning team. So, tell them.

5. **Is interpersonal conflict acknowledged and productively resolved with the assistance of managers?** Make sure your managers are not co-opted into siding with employees on issues nor are handling the situation themselves. You also need to ensure that your managers aren't ignoring these situations and that the issues are proactively resolved. Training in conflict resolution and in how to have difficult conversations for your managers can help. So can training your rank and file on how to raise issues productively and avoid resentment.

6. **Is debate encouraged, even when opinions run contrary to leadership's point of view?** I don't suggest playing the devil's advocate just to slow down the process. They hold those views for a reason. Dig deep. Find the why behind the why. Divergent views and discussion are how you can create something better. It can uncover something new. My friend and collaborator, Professor Laurence Minsky, calls the approach "creating a genius." In this approach, "everyone on the team contributes their strengths and unique perspectives and, when done right, eliminates their weakness."[215]

7. **Is holding a contrary view or questioning something seen as a potentially dangerous career-limiting move?** Your employees need to be able to speak freely. But it can't happen unless debate is encouraged in a safe environment where questioning and

disagreeing is rewarded. This is similar to the story I shared in the introduction about my experience in the early days of my career at Hewlett Packard. If they feel like a comment will come back to haunt them, they will hold back, and you won't have the rigorous debate that can lead to something new and better—or the warning that you're going down the wrong road.

8. **Do managers admit when they make mistakes, and do they apologize?** It's okay for a manager to show her or his humanity. We all make mistakes. But so few apologize, and this is a very powerful tool for leaders to use. It shows strength and a depth of caring.

9. **Does leadership often express gratitude and praise?** We couldn't do our job as leaders if the team that supports us isn't doing theirs. Let them know what they're doing right and that their efforts are seen and appreciated. Be specific and timely and thank them in public whenever possible for others to see.

10. **Do your managers handle customer issues with focus and resolve and, when appropriate, stand up for their employees?** Customers and clients are our lifeblood. Your managers need to make sure that clients are more than just "satisfied" but are brand advocates. When issues arise, your managers need to take it personally and work to resolve it. However, the customer isn't always right. They can have a bad day too and take it out on one of your team members. And when that happens, you need to intervene and protect your people while reinforcing your values to the client. They too will appreciate your level-headed support for your employees and clear articulation of acceptable norms.

11. **What kind of language is used by leadership when discussing customers, especially difficult ones?** Is it respectful, caring, and reflective of the stated ethics of your company? If your team does not value or respect a customer and cannot treat them with the

same professionalism afforded others, then they shouldn't be your client. Period.

12. **What happens when a big deal is lost to a competitor?** Does leadership speak disparagingly of them, tear down the internal team for the failure, or hold a review in order to be accountable and learn from the experience?

13. **Are subordinates treated with respect and made to feel valued?** They enable us to do what we do best. They are appreciated for their important contributions and given credit for their achievements. They are given shout-outs for helping others out and know that their work matters.

14. **Is there a desire to teach, coach, groom, and grow team members?** Your managers don't only care about your teams hitting their numbers; they feel responsible for the technical proficiency of their teams and for ensuring the development of the next generation of leaders. They are proud of their role as coaches and mentors and take that responsibility seriously.

Can you and your managers answer these fourteen questions in the affirmative? If not, ask why for each one and listen to what is inhibiting your managers. You'll learn a lot if you keep an open mind and provide time for the free flow of this kind of meaningful discussion. It's a great exercise to do as a leadership team. Just run through the questions and go around asking for people to provide examples of both successes and areas that are in need of improvement as well as what would need to change at the company to enable that change. It is a simple yet effective way, as a team, to check in on the health of your leadership, and maybe even do something to improve upon it.

Creating an Employer Brand Based on the Employee's Hierarchy of Needs

A Guest Perspective by Christine Buck, Global Head of Marketing & Brand, Talent & Culture, Morningstar

We all form emotional connections to brands, and increasingly today, we look to them to amplify our own personal image or brand. In the business landscape, the importance of developing and protecting a brand image has grown beyond the traditional client or consumer relationship. Brands are as much about the people inside of the company as they are the buyers outside. And just as organizations manage their external brands to consumers, they need to manage the internal one to their employees. But what does it take to intentionally create an authentic employer brand that reflects the culture of a company? To find out, we asked Christine Buck, who led the effort to create a defined, managed employer brand at Morningstar, a global financial services and technology firm that provides both investment research and investment management services. Prior to serving as Morningstar's global head of marketing & brand, talent & culture, Christine was the senior director, head of global marketing, capital markets, and investor services at CBRE. She was global brand manager at Accenture after having started her career with Microsoft. Here's is what she had to say:

"Morningstar was in a unique situation. We started over thirty-five years ago with a printed binder of mutual fund research and went on to become a technology company providing investment research, analytics, and data in the form of research to investors. We just kept evolving and growing. Our company was special from the beginning, with our founder, Joe Mansueto, building the organization around an inclusive environment and establishing a culture that celebrates diversity of thought and this enduring idea of transparency and objectivity that extends to our mission, Early on, the company started offering programs and benefits that predate start-ups like Google and a focus on a workplace environment that did not have the typical corner-office or hierarchy you'd see in the typical banking or investment management. One example of an enduring cultural benefit is the Morningstar Sabbatical program, which offers full-time employees a paid six-week leave for every four years of service. And we are always innovating and modernizing our programs. Our team developed a policy to help people transition and protect those individuals with a safe working environment. We were among the first companies in the fintech space that had open conversations about how to support our people and what diversity and inclusion means for us. In the last year, we are using our data, research, and talents to bring more insights to equitable access to investing and wealth creation. Morningstar has always had a very special culture, yet somewhere, we just took it for granted and didn't tell our story to our people or the outside world. And I think that led to our people taking it for granted too.

"While we have a great external brand that represents transparency connected to a very credible mission—empowering investor success— internally we became stale. We were not paying attention to social media and crowd-sourced reviews and comments from an employer brand or reputation perspective. And we started to lose ground. We just weren't attending to this emerging media format, meaning that we were missing opportunities to tell the story about our culture, our view on innovation, and even the story of our place in the global investment community. We started competing with companies who were also hiring the best technologists. Meanwhile, the world changed, with millennials and Gen Z coming on board. It went from employees and new hires saying, 'I'm grateful to have this job' to one where they said, 'I have fifty different companies to choose from, and I'm shopping. I want to make sure you are the best employer for me, and you provide the best benefits, best environment, and best opportunity for growth.' We missed that opportunity and were about six years behind in how we were designing, setting up, and packaging our programs for our people.

"We went through a transformation to develop and launch an employer brand by executing lots of different projects at once. I worked with our CHRO, Bevin Desmond, our CEO, Kunal Kapoor, and a small team to define what we thought Morningstar's employee experience should be. Using his perspective, I looked at our satisfaction data, engagement, and audited how we are talking to our people. I benchmarked us against other best-in-class firms and looked at our total rewards, including our key compensation programs as well as our cultural programs. Bringing in the customer voice was key—in this case, our employees—we uncovered what engagement meant to them. With our chief technology officer, technologists, workplace team, designers, and my small marketing and brand strategy team, we developed a new mission, defined the employer brand connected to our corporate brand, and solidified how we express our employee value proposition: 'Morningstar is a place where talented, driven people can grow.' We then packaged it all up in a way that would help our people see the bigger picture, but most crucial was building a brand that put our people—their stories and experiences—at the center. And it worked. Within three years, we noticeably increased employee satisfaction. Our Glassdoor rating, which had sunk to 3.2, was back to a best-in-class range of 4.1. We started receiving workplace and DEI-focused accolades again, including one from the Human Rights Campaign Equality Index (HRC100).

"Before we had established our employer brand expression and strategy, our social media was all about our research, our intellectual property, and our software—things that are a little bit more esoteric. We created a strategy that brought our people to the center and developed a platform or media channel we call *MorningStories*. We have a TV studio inside of our major offices, and I just started experimenting, interviewing colleagues around the world so they can tell their stories, why they work here, and what they believe. We needed a vehicle to communicate and share these stories, so we launched our first eZine, *Experience Morningstar*. We launched a pilot podcast series. And we even created our first D&I advertising campaign,

Free to Be Who You Are. We created a recruiting campaign on Instagram to show a day in the life of colleagues from our offices around the world. We found that by putting people at the center, focusing on the experience of what it means to be a part of Morningstar, the results were encouraging. It seems straightforward, but this work proved that people-centered messaging is much more powerful, with the data showing that people both inside and outside of the company were engaging with it more than just our average product content.

An example from Morningstar's Instagram-based recruitment campaign.*

*   Designed by Matthew Terdich, Morningstar. Used with permission.

Our Mission | Why We're Here

Empowering Investor Success

Our Values | What We Believe

| Great Products | Entrepreneurial Spirit | Uncompromising Ethics |
| Great People | Investors First | Financial Success |

Our Commitments | How We Work

Build Bridges	**Commit & Deliver**	**Create the Future**
Embrace new perspectives	Prioritize for impact	Think bigger
Dare to disagree	Make it happen	Investigate unknowns
Foster understanding	Own the outcome	Experiment to grow

Morningstar's cultural pillars.

"We also localize content to the best of our ability, which we found to be important with our employees. We created what I call the Global Partnership Network, wherein we give our partners around the world in different offices a concept and let them share the Morningstar perspective in their own words, and then disseminate it. We found it to be very powerful, and it shows that we care as a company and that we are sensitive to creating a global brand approach that can be localized to reflect the culture and customs of that office. While English is spoken by 99.9 percent of the people in our organization, because we're software engineers, researchers, and investment analysts in financial services, we take the extra step of localizing content to make all employees feel seen and included. When we start to feel like we're too Chicago-focused or U.S.-centric or too homogenous, we quickly rein it in. We don't ever put something out unless we consider the perspective of our offices, what it sounds like, or how it will be received by our colleagues in every one of our twenty-seven offices from Mumbai to Hong Kong.

"We use lots of research. We have an employee survey or what we call a listening program that we set up about three years ago that's run through Qualtrics. First, we ask about psychological safety and engagement as a standard set of questions. We then change and add other questions each quarter such as: Did our new mission resonate with you? How are you feeling about the company? What should we be doing differently? We then publish the findings, insights, how we can improve, and what we are planning to do differently in what we call our Organizational Health Report. Data is also used as part of our talent development process, showing us where we should invest in programs, learning tools, and so on. Finally, we use data to inform our operations and to make further investments.

"If I were to advise someone on creating or refreshing an employer brand, I would suggest starting with your corporate strategy and business goals as an organization. Next I'd turn to employee survey data. Most companies have some kind of internal survey data or a third-party survey like *Best Places to Work* to look at the key drivers of engagement. They can help you identify what is strong in your organization as well as the gaps and where you are falling short. And I would look at benchmarking the tactics and brand approach to best-in-class companies. What do they look like? What is the benchmark for companies in my category? I'd also look at companies outside of my category to see what they're doing. For example, a global manufacturing company might want to look at eBay, Netflix, or Patagonia and find what they've done. What is special about them that makes their people happy? What accolades have they received? What makes their culture attractive? Innovative?

The employer brand experience hierarchy of the key attributes.

"One way you can look at the employee experience is by using Maslow's hierarchy of needs as a way to understand the relationship of key attributes present in an employer brand and the employee brand experience. Just like Maslow's hierarchy, it starts on the bottom of a pyramid with the most basic needs and progresses up to the complete fulfillment of the organizational mission. For instance:

- At the bottom, you will find the basics: Do you offer equitable pay? Are your benefits what your employees want and need? Do they have the basic tools such as a desk, chair, equipment, and software to carry out their job? And do you have the right talent? Is your mission and culture accessible by all?
- The next level covers your workplace environment: Are your employees able to easily collaborate? Does the office space

reinforce the corporate culture, values, and principles? Do employees feel safe? Are they physically comfortable? Does the space reinforce collaboration and innovation?

- The third level is your culture: Do your employees feel psychologically safe, comfortable, and accepted? Do they feel like they are enabled to do their best work? Does their boss have their back? Are they included? Do they feel they can express a diversity of thought? (At Morningstar, we have this in spades. Our people are contrary. They are skeptics and vocal about what they like or don't like. And it is openly welcomed.) Can they explore ideas or opinions without being hurt in some way or held back as a result?

- At the top is agility: Can your employees experiment through testing and iterating? Do you have a culture of innovation? Do you have a mindset of continuous improvement?

"From consulting to manufacturing to retail, this model can be very helpful in developing an employer brand and experience that is connected to your people. And now more than ever, putting your people at the center is key. The pace of change is incredible—agile retailers were able to more easily pivot during the early days of the pandemic, quickly going from brick-and-mortar to a range of digital distribution options, and it was their workforce who delivered innovative tools and process to make that pivot. The same goes for manufacturing businesses—your people are building and delivering your products. You want them to take great pride in it and to believe in your brand, and at the same time, your employer brand should reinforce the kind of people you want to attract. You want great thinkers and great doers, people who make connections and are able to develop products that anticipate the needs of our clients in ways that are different. And to recruit and retain these great thinkers and doers, they need to feel good about their employer and that they're able to do their best work. It is not about putting what the corporation wants first. Instead, it is putting your people at the center of the story.

"For the scaffolding to make the business case, you have to work backwards from the voice of the customer or client. Then you backtrack into what drives innovation and allows people to do their best work. Your enablement data must be strong, answering such questions as, Can your people find a place here? Will they be intellectually challenged and enabled to make a difference for the customer? If you have a company that's taking the voice of the customer into consideration and can marry it with a highly engaged, highly enabled environment, you will see positive results and higher Net Promoter Scores. And that's what a CFO should be seeking. They should be reminded that it's not just the sales numbers, marketing efficiencies, or product innovation. It's everyone. A strong Net Promoter Score indicates happy and highly enabled employees. The client is saying, 'I will work with you again. I'm not a detractor. I will promote you, and I will buy your services, and I'll bring my friends along too.' There's a direct tie between the two. You can't have happy, loyal customers without happy, engaged employees. It's that simple."

Chapter 10:

A VISION OF THE FUTURE

I consistently hear from executives across the globe that they want to be more joyful and caring in their work. They feel that maintaining the status quo is neither fun nor easy anymore and that they are being tugged in opposite directions by competing forces. On the one hand, they are trying to manage the day-to-day operations of their enterprises in uncertain times, and on the other, they are seeking personal inspiration and even a higher state of awareness and presence from which they can experience more gratitude, happiness, and sense of having a positive impact on their companies, colleagues, families, and communities. While these executives are struggling to find a source of inspiration, ironically their teams are looking to them (now more than ever) to feel reassured and inspired, and many executives feel like outright frauds pretending to be visionary leaders with the answers. In fact, today's CEOs operate in an often-soulless corporate desert they inherited from predecessors who did not value the lives and struggles of the people who toil to deliver the products and services that are at the core of the company.

We are still haunted by Six Sigma certification training,[216] with its white- to black-belt skill levels, which was created by an engineer at Motorola to better identify and root out defects in hardware devices, not to groom and nurture the next generation of visionary leaders. Firing the employees performing in the bottom 10 percent each year, which we mentioned in the previous chapter, was a practice made famous by Jack Welch, the former CEO of GE. It was called managing "the vitality curve," but was better known by its euphemism "rank and yank." This antiquated rule-by-fear 1980's Welchian system of rigorously reducing employees down to a stack ranked number based upon annual performance reviews and rooting out the lowest 10 percent like menacing weeds from a garden was considered the epitome of enlightened leadership at the time. But it did not work out and actually made teams less cooperative and cohesive.[217] GE has evolved tremendously since then[218,219] and abolished the practice over a decade ago, in favor of a more nurturing and people-centric approach to developing their younger workforce with frequent feedback and a more positive career management philosophy. As one executive shared, "Command and control is what Jack was famous for. Now it's about connection and inspiration."[220] Performance at all cost, however, continues to permeate corporate America, and many modern CEOs are still recovering from it and trying to figure out how to move beyond it.

The post-WWII-era CEOs who built up the industrial and manufacturing giants of the last century like GE, Boeing, and Ford Motor Company were understandably attracted to inculcating simple, top-down, and quite militaristic principles into their organizational leadership principles. The U.S. military even adopted Six Sigma training[221] because defects cost lives, and in battle, it is essential that all troops are trained to react in exactly the same way at the same time every time without risking creativity, uncertainty, or dissension.[222] This also explains how companies inherited the platitude-filled corporate values statements and widely accepted old-school business practices from quite literally another era, and why today's CEOs and more diverse and inclusive workforces no longer believe in it either. These modern-day CEOs are in a genuine bind. They have ascended to the top spots after decades of proving themselves, at great personal sacrifice, on a field of play where they mastered the rules of the game but no longer buy into them. So, what do they do now that they are in charge? How much dare they risk in order to institute the changes that will fuel their souls and transform the cultures, behaviors, and norms for the workforces entrusted to them?

While many Silicon Valley investors have embraced microdosing with psilocybin[223] to try and spark their creativity, break down the barriers between themselves and others, and attempt to feel more connected to the collective consciousness in order to find their elusive path forward, there are far less extreme and ego-filled methods of rediscovering one's feeling of connection to humanity. In truth, the surest way to tap into this lost ability to harness your innately caring nature is to simply tap into yourself. The great irony of modern management is that after fifty years of top-down corporate constructs created to groom the aspiring CEO in the fine art of squeezing every last ounce of productivity out of each worker, the visionary leader of tomorrow will only succeed by inspiring creativity and loyalty as a direct consequence of their unique brand of empathy. And so, you must unlearn much of what got you to where you are today and trust your natural instincts in order to rebuild and reassert the corporate good for good. Let me explain.

Hack the system

Let's start with our most recent history. Isn't it interesting that as we settled into the social distancing routine during the early days of the COVID-19 pandemic, we quickly sought creative ways to work around the system? Humans are innately social creatures, so it's only natural for us to exploit loopholes to allow us to be (or at least feel) closer together. When county-wide shelter-in-place orders were instituted, and we couldn't offer hand-shakes or hugs, or even come within six feet of non–household members, we identified clever ways of maintaining some form of intimacy with the people outside of our homes. The spectrum ranged from attending vir-tual business meetings via video apps while occasionally flashing colorful pajama bottoms, to leaving cheerful chalk messages for neighbors in their driveways. Both examples count on the connection continuum. We didn't want to lose that authentic, personal touch we'd been missing so much just then. And if you think about it, our yearning for connection extends in a surprisingly consistent way whether it is between colleagues, siblings, work friends, or neighbors. That's why these little moments of connection and delight can be so powerful.

On the home front, families were finding ways to get together—doing curbside drive-bys, honking car horns for children's birthdays, or having backyard visits while maintaining touch-free social distancing. To keep the family entertained during spring break, my brother created an obstacle course in his backyard. His kids competed against themselves for their own personal records and then raced against their parents in a mini family Olympics—and they filmed it! The best part for me? My brother came over to my house with my nieces and nephew and stood at the curb so we could talk about their obstacle course in person, albeit at a distance.

Similarly, many companies were looking beyond the (now) standard methods of remote collaboration—aiming to support employees' whole lives, not just work lives. Tools like Zoom video conferencing and Slack messaging keep us connected to coworkers day in and day out, whether we're meeting to talk business or share casual jokes. But these tend to stop short of providing personal support of the more warm-and-fuzzy variety. As discussed in chapter 4, when deciding how best to reinsert humanity into your approach to human capital, as CEO or a management team member, you must first look inward to assess what you truly stand for as a person and a leader, then intentionally connect this to your company and commit to it. Then you need to set the example and hack the system, from the top down.

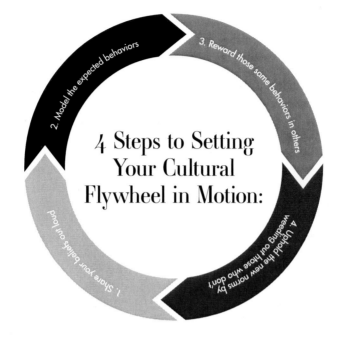

4 Steps to Setting
Your Cultural
Flywheel in Motion:

2. Model the expected behaviors

3. Reward those same behaviors in others

4. Uphold the new norms by weeding out those who don't

1. Share your beliefs out loud

Create cultural momentum to ensure your caring cultural shift
permeates your entire organization.

Setting the flywheel in motion

Like any chain reaction, to ensure your caring cultural shift permeates your entire organization and becomes self-reinforcing, you need to set it into motion with a number of self-amplifying reactions that all follow the same virtuous path, thereby creating positive cultural inertia. Think of it as setting a cultural flywheel in motion, and all it takes are four simple steps, which echo the steps outlined by Dr. Akilah Cadet in her Guest Perspective in chapter 7: 1) share your beliefs out loud and employ effective storytelling to make it personal; 2) model the expected behaviors; 3) reward those same behaviors in others; and 4) uphold the new authentic, caring cultural norms by weeding out those who do not. Showing by doing is the only effective means by which leadership can transform culture, and it cannot be delegated. While we have touched on this in previous chapters, it's valuable to briefly look at these steps again:

1. **Sharing is caring:** As the leader, or being a member of the leadership team, you have the obligation and the vantage point from which to change the narrative. But you cannot borrow the storyline. Rather, you must write it yourself. What are the beliefs you hold and wish to impart? Where did they come from and why do they matter to you? If you can share your origin story authentically and connect the beliefs that emanated from your personal experience to both the purpose and the values of the company you are currently committed to, then others will understand you and your passion and will have the opportunity to decide if they want to join you on whatever inspiring mission you outline. By building a common foundation out of your and every other leader's unique human experience and concretely tying it to the overarching goals and raison d'être of your company, you create a shared platform that feels differentiated in myriad ways, where the whole is truly greater than the sum of its parts.

   In some ways this may feel like an unnatural act. After all, you've been trained to compartmentalize the personal and suit up in your professional armor to ensure you do not betray any signs of weakness. But your true power is in the personal. You get to decide how you want to show up in this new work world, and it doesn't need to be in the image of every conservative, navy-blue-suited, middle-aged male CEO you worked for in the past. You have the privilege and the potential to approach your leadership and legacy courageously, so don't squander the opportunity. Lead boldly from the front by sharing your truth generously and making it clear both why you are committed to the corporate purpose as well as how you see the company evolving. By setting the example and revealing the nexus between your life experience and the company mission, vision, and values, you will be giving others permission to follow in your footsteps.

2. **The eyes have it:** Whether or not they are conscious of it, your team is constantly watching you and modeling their behavior on yours. In fact, the casual observation of your interactions with peers, superiors, and subordinates will dictate how your employees conduct themselves irrespective of what is emphasized during new employee training or written in your employee handbook. According to social learning theory, there are two main ways in which people learn new behaviors: 1) they observe others, and 2) they see or experience the consequences of their behavior.[224] As a leader, you have disproportionate influence on others' behavior because individuals are more likely to adopt a modeled behavior if the model "has admired status and the behavior has functional value."[225] And while all teammates pay a lot of attention to the actions of superiors, it is through the reinforcement of their memory of the behaviors and the motivation created by the observed positive or negative consequences of those behaviors that those same observed behaviors become encoded and propagated. Essentially, the eyes have it. What you see, what you recall seeing, and what you experience (directly or indirectly) as the result of what you saw shapes your behaviors and actions.

So, you really do need to be a model corporate citizen, and it is more important for the most senior members of a company to behave unflinchingly in the desired manner and in keeping with the values the company wishes to inculcate in the culture. Equally important is the need for these senior leaders to call attention to and apologize when they err in this modeling. We can't be perfect, but we can be human, and acknowledging when mistakes are made is essential to effectively shepherding this process. While written aids such as value statements prominently hanging on walls can certainly help reinforce rapid recall of desired behaviors, unless leadership is consistently modeling the right behaviors and both rewarding those same behaviors in others as well as taking corrective action when those behaviors are contravened, those corporate values posters won't be worth printing. As a leader you must not only model behavior but be a supermodel for the behaviors you want others to emulate. "Do as I say" just doesn't cut it in the real world.

3. **Reward consistently and generously:** As we just explored in the previous chapter, public praise and incentives, ranging from experiential to financial rewards, are essential to inculcating and retaining the behaviors you want. And they must be frequent, especially at first, when trying to introduce new behavioral norms. Two other critical factors required for incentives to be effective are for them to be 1) valuable or important to the targeted individuals, and 2) attainable enough to be motivating. The greater the perceived value of the reward and confidence in its attainability, the more strongly people will be motivated to pursue it. This is why being consistent in your application of rewards and reinforcement of positive behavior is so critical. An example of a highly effective incentive at Grokker is a twenty-five-dollar gift card to a favorite local coffee roaster. When our head of Business Solutions wants to enlist the teammates to participate in a brainstorm or help him solve a challenging customer problem, he simply offers a gift card to the individual who submits the most ideas or comes up with the winning solution. Our team is highly coffee motivated and frugal, and the odds are pretty favorable that you may win if you participate. What's more, since the team is already aligned with the greater corporate mission of helping

enable physical and emotional wellbeing for our customers and their employees, there is an inherent tendency to want to assist, and the incentive merely super charges it.

4. **Weed your garden:** Much as we'd like to believe that articulating and reinforcing the positive is all we need to do to assure upstanding corporate citizenry, there are always going to be a few bad actors who need to be dealt with. This requires extra vigilance and a willingness to act quickly, because no number of healthy apples can prevent even one rotten interloper from spoiling the whole barrel. People are obviously not pieces of fruit, but the effect is the same: one person making sexist, bigoted, or racist comments (especially if they are the manager) permeates and contaminates the entire team. Too often we ignore troubling actions or any obvious signs of inappropriate cultural behavior on the part of erstwhile star performers in particular. They crushed their sales goals, they are a lead developer, they saved a key client, and so we relax our standards and allow the proverbial fox into the cultural henhouse by failing to address their behavior. This is akin to how weeds overtake a garden. Weeds don't just take up space, they compete for the soil nutrients and sunlight your lawn and flowers need to thrive. Failing to introduce a structured approach to weeding regularly, as well as methods to properly dispose of the pulled weeds to ensure they cannot reroot, will result in stunting the growth of the rest of your garden. This is precisely what happens with unaddressed employee contraventions of behavioral norms. The unwanted, often toxic behaviors left unchecked will compete and overrun your organization as teammates recognize that such behaviors are accepted and even encouraged as evidenced by the continued presence and promotion of bad actors who excel in other areas. What really matters becomes evident through this inaction, thereby preventing the

adoption of the behaviors you may wish to advocate. You need to weed, proactively—ideally in an ongoing manner with consistent application across the board. But if push comes to shove and all else fails, twice a year, hire a goat!

Reimagining a better future

Let's envision the results of a more caring environment by revisiting Laura, Dan, and Barbara, whom we briefly met in chapter 1 and again in chapter 8. By feeling that their employers care for them and are providing the on-demand tools to overcome their concerns, how might their stories be changed for the better?

Laura was comfortable sharing her logistical challenges with her boss prior to her maternity leave, and he now schedules an 8:00 a.m. call on Monday, Wednesday, and Friday for dealing with emergent issues. Laura is now able to leave the office at 5:00 p.m. daily, without feeling the need to sneak out, to pick up her daughter from child care as well as make her twice-weekly evening reformer class while attending the early-morning team meetings that fit more easily into her and her colleagues' schedules.

Dan was able to discuss his commuting woes with his manager, who greenlit Dan's request to continue with his work-from-home schedule initiated during the lockdown. Dan is able to work remotely most days and, now that he and his husband have completed the adoption process, is basking in the joy (and occasional anguish) of raising a family without spending three hours on the corporate shuttle each day.

Barbara explained her predicament to her supervisor, who assured her he knew how committed she was to her work and the business. She is taking advantage of being able to schedule her shifts more flexibly and has started speaking to a company-sponsored counselor about her elevated stress level. She is relieved to have the time to help her aging parents, particularly her father with dementia, without fear of reprisal at work. What's more, she has reduced her evening wine consumption and as a result has even lost the fifteen pounds she had gained. She began seeing a counselor through the company's EAP and learned and learned cognitive behavioral therapy techniques that have helped alleviate her panic attacks, reducing her reliance on the company-sponsored insurance plan.

In all, Laura, Dan, and Barbara are happier, healthier, more focused, and, as a result, more productive. Not only were their employers able to retain their valuable services, but in so doing the companies avoided expensive replacement recruitment and training costs. As Susan Shuman pointed out in chapter 3, when managers are empowered and encouraged to be creative with employee management, the entire organization becomes more empathetic, flexible, and adaptable. This in turn positions the company well to face the constant need for transformation required of all companies today. They and their subordinates feel freer to put more of themselves into their work, which can bring greater energy and innovation to fuel their organization's future growth. But I'm not arguing for a purely financially motivated approach. Even if leading with empathy and connection were not obviously good for the business, it's the right thing to do. You'll be happier, less distracted, and more focused and joyful, and so will your employees!

♥ ♥ ♥

How My Life Experience Set Me on the Path of Caring and Diversity

A Guest Perspective by Stedman Graham, Chairman and CEO of S. Graham and Associates and New York Times Best-Selling Author

In addition to being CEO of S. Graham and Associates, a management and marketing consulting firm, Stedman Graham is the author of twelve books, including two *New York Times* best sellers and one *Wall Street Journal* bestseller. As a businessman, educator, and speaker, Graham lectures and conducts training and development programs for communities, corporations, and educational institutions worldwide on the topic of "identity leadership," which is based on the philosophy that you cannot lead anyone else until you first lead yourself. He served in the United States Army and played professional basketball in the European League. Graham holds a bachelor's in social work from Hardin-Simmons University, a master's in education from Ball State University, and has been awarded three honorary doctorates. Now let's hear his thoughts:

"I don't remember exactly when I became aware of differences, but I was pretty young. Around nine or ten, I began to feel like I was a second-class person because of the color of my skin. We lived in an all-black community surrounded by a white county. Most of the issues we dealt with were racially motivated. How does a child build self-esteem with people telling him that he's not good enough because of the color of his skin? Having this label as a part of my conditioning, both consciously and unconsciously—especially unconsciously—didn't give me a strong sense of myself. A person growing up in these conditions ends up for a lifetime trying to find ways to prove that they're just as good as anybody else.

"The good that I experienced came directly from caring. It's hard to accomplish anything without it. The way I gained self-esteem was through sports in school. Kids clapped and cheered me on, giving me a positive sense of myself for the first time. As an adult, I played college and European professional basketball.

"Playing sports has taught me a lot about being a CEO. Team sports offers lessons in developing caring, inclusiveness, equitable corporate ecosystems. It is a metaphor for being an effective leader. Better than anything else in life, it taught me discipline and how to show up—and on time. I also learned other life skills that transferred to the work world, such as practicing the power of determination—you're trying to win; exercising a healthy sense of competitiveness—you're competing against others; mastering how to work together with other folks for a common cause—you're trying to win as part of a team.

"Due to my early experiences, I have come to prefer the word 'equality' over 'diversity.' 'Equality' gives people more of a chance to understand their own empowerment rather than being defined and labeled by the outside world. I want people to be free and to have self-determination. My passion is giving them the tools they need to find out who they are, to define themselves and improve lives. I've made it my life work to teach people what I've learned and what I am still learning.

"Achieving equality in the workplace is easier now than before. Today, it's a skill-based strategy. Companies are less likely to look at color or gender or nationality or religion. They are more interested in finding people who are highly skilled. However, young people have not been prepared for twenty-first-century thinking. Besides being skilled, they must be able to think critically to be relevant, and they need to continually learn so they can keep pace with changing circumstances. While the skill-based strategy opens the door for equality, we are still far from achieving it.

"I don't know a business leader who doesn't want to show caring and practice equality in their workplace. They find it very difficult, though, because they have to rise above the systems in our society. It can feel hopeless for them to reach beyond them, because these systems define their existence. Oftentimes, CEOs don't have the tools or the know-how to show care and practice equality, but there is a lot they can do. A leader's role is to look at the big picture—where they want to go and how they're going to get there. However, they can't get to their vision without empowered people, and for that, caring is imperative. When it comes to caring, we're really talking about a leader's ability to first understand and care for themselves. In fact, as far as I am concerned, the number-one issue is self-leadership— the ability to lead oneself. How can anyone care for others unless they care for themselves? The best thing a leader can do is work on him- or herself to know who they are. That's the philosophy of my work in identity leadership. The highest form of leadership is self-leadership. When they can be of service to themselves, leaders can be of service to others. They've increased their capacity to care. In turn, their self-confidence and self-esteem grow, enabling them to continue to grow into the future.

"Why now? Because we are experiencing the perfect circumstances to set caring into motion. Due to the virus, we are unable to fly around or meet in person. We've had to learn how to work effectively from a distance.

Whether it's pandemics, climate change, or social and political upheaval, caring saves us from wear and tear from constant exhaustion, stress, and uncertainty, and will continue far beyond the virus. While we have the technology, and we are using the skills of caring for each other, we've learned the social skills and communication skills, and we are on the same page. But technology also has the ability to take time away. It can become about the shiny gear we love rather than strategy about transformation of lives, feelings, and energy. We have to be careful. "Who's Zooming who?" Does technology use you, or do you use it? If it uses you, then you are the product for sale.

"Even while leaders are saying that caring and equality are important, I've been asked, many times, 'Can't we just sneak by all this? That takes a lot of extra work! Things aren't so bad. With time, any problems we have will go away.' This points to short-term thinking. Ones who ask these questions likely believe that by hiring a few women and some people of color, equality will kick in, and boom!—everyone will start to care. This is false hope. When different folks are put together, they don't automatically care long term. Rather, caring and equality happen by intentionally looking holistically at everything—talent, differences, and the needs of the marketplace. It can happen when talented leaders improve upon how to be their best in the world. As a leader continues to work on him- or herself, they make more intentional decisions, foster an increasingly productive attitude, and feel better and better about who they are—all of which makes it easy for the leader to care about and believe in others.

"A doubting CEO may say, 'Okay, but so what? What could happen if I don't really care?' But any time 'so what' is asked, it says, 'I don't care.' Any cavalier leader will find themselves in trouble—whether it's with their family, keeping their job, or leading their people. An attitude of not caring spreads like a virus. It takes courageous effort to turn not caring into caring, because it's personal. But it's worth it. Leaders continually need to ask: 'How do I improve? How do I keep developing myself and creating opportunities that benefit the people and the organization?' Every CEO and leader who learns to care, in fact, sees their own lives start to improve in some way. Seeing that turnaround is a relief. It is exceptionally motivating. But for the leader who is not strong and doesn't care, everything around him or her is disappointing.

"A caring workplace is easy to recognize by its energy. Early benefits include notable increases in productivity, passion, performance, and a living, energized ecosystem. The workforce feels healthy and happy, and they have a palpable desire to excel. They are proactive. They don't wait to be told what to do—they initiate solutions. When I walk into a place that cares, the spirit is alive, open, and warm. The structure shows a clarity of vision at its base. People are busy, not stressed. They are visibly effective and share a common page. They are empowered—performing together in teams at their highest skill levels, growing in wisdom, and doing what they do best. A CEO or leader cannot achieve that unless he or she is authentic and engaged. It shows. Whatever they give out, they get back. When caring is there, it shows up in everything. It's obvious in the way they attract the talent that drives their revenues, demonstrates good will, and creates shareholder value, especially for a public company. It means thinking long term about where they're going, what that looks like, and how it will impact their organization. It's all in their vision, the planning, and structural design—with inclusion, equality, and caring.

"Good CEOs and executives also try to serve the whole community. It's a team effort—one that requires balance, constant improvement, innovation, and ideas about how they should enter the market. What does that look like? How should they present themselves? What's their brand image? What will their brand identity become? How do they begin to execute all of that? It takes someone highly skilled with an ability to look at the complexity of the company and how it fits into the global marketplace. Leaders institute a collective consciousness in their present-day moments within the twenty-four hours that they have every day, the same twenty-four hours that make everyone equal. This way, the CEO can all at once be present and focused on their vision of the future, by first understanding what vision really is, then by seeing how to employ it in every aspect of life and work. That's being present.

"What's more, caring and equality apply to managers, executives, and even frontline employees. Individuals at all levels need to assess their skills, talents, and abilities. They need to work on themselves—who they are, who they want to be, where they're going, and how to execute—goals, clarity, self-empowerment, attitude, contribution to the organization, family, community, and so on. They must equip themselves with skills that empower them to do the things that make the difference they seek. They need to learn how to base them on their identity and leadership aims and to reinforce them. They grow over time by constantly reading, self-directing, taking charge, and motivating themselves to execute what matters to them and their constituents.

"It takes exceptional understanding to navigate the rough terrain of leadership, yet still care. Leaders need a courageous approach to create equality in their organizations. From my perspective, I suggest identity leadership. I love identity leadership because it starts with the ability to recognize one's own influence. It gives a leader the ability to make a difference, because they improve their skills, their self-leadership, and their acumen. They are energized to become more disciplined and to look at things differently. They continuously work on themselves. The most important thing about identity leadership is that it internalizes how to learn and how to organize life. The leader realizes the true value of information and knowledge and how to apply it to their own development. They gain an ability to stay in the present and to be conscious of their consciousness—'conscious consciousness'—awareness of themselves and of what's going on around them. You can call it engagement.

"Ask yourself: are you engaged in the world you're in, every single day? Do you understand how to make decisions based on being in the present? Identity leadership teaches CEOs and leaders how important that is and how to do it. It also gives them a framework for improving themselves, so they're focusing on performance, performance, performance.

Practicing identity leadership means that a CEO forms authentic relationships, lays out how to plan, sets goals in new ways, and develops a working value system—all for him- or herself—and that's before the CEO even gets to the office! This CEO considers how to develop him- or herself to be more beneficial to the world they inhabit. Anyone can do this, because the process for success is the same for everybody. The only difference is that some already understand how, while others don't. As Einstein said, 'You can't solve the problem with the same mind that caused it.'[226] Change your mindset, starting today, and you can create solutions that will change the world for tomorrow."

AFTERWORD: A CALL TO ACTION

It's time to start right now! So, what can you do for your employees today? When I began writing this book in January of 2020, my goal was to help executives in need of assistance with developing business cases to sell in the idea of creating more caring environments at their organizations. The global coronavirus pandemic has significantly increased the importance of building caring cultures and developing deeper connections with employees who are more distanced, stressed, and in need of employer support to cope with the new realities of life. Seventy-four percent of employees are concerned about at least one aspect of their wellbeing as a result of COVID-19,[227] and 32 percent are craving help with work-life balance and physical wellbeing. Yet, 40 percent of global employees report that no one at their company had asked them if they were doing okay since the outbreak began.[228]

At the same time, employers have had something of an awakening to the imperative of understanding the struggles of their workforce and both helping them as well as making them feel seen and heard if they want their businesses to survive economic turmoil. It is viscerally understood now that people matter, and we cannot turn a blind eye to their reality and expect them to figure it out on their own. The stakes are just too high. Employees are in need of an employer mindset of caring and compassion that offers them the digital resources they need to take control and care for themselves and their families as well as one that focuses on fostering community and culture.

Emphasize connection

I believe that employers are now, more than ever, responsible for helping employees feel cared for within the context of their new normal. This includes the physical, emotional, social, and financial stress that employees face when we view and appreciate them in a realistic fashion as whole people. This may mean curbing the loneliness and sense of isolation that can naturally occur from living alone or providing greater support for working parents as they grapple with finding adequate childcare. Turning our work colleagues into a virtual community of caring as well as a much-needed source of fun is a relatively easy way to expand our emotional worlds in difficult times. Obviously, employers can't manufacture meaningful connections out of thin air for people any more successfully than they could before the global COVID-19 outbreak. That's not an employer's "job." But caring for your employees and providing a sense of purpose, belonging, and balance is.

By emphasizing connection, practicing humanity, and promoting resilience, you will inspire your employees by creating an authentically caring culture that makes them feel valued while engendering their loyalty and future proofing your company from the talent wars and economic downturns that no doubt lie ahead. Today's employees want to be heard, understood, and given the tools they need to live their best lives, inside and out of the workplace.

Necessity is the mother of invention. And while from the very beginning, I created Grokker as a wellbeing resource for people to be transformed through connection, I watched our clients invent new, fun ways I had never imagined of using our platform to keep their employees engaged and connected to each other while working from home—or even while furloughed. While engagement has always been relevant, we're in a whole new world—one that isn't likely to go back to the way things were, at least not anytime soon.

As mentioned earlier, one company launched a "Social Distancing Challenge," at the height of the COVID-19 lockdown in their state, during which participants shared their daily at-home wellbeing activities by posting photos with captions of themselves with their family members working out, doing yoga, or cooking together. Another ran a "Healthy at Home" initiative that provided employees with resources to help them create and share a variety of healthy home-based routines to feel their best. Yet another hosted a daily five-ingredient in under thirty minutes healthy dinner recipe challenge, while another instituted group Mindfulness Moments scheduled at set times during the week, where they watch stress reduction and resiliency training videos together and discuss how they are feeling before and after the video plays.

These efforts help put a more personal and positive face on a difficult time when we can't depend on our usual social outlets. Kids can't invite their friends over to watch movies or even meet at the park for Little League, and adults aren't going out with friends for dinner or date night like they used to. It's hard on everybody. So, when employers can help individual employees and their families make the best of a challenging situation, it's a win-win that can make a big difference to an employee's experience during this strange, stressful time. Instead, employers need to adapt—and quickly—by offering employees the tools that meet them where they are today. That means ways to stay connected outside of Slack and Zoom, but on the employee's own terms.

At Grokker this week, we sent a home delivery of fresh-baked cookies to each of our employees just to let them know we were thinking of them and wanted them to have a little comfort food within reach. It was a small gesture but an important one that said: we see you and we care. Because that is what our employees need more than ever, to be seen and to feel cared for.

That means content that feels personal to their situation without putting limits on what they might need and accounts for everything from workouts they can do from the discretion of their own home to helpful resources for navigating financial fragility. These are highly emotional, fraught times, and employees need to feel valued and cared for, in order to do their best work. Because when employees feel connected to their employer—and colleagues—on a human level, they become better able to cope with uncertainty, handle stress, and take control of their health and wellbeing. These are employees who are less likely to tune out or burn out, able to remain engaged and stay resilient despite the circumstances.

While this may sound like a daunting task, the good news is that there is nothing stopping you from creating small actions right now. Share some fresh-baked cookies. Make sure all voices in your organization are heard. Recognize the little wins. Empower your people to reach out to colleagues and support one another. At the outset of the COVID-19 outbreak in Asia, one hotel group did just that by asking managers to touch base weekly with their direct reports and simply ask them how they are doing. This led to a postcard campaign where managers mailed out handwritten cards to employees just to let them know they care.

Give employees the time, space, and means to fully address their physical, financial, and emotional wellbeing. Extend support to their immediate family as well, because when one is not doing well, our entire support system is affected. Richard Branson, renowned entrepreneur and founder of The Virgin Group, is credited with the famous saying, "Clients do not come first. Employees come first. If you take care of your employees, they will take care of the clients."[229] Taking care of your employees means more than just paying a fair wage or providing basic medical insurance, it means caring for the whole person, and providing them with an inclusive environment where they can belong. In fact, if you visit the Careers page on the company website, you will read the following: "The Virgin Group believes that when people feel they have a genuine sense of belonging to an organisation, they thrive."[230] Branson's long-held belief, prior to it being fashionable, is that people are a company's true competitive advantage. As long as you are meeting their needs, they will make the magic happen.

And be sure to take care of yourself and address your wellbeing. Remember, it starts with you. Susan Lyne, whom you met in chapter 8, told me that even back at the start of her career before laptops and connectedness, she'd escape to a coffee shop to read, to write, and to think. As she told me, "You have to carve out a space that is yours—a place where you can spend time with your own thoughts and kind of regenerate whatever it was that got you excited about doing this in the first place."[231] As she explained it, at the coffee shop, "I'd capture any ideas I had—or even germs of an idea, however small—so that I could go back to them at some point. It was also a way to just quiet the noise because the thing that kills creativity ultimately is just having too many voices in the room and too many people who are giving their opinion. When you book every minute of every day, you really run the risk of losing sight of your own voice." As you might recall I mentioned the 8-3-3-1 Stability Framework in chapter 4, and shared that my personal wellbeing routine consists of 8 hours sleep nightly, 3 sweaty workouts per week, 3 nutritious meals daily, and 1 fun thing to look forward to each week; that's what keeps me balanced. What is your wellbeing routine? If you don't have one, create one or adapt mine to suit your life. You'll notice the difference.

Once you start your organization's transformation to a more caring environment and are seeing the results, please let me know about them. Tell me how the wellbeing of your employees has improved. I'd love to share your successes with the world! I can be reached at lorna@caseforcaring. com. I look forward to hearing about your vision, values, and the employee brand you are creating through the experience you are crafting. As I mentioned above, the time to start is now. So, I won't keep you any longer. Onward! After all, it's the right thing to do, and now that you have an airtight business case at your fingertips, you are ready to give your employees the sense of purpose, belonging, and balance they crave.

ACKNOWLEDGEMENTS

I want to thank those who enabled the development of *It's Personal*, including Jennifer Aaker, Patrick Aylward, Jim Ambach, Milagros Arrisueño, Amy Banse, Bruce Bendinger, Bonnie Bernell, Marc Borenstein, Marianne Borenstein, Richard Borenstein, Sylviane Borenstein, Chloe Borenstein-Lawee, Justin Borenstein-Lawee, Livvy Borenstein-Lawee, Christine Buck, Jon Burbage, Barbara Burlington, Dr. Akilah Cadet, Becky Cantieri, David Coats, Ron Conway, Marcella David, Juliet deBaubigny, Sue Decker, Keval Desai, Jennifer Dulski, Emerita Duran, Natalie Fair, Jennifer Fonstad, Eric Freedman, Zachary George, Chavah Golden, Blanche Gonzalez, Dan Graovac, Stedman Graham, David Houle, Dr. David Kaplan, Avery Kaufman, Kwang-Wu Kim, Chris Kirmse, Fil Konaka, Josh Kopelman, Chris Kurose, Daniel Lawee, David Lawee, Suzanne Lawee, Geraldine Laybourne, Zander Lurie, Susan Lyne, Drew Marich, Jessica Marks, Caryn Marooney, Mary Mattucci, Suzanne McBride, Corrie Mieszczak, Jorie Minsky, Kay Mooney, Colleen Moorehead, Lakshmi Mudlapur, Marko Navala, Rachel Paris, Ryan Picerella, Rhonda Present, Christa Quarles, Linnea Roberts, Amy Rosenberg, Dan Rosensweig, Libby Sartain, Hilary Schneider, John Schoenstein, Meghan Scudero, Georgia Sievwright, Craig Sigele, Joyce Smith, Susan Schuman, Missy Stein, Chad Walker, Maynard Webb, David Weiden, and Marefia Yisa.

ABOUT THE AUTHORS

Lorna Borenstein is CEO and founder of Grokker, the enterprise wellbeing engagement solution that enables physical, emotional, and social wellbeing for everyone. By providing millions of employees globally—from full-time to oft-overlooked hourly and "gig" employees—access to holistic, digital wellbeing anytime, anywhere, on any device, Grokker restores a much-needed sense of purpose, belonging, and balance into today's workforce.

An expert on innovation and driving transformational change in nascent markets, Lorna honed her consumer technology product and marketing skills at Hewlett Packard, eBay, and Yahoo!, giving her a front row seat at some of the most iconic and disruptive companies. She is an inventor of various patents including a distributed collaborative knowledge generation system and a video filming and discovery system. Her unique experience resulted in her ability to translate employee needs into cutting-edge technologies and experiences, inculcating cultures that inspire, differentiate, build resilience, and lead to long-term individual and business success.

Lorna's purpose-driven approach in transforming work through wellbeing also aims to revolutionize the role of organizational leadership into being more human-led and caring. Her fundamental belief is that businesses must acknowledge and support employees' whole lives.

She seeks to help solve the complex challenges that CEO's and their leadership face—juggling dispersed and increasingly remote workforces, cross generational teams, competing individual needs, along with corporate objectives—by paving the path with a uniquely personal and practical approach, ultimately leading to happier and healthier employees, as the foundation for the high performing enterprise of the future.

Lorna has been recognized as a woman of influence by the Silicon Valley Business Journal, a Human Resource Executive Top 100 HR Tech Influencer, and in 2020 her company Grokker was named a 100 Best Small

Workplaces by Fortune Magazine. She is a sought after speaker at conferences and regular contributor to Forbes. Lorna is a founding member, signatory and mentor of The Boardlist, Female Founders Office Hours, and Founders for Change, established to promote gender diversity, inclusion, and equality in the business world. In addition, she has served as a Board Director of Icebreaker, the sustainable Merino fashion brand, which was later acquired by VF Corporation in 2018.

Lorna grew up in Montreal, Canada, the daughter of European immigrants who valued education, hard work, and community volunteerism. She holds multiple degrees in law from McGill University as well as a degree in business from the American College in London. She is an avid yogi, hiker, cyclist, adventure traveler, gluten-free bread baker, supporter of women's empowerment, adolescent mental health, civil liberties, and LGBTQ+ rights. She is a dual citizen of the U.S. and Canada, speaks five languages, and has three children with her husband.

Laurence Minsky is an associate professor in the Communication Department of the School of Media Arts at Columbia College Chicago and a marketing and advertising consultant for leading ad agencies, corporations, and nonprofits across the globe. His books include *Global Brand Management: A Guide to Developing, Building and Managing an International Brand* (Kogan Page, 2020); *Advertising Under One Hour* (Under One Hour, 2018); *Audio Branding: Using Sound to Build Your Brand* (Kogan Page 2017); *The Activation Imperative: How to Build Brands and Business by Inspiring Action* (Rowman & Littlefield, 2017), *The Get A Job Workshop: How to Find Your Way to a Creative Career in Advertising, Branding, Collateral, Digital, Experiential & More* (Copy Workshop, 2013); *Advertising and the Business of Brands Media Revolution Edition* (Copy Workshop, 2009), and *How to Succeed in Advertising When All You Have Is Talent* (Copy Workshop, 2007). He has also been published by the *Harvard Business Review*, the *European Business Review*, MarketingProfs, and many others.

NOTES

1 J. Stanier, "Is the HP Way Still Relevant Today?," Medium, 2018, accessed October 27, 2020, https://medium.com/swlh/is-the-hp-way-still-relevant-today-3603432563b8.

2 R. Heinlein, Stranger in a Strange Land (New York: Penguin Random House, 1968).

Chapter 1

3 "Deeper Dive into the Employee Experience Implications of COVID-19," Willis Towers Watson, 2020, 2, accessed 1 December 2020, https://www.willistowerswatson.com/assets/covid-19/NA-COVID-19-ClientWebcast-April-22-Final.pdf.

4 "Workplace Stress," The American Institute of Stress, 2020, accessed October 28, 2020, https://www.stress.org/workplace-stress.

5 "Cost of Sleepiness Too Pricey to Ignore," PR Newswire, 2018, accessed October 28, 2020, https://www.prnewswire.com/news-releases/cost-of-sleepiness-too-pricey-to-ignore-300610582.html.

6 S. Agrawal and B. Wigert, "Employee Burnout, Part 1: The 5 Main Causes," Gallup, 2018, accessed August 5, 2020, https://www.gallup.com/workplace/237059/employee-burnout-part-main-causes.aspx.

7 "The Employee Burnout Crisis: Study Reveals Big Workplace Challenge in 2017," Business Wire, 2017, accessed July 13, 2020, https://www.businesswire.com/news/home/20170109005377/en/Employee-Burnout-Crisis-Study-Reveals-Big-Workplace.

8 "Economics New Release," US Bureau of Labor Statistics, accessed July 13, 2020, https://www.bls.gov/news.release/jolts.t04.htm.

9 M. Karpman, S. Zuckerman, and D. Gonzalez, "Material Hardship among Nonelderly Adults and Their Families in 2017," Urban Institute, 2018, accessed August 5, 2020, https://www.urban.org/research/publication/material-hardship-among-nonelderly-adults-and-their-families-2017.

10 M. Toossi, "A Century of Change: The U.S. Labor Force, 1950–2050," Monthly Labor Review, 2002, 16, accessed August 5, 2020, https://www.bls.gov/opub/mlr/2002/05/art-2full.pdf.

11 Toossi, "A Century," 15.

12 A. Duncan, "Surprising Facts and Research about Stay-at-Home Moms," Verywell Family, 2019, accessed August 5, 2020, https://www.verywellfamily.com/research-stay-at-home-moms-4047911.

13 L. Stone, "Beyond Simple Multi-Tasking: Continuous Partial Attention," Linda Stone (blog), November 30, 2009, accessed August 5, 2020, https://lindastone.net/2009/11/30/beyond-simple-multi-tasking-continuous-partial-attention/.

14 "Is Your Attention Span Shorter than a Goldfish's?," NeuroTracker, 2017, accessed August 4, 2020, https://neurotracker.net/2017/05/24/humans-attention-span-shorter-than-goldfish/#:~:text=The%20findings%20revealed%20that%20the,attention%20

span%20of%20nine%20seconds.

15 J. Harter, "Employee Engagement on the Rise in the U.S.," Gallup, 2018, accessed January 20, 2020, https://news.gallup.com/poll/241649/employee-engagement-rise.aspx.

16 "From Wellness to Wellneing: Employers Moving beyond Physical Health," *MI Blues Perspective*, accessed October 28, 2020, https://www.mibluesperspectives.com/2018/08/30/from-wellness-to-well-being-employers-moving-beyond-physical-health/.

17 L. Solow, "The Scourge of Worker Wellness Programs," *The New Republic*, 2019, accessed November 3, 2020, https://newrepublic.com/article/154890/scourge-worker-wellness-programs.

18 J. Brooks, "Why Anti-Smoking Ads Make You Smoke More, Waste Money, and Gain Weight," *Comfort Pit* (blog), 2014, accessed October 30, 2020, https://comfortpit.com/anti-smoking-ads/.

19 "Burnout is Sabotaging Employee Retention Efforts," *501(c) Services* (blog), 2017, accessed August 4, 2020, https://www.501c.com/new-study-says-burnout-is-sabotaging-employee-retention-efforts/.

20 "Millennials and Generation Z, The New World of Work," Capital-Global Employment Solutions, 2018, accessed August 4, 2020, https://www.capital-ges.com/millennials-and-generation-z-the-new-world-of-work/.

21 "How Millennials Want to Live and Work," Gallup, 2016, 18, accessed August 4, 2020, https://enviableworkplace.com/wp-content/uploads/Gallup-How-Millennials-Want-To-Work.pdf.

22 "How Millennials Want," 19.

23 "How Millennials Want," 20.

24 "2018 Deloitte Global Millennial Survey," Deloitte, 2018, 18, accessed August 4, 2020, https://www2.deloitte.com/content/dam/Deloitte/global/Documents/About-Deloitte/gx-2018-millennial-survey-report.pdf.

25 R. Chetty et al., "The Fading American Dream: Trends in Absolute Income Mobility Since 1940," NBER Working Paper Series, 2016, no. 22910, 9, accessed October 28, 2020, http://www.equality-of-opportunity.org/papers/abs_mobility_paper.pdf.

26 "How Millennials Want," 7.

27 C. Cakebread, "These Are the 47 Things Uber Had Agreed to Do to Change Its Company Culture," *Business Insider*, 2017, accessed August 4, 2020, https://www.businessinsider.com/47-ways-uber-is-changing-its-culture-2017-6#changes-to-leadership-1.

28 D. Johnson, "McDonald's Goes for a Culture Change," *Industrial Safety and Hygiene News*, 2016, accessed August 4, 2020, https://www.ishn.com/articles/104797-mcdonalds-goes-for-a-culture-change.

29 A. Nossiter, "3 French Executives Convicted in Suicides of 35 Workers," *New York Times*, December 20, 2019, accessed February 20, 2020, https://www.nytimes.com/2019/12/20/world/europe/france-telecom-suicides.html.

30 "Press Release: Poor Health Costs US Employers $530 Billion and 1.4 Billion Work Days of Absence and Impaired Performance According to Integrated Benefits Institute," Integrated Benefits Institute, 2018, accessed February 6, 2020, https://www.ibiweb.org/poor-health-costs-us-employers-530-billion-and-1-4-billion-work-days-

of-absence-and-impaired-performance/.

31 "Press Release: Poor Health."

32 "Press Release: Poor Health."

33 "Cost of Sleepiness Too Pricey to Ignore," Cision, PR Newswire, 2018, accessed August 5, 2020, https://www.prnewswire.com/news-releases/cost-of-sleepiness-too-pricey-to-ignore-300610582.html.

34 K. Proper and W. van Mechelen, "Effectiveness and Economic Impact of Worksite Interventions to Promote Physical Activity and Healthy Diet," *World Health Organization*, 2008, accessed August 5, 2020, https://www.who.int/dietphysicalactivity/Proper_K.pdf.

35 T. J Walker, et al. "Association of Self-Reported Aerobic Physical Activity, Muscle-Strengthening Physical Activity, and Stretching Behavior with Presenteeism." *Journal of Occupational and Environmental Medicine*, 59, no. 5 (2017), doi:10.1097/JOM.0000000000000978.

36 N. Otto, "Avoidable Turnover Costing Employers Big," *Benefit News,* 2017, accessed August 5, 2020, https://www.benefitnews.com/news/avoidable-turnover-costing-employers-big.

37 G. Willard, "How to Really Calculate the Cost of Employee Turnover," ERE Recruiting Intelligence, 2014, accessed August 5, 2020, https://www.ere.net/how-to-really-calculate-the-cost-of-employee-turnover/.

38 P. Petrone, "How to Calculate the Cost of Employee Disengagement," LinkedIn, 2017, accessed August 5, 2020, https://learning.linkedin.com/blog/engaging-your-workforce/how-to-calculate-the-cost-of-employee-disengagement.

39 S. Crabtree, "Worldwide, 13% of Employees Are Engaged at Work," Gallup, 2013, accessed August 5, 2020, https://news.gallup.com/poll/165269/worldwide-employees-engaged-work.aspx.

40 T. Jane, "An Open Letter to My CEO, *Medium* (blog), February 19, 2016, accessed October 15, 2020, https://medium.com/@taliajane/an-open-letter-to-my-ceo-fb73d-f021e7a.

41 "2020 Trends in Employer Wellbeing Offerings," Business Group on Health, 2020, accessed October 28, 2020, https://www.businessgrouphealth.org/get-involved/events/2020-trends-in-employer-well-being-offerings.

42 Personal conversation, February 11, 2020.

43 B. Kimmel, "Building a Healthy Workplace Goes beyond Wellness," SmartBrief, accessed February 7, 2020, https://www.smartbrief.com/original/2020/02/building-healthy-workplace-goes-beyond-wellness.

Chapter 2

44 R. Kroc, *Grinding It Out* (New York: St. Martin's Publishing, 2016).

45 V. J. Cannato, "A Home of One's Own," *National Affairs,* 2010, accessed August 6, 2020, https://www.nationalaffairs.com/publications/detail/a-home-of-ones-own.

46 H. Berkowitz and H. Dumez, "The Gribeauval System, Or the Issue of Standardization

in the 18th Century," Research Gate, English Language Online Edition, 2017, https://www.researchgate.net/publication/319664722_The_Gribeauval_system_or_the_issue_of_standardization_in_the_18th_century.

47 A. Bloomberg and A. Davidson, "Accidents of History Created U.S. Health System," *All Things Considered*, NPR, 2009, accessed February 24, 2020, https://www.npr.org/templates/story/story.php?storyId=114045132.

48 E. Rosenthal, *An American Sickness* (London, Penguin, 2018)14, accessed November 3, 2020, https://stanmed.stanford.edu/2017spring/how-health-insurance-changed-from-protecting-patients-to-seeking-profit.html.

49 Rosenthal, *An American Sickness*, 18.

50 Rosenthal, *An American Sickness*,16.

51 Institute of Medicine et al., *Employment and Health Benefits: A Connection at Risk* (Washington DC: National Academy Press, 1993).

52 A. Khoury, "The Evolution of Worksite Wellness," *Corporate Wellness*, accessed February 24, 2020, https://www.corporatewellnessmagazine.com/article/the-evolution-of.

53 M. Phipps, "The History of the Pension Plan," The Balance, 2020, accessed February 24, 2020, https://www.thebalance.com/the-history-of-the-pension-plan-2894374.

54 Phipps, "The History."

55 "Where Did All The Pensions Go?," *Forbes*, 2018, accessed February 24, 2020, https://www.forbes.com/sites/impactpartners/2018/02/09/where-did-all-the-pensions-go/#-59feaab13aab.

56 "Where Did All The Pensions Go?."

57 M. Friedman, "The Social Responsibility of Business Is to Increase its Profits," *New York Magazine*, 1970, accessed February 24, 2020, http://umich.edu/~thecore/doc/Friedman.pdf.

58 Friedman, "Social Responsibility," 2.

59 Friedman, "Social Responsibility," 1.

60 Friedman, "Social Responsibility," 3.

61 "Business Roundtable Redefines the Purpose of a Corporation to Promote 'An Economy That Serves All Americans,'" Business Roundtable, 2019, accessed August 7, 2020, https://www.businessroundtable.org/business-roundtable-redefines-the-purpose-of-a-corporation-to-promote-an-economy-that-serves-all-americans.

62 "Statement on the Purpose of a Corporation," Business Roundtable, accessed August 6, 2020, https://opportunity.businessroundtable.org/ourcommitment/#:~:text=Americans%20deserve%20an%20economy%20that,and%20economic%20opportunity%20for%20all.

63 "About Us," Business Roundtable, accessed August 6, 2020, https://www.businessroundtable.org/about-us.

64 "Business Roundtable Redefines."

65 R. Chetty et al., "The Fading American Dream: Trends in Absolute Income Mobility Since 1940," *NBER Working Paper Series*, 2016, no. 22910, 18, accessed October 28, 2020, http://www.equality-of-opportunity.org/papers/abs_mobility_paper.pdf.

66 M. Dimock, "Defining Generations: Where Millennials End and Generation Z Begins," Pew Research Center, 2019, accessed August 6, 2020, https://www.pewresearch.org/fact-tank/2019/01/17/where-millennials-end-and-generation-z-begins/.

67 K. Parker and R. Igielnik, "On the Cusp of Adulthood and Facing an Uncertain Future: What We Know about Gen Z So Far," *Pew Research Center,* 2020, accessed August 6, 2020, https://www.pewsocialtrends.org/essay/on-the-cusp-of-adulthood-and-facing-an-uncertain-future-what-we-know-about-gen-z-so-far/.

68 Parker and Igielnik, "On the Cusp."

69 J. M. Grow and S. Yang, "Generation-Z Enters the Advertising Workplace: Expectations through a Gendered Lens," *Journal of Advertising Education* 1, no. 22 (2018), https://doi.org/10.1177/1098048218768595.

70 Personal conversation, February 27, 2020

71 C. O'Boyle and S. K. Hogan, "Engaging Workers as Consumers," *Deloitte Review* 8 (2019), 146, accessed August 6, 2020, https://www2.deloitte.com/content/dam/insights/us/articles/4731_Engaging-workers-as-consumers/DI_DR24_Engaging-workers-as-consumers.pdf.

72 C. Quarles, "Culture Lessons from OpenTable: Secrets from Silicon Valley," interviewed by Lorna Borenstein, accessed November 3, 2020, https://go.grokker.com/lessons-from-opentable-takeaway.

73 "Global Wellness Economy Monitor," *Global Wellness Institute* (2018), 3. https://globalwellnessinstitute.org/wp-content/uploads/2018/10/Research2018_v5FINALExecutive-Summary_webREVISED.pdf.

74 "Global Wellness Economy Monitor," 8.

75 Dr. J. West, "The Truth about Job Satisfaction and Friendships at Work," National Business Research Institute, accessed August 7, 2020, https://www.nbrii.com/employee-survey-white-papers/the-truth-about-job-satisfaction-and-friendships-at-work/.

76 West, "The Truth."

77 "2020 Employee Wellbeing Mindset Study," Business Group on Health, 2020, accessed November 3, 2020, https://www.businessgrouphealth.org/resources/2020-employee-well-being-mindset-study.

78 "Social Connectedness and Wellbeing," Ministry of Social Development, accessed August 7, 2020, https://www.msd.govt.nz/about-msd-and-our-work/publications-resources/literature-reviews/social-connectedness-and-well-being.html#:~:text=Social%20connectedness%20is%20a%20key,the%20problems%20they%20are%20facing.

79 "American Time Use Survey," US Bureau of Labor Statistics, accessed August 7, 2020, https://www.bls.gov/tus/.

80 "Job Satisfaction: From Research to Action," Business Group on Health, 2020, accessed August 7, 2020, https://www.businessgrouphealth.org/en/resources/job-satisfaction-from-research-to-action.

81 "Job Satisfaction."

82 "Can Wellbeing Programs Supercharge Employee Engagement?," Optum, 2017, 5, accessed August 12, 2020, https://www.optum.com/business/resources/library/nbgh-survey.html.

83   "Rethinking Rewards: How to Compete with Technology Companies for the In-Demand Digital Workforce, Aon, 2019, 1, accessed August 7, 2020, https://insights. humancapital.aon.com/talent-rewards-and-performance/aon-rethinking-rewards-white-paper.

84   "Benefits and Trends Survey," Aon, 2019, 6, accessed August 7, 2020, https://www.aon. com/unitedkingdom/insights/benefits-and-trends-survey-2019.jsp.

85   J. C. Ramirez, "Creating a Compelling Employee-Value Proposition," *Human Resource Executive,* 2018, accessed August 7, 2020, https://hrexecutive.com/creating-compelling-employee-value-proposition/.

86   R. L. Pardee, "Motivation Theories of Maslow, Herzberg, McGregor & McClelland A Literature Review of Selected Theories Dealing With Job Satisfaction and Motivation," Eric, 1990, 7, accessed August 7, 2020, https://files.eric.ed.gov/fulltext/ED316767.pdf.

87   Pardee, "Motivation Theories," 10.

88   "Yelp Careers," Yelp, accessed August 7, 2020, https://www.yelp.careers/us/en.

89   "Morningstar Careers," Morningstar, accessed October 28, 2020, https://www.morningstar.com/careers.

90   "Trader Joe's Careers," Trader Joe's, accessed August 7, 2020, https://www.traderjoes. com/careers.

91   J. Miller-Merrell, "9 Employer Examples of EVPs," Workology, 2018, accessed August 7, 2020, https://workology.com/employee-value-propositions-evp/.

Chapter 3

92   J. Medina, K. Benner and K. Taylor, "Actresses, Business Leaders, and Other Wealthy Parents Charged in U.S. College Entry Fraud," *New York Times,* 2019, accessed August 11, 2020, https://www.nytimes.com/2019/03/12/us/college-admissions-cheating-scandal.html.

93   J. Buchanan et al., "How Teens Do Research in the Digital World," Pew Research Center, 2012, accessed October 28, 2020, https://www.pewresearch.org/internet/2012/11/01/how-teens-do-research-in-the-digital-world/.

94   M. Anderson and J Jiang, "Teens and Their Experiences on Social Media," Teens' Social Media Habits and Experiences, Pew Research Center, 2018, accessed August 12, 2020, https://www.pewresearch.org/internet/2018/11/28/teens-and-their-experiences-on-social-media/.

95   "Full Report: Generation Z in the Workplace," Workforce Institute, Kronos, 2019, 4–5, accessed August 12, 2020, https://workforceinstitute.org/wp-content/uploads/2019/11/ Full-Report-Generation-Z-in-the-Workplace.pdf.

96   J. Anderson and L. Rainie, "Main findings: Teens, Technology, and Human Potential in 2020," Pew Research Center, 2012, accessed October 28, 2020, https://www.pewresearch.org/internet/2012/02/29/main-findings-teens-technology-and-human-potential-in-2020/.

97   "How the Great Recession Has Shaped Generation Z," *Harland Clarke,* 2017, 3, accessed August 11, 2020, https://insight.harlandclarke.com/wp-content/uploads/2017/05/HC-How-Great-Recession-Shaped-GenZ-white-paper-2017-01.pdf.

98 *Mind Share Partners' 2019 Mental Health at Work Report,* Mind Share Partners, 2019, 9, accessed August 12, 2020, https://www.mindsharepartners.org/mentalhealthat-workreport.

99 *Mind Share Partners',* 9.

100 *Mind Share Partners',* 11.

101 *Mind Share Partners',* 4.

102 A. Sraders, "The New PPP Loan Forgiveness Application Is Causing lots of Confusion," *Fortune,* 2020, accessed August 11, 2020, https://fortune.com/2020/05/20/sba-ppp-loan-forgiveness-application-confusion/.

103 N. Vardi, "Public Companies Rush to Repay Paycheck Protection Program Loans amid Government Pressure," *Forbes,* 2020, accessed August 12, 2020, https://www.forbes.com/sites/nathanvardi/2020/04/23/some-companies-repay-payment-protection-program-loans-amid-government-pressure/#148f26c151e7.

104 R. Winkler and Y. Chernova, "Silicon Valley Debate: Should Venture-Backed Firms Take Stimulus Money?," *Wall Street Journal,* 2020, accessed August 11, 2020, https://www.wsj.com/articles/startup-world-wrestles-with-taking-small-business-loans-11587470400.

105 D. Abril, "Instacart to Hire 250,000 More Workers amid Soaring Demand during the Coronavirus Pandemic," *Fortune,* 2020, accessed August 12, 2020, https://fortune.com/2020/04/23/instacart-hiring-250000-workers-wellness-checks-coronavirus-covid-19/?utm_source=email&utm_medium=newsletter&utm_campaign=data-sheet&utm_content=2020042414pm.

106 J. Elias, "Google to Cut Marketing Budgets by As Much As Half, Directors Warned of Hiring Freezes," CNBC, 2020, accessed August 12, 2020, https://www.cnbc.com/2020/04/23/google-to-cut-marketing-budgets-hiring-freeze-expected.html.

107 Business of Fashion Team, "Keeping Track of Fashion's Layoffs," Business of Fashion, 2020, accessed August 12, 202, 0https://www.businessoffashion.com/articles/news-analysis/keeping-track-of-fashions-layoffs.

108 Alex K, "Google's 20% Time in Action," Google (blog), May 18, 2006, accessed August 12, 2020, https://googleblog.blogspot.com/2006/05/googles-20-percent-time-in-action.html.

109 "Volunteerism," Genentech, accessed August 12, 2020, https://www.gene.com/good/giving/volunteerism.

110 "Work Perks and Benefits: What Employees and Candidates Want," Randstad, Workforce Insights, 2018, accessed August 12, 2020, https://www.randstadusa.com/workforce360/workforce-insights/work-perks-and-benefits-what-employees-want/604/.

Chapter 4

111 B. Groysberg et al., "The Leader's Guide to Corporate Culture," *Harvard Business Review's 10 Must Reads,* 2019, accessed August 13, 2020, https://stingrayresearch.com/wp-content/uploads/2019/10/HBRMustReads2019.pdf.

112 Groysberg et al., "The Leader's Guide."

113 *Pinterest's Head of CPG Strategy Discusses the New Digital Shopper,* online video,

presenter A. Sevilla, Santa Monica, California, Noshlive, 2019, accessed August 13, 2020, https://www.nosh.com/events/noshlivewinter19/Pinterests-Head-of-CPG-Strategy-Discusses-The-New-Digital-Shopper.

114 Enid H, "Knit Con: Inspiration from the Inside Out," Pinterest Newsroom, 2019, accessed August 13, 2020, https://newsroom.pinterest.com/en/post/knit-con-inspiration-from-the-inside-out.

115 "Pinterest Mission, Vision, & Values," Comparably, accessed August 13, 2020, https://www.comparably.com/companies/pinterest/mission.

116 *7 Steps to Creating Culture*, online video, San Jose, California, Grokker, accessed December 2 2020.

117 *Culture Lessons from Facebook*, online video, presenter C. Marooney, San Jose, California, Grokker, accessed August 13, 2020, https://go.grokker.com/culturetipsfacebook.

118 "The Judy Project," Rotman School of Management University of Toronto, accessed August 13, 2020, https://www.rotman.utoronto.ca/ProfessionalDevelopment/InitiativeForWomenInBusiness/Programs/Judy-Project.

119 "The Judy Project."

120 C. Moorehead, *The Collective Wisdom of High-Performing Women: Leadership Lessons from the Judy Project* (Toronto, Canada: Barlow, 2019).

121 P. Crowe, "An Acquisitive Software-Security Company Just Made a $2.3 Billion Deal in Another Example of the Frenzy That's Sweeping the Tech Industry," *Business Insider*, 2016, accessed August 14, 2020, https://www.businessinsider.com/symantec-to-buy-lifelock-2016-11.

122 *How Lifelock Cultivates an Amazing Culture*, online video, presenter H. Schneider, San Jose, California, Grokker, accessed August 14, 2020, https://go.grokker.com/culturetipslifelock.

123 F. Giovanetti, "Women in Wellness: Working Out before the School Run with Lorna Borenstein from Grokker," Medium, 2019, accessed August 14, 2020, https://medium.com/authority-magazine/women-in-wellness-working-out-before-the-school-run-with-lorna-borenstein-from-grokker-a1c098ad412b.

Chapter 5

124 J. P. Kotter, *Power and Influence* (New York: Free Press, 1985), 3.

125 Kotter, *Power and Influence*.

126 W. Rosen and L. Minsky, *The Activation Imperative* (Lanham, Maryland: Rowman and Littlefield, 2016), 153.

127 Rosen and Minsky, *The Activation Imperative*, 153.

128 R. Thaler and C. Sunstein, *Nudge: Improving Decisions about Health, Wealth, and Happiness* (New Haven, CT, Yale University Press, 2008), 6, file:///Users/MeghanScudero/Downloads/Richard_H._Thaler_Cass_R._Sunstein_Nudge_Improv..pdf.

129 "Path of Least Resistance in 401(k)," *The Digest*, no. 4 (2002), NBER, accessed October 29, 2020, https://www.nber.org/digest/apr02/w8651.html.

130 A. Ferrier, *The Advertising Effect* (South Melbourne, Victoria, Australia, Oxford Uni-

versity Press, 2014).

131 K. T. May, "10 Brand Stories from Tim Leberecht's TED Talk," *TED* (blog), 2012, accessed August 18, 2020, https://blog.ted.com/10-brand-stories-from-tim-leberechts-tedtalk/.

132 "Enron's 'Code of Ethics,'" The Smoking Gun, 4, accessed November 3, 2020, http://www.thesmokinggun.com/file/enrons-code-ethics?page=2.

133 "The Fallout of Arthur Andersen and Enron on the Legal Landscape of American Accounting," HG.org Legal Resources, accessed August 17, 2020, https://www.hg.org/legal-articles/the-fallout-of-arthur-andersen-and-enron-on-the-legal-landscape-of-american-accounting-31277.

134 Associated Press, "A Look at Those Involved in Enron Scandal," *Chicago Tribune*, 2006, accessed August 17, 2020, https://www.chicagotribune.com/sns-ap-enron-trial-glance-story.html.

135 "Kill All Your Darlings," *Book Architecture* (blog), 2018, accessed August 17, 2020, https://bookarchitecture.com/kill-all-your-darlings/.

136 J. S. Lerner et al., "Emotion and Decision Making, "*Annual Review of Psychology*, 2015, 4, accessed August 17, 2020, https://scholar.harvard.edu/files/jenniferlerner/files/annual_review_manuscript_june_16_final.final_.pdf.

137 "La Salle Network Publishes Report Based on 5,000 Survey Responses: Hiring Millennial Talent in 2019," La Salle Network, 2018, accessed August 18, 2020, https://www.thelasallenetwork.com/press-releases/lasalle-network-publishes-report-based-5000-survey-responses-hiring-millennial-talent-2019/.

138 "The Benefits of Benefits: Why Employers Can't Afford Inadequate Workplace Perks," Randstad, 2018, accessed August 18, 2020, https://rlc.randstadusa.com/press-room/press-releases/the-benefits-of-benefits-why-employers-cant-afford-inadequate-workplace-perks.

139 "The Benefits of Benefits."

140 "The Benefits of Benefits."

141 "The Benefits of Benefits."

142 "Survey: 73 Percent of Workers Consider Health and Wellness Offerings When Choosing A Job," Robert Half, 2019, accessed August 18, 2020, http://rh-us.mediaroom.com/2019-01-07-Survey-73-Percent-Of-Workers-Consider-Health-And-Wellness-Offerings-When-Choosing-A-Job.

143 "Investment in a Company's Internal Culture of Health Is Good for Health and Good for Business," Academy Health, 2019, accessed August 18, 2020, https://www.academyhealth.org/sites/default/files/int_ext_health_june_2019.pdf.

144 "The Executive's Guide to Engaging Millennials," Great Place to Work, 2018, 8, accessed August 18, 2020, https://www.greatplacetowork.com/images/media/2018_millennials_report_3.0.pdf.

145 J. A. Goodby, "The Gossage Galaxy: A Few Words about Howard Luck Gossage, the 'Socrates of San Francisco,' for Whom Advertising was Frequently a Cup of Hemlock," *Ad Age*, 1995, accessed August 18, 2020, https://adage.com/article/news/gossage-galaxy-a-words-howard-luck-gossage-socrates-san-francisco-advertising-frequently-a-cup-hemlock/93841#:~:text=%22In%20baiting%20a%20trap%2C%20

always,up%20to%20more%20credible%20sources.).

146 L. Minsky and K. A. Quesenberry, "How B2B Sales Can Benefit from Social Selling," *Harvard Business Review*, 2016, accessed August 18, 2020, https://hbr.org/2016/11/84-of-b2b-sales-start-with-a-referral-not-a-salesperson.

147 R. Cialdini, *Influence: The Psychology of Persuasion* (New York: HarperCollins, 1993), 114.

148 A. Lee, "30 Legendary Startup Pitch Decks and What You Can Learn from Them," Piktochart, 2016, accessed August 18, 2020, https://piktochart.com/blog/startup-pitch-decks-what-you-can-learn/.

Chapter 6

149 A. Fisher, "Giving a Speech? Conquer the Five-Minute Attention Span," *Fortune*, 2013, accessed September 2, 2020, https://fortune.com/2013/07/10/giving-a-speech-conquer-the-five-minute-attention-span/.

150 D. Mendel, "User Attention Span on the Internet Contracting," Anagard, 2013, accessed September 2, 2020, http://www.anagard.com/blog/2013/12/04/user-attention-span-on-the-internet-contracting/.

151 N. Zandan, "The Science of Audience Engagement," Quantified Communications, accessed September 2, 2020, https://www.quantifiedcommunications.com/blog/the-science-of-audience-engagement/.

152 M. Nossel, *Powered By Storytelling: Excavate, Craft, and Present Stories to Transform Business Communication* (New York: McGraw-Hill, 2018), accessed November 3, 2020, https://narativ.com/powered-by-storytelling-book/.

153 H. Monarth, "The Irresistible Power of Storytelling as a Strategic Business Tool," *Harvard Business Review*, 2014, accessed September 2, 2020, https://hbr.org/2014/03/the-irresistible-power-of-storytelling-as-a-strategic-business-tool.

154 S. Mcfeely and B. Wigert, "This Fixable Problem Costs U.S. Businesses $1 Trillion," Gallup, 2019, accessed September 2, 2020, https://www.gallup.com/workplace/247391/fixable-problem-costs-businesses-trillion.aspx.

155 Mcfeely and Wigert, "This Fixable Problem."

156 L. Schwartz, "'Great' and 'Gretzky' Belong Together," ESPN, accessed September 2, 2020, http://www.espn.com/sportscentury/features/00014218.html.

157 A. Moazed, "5 Things You Can Learn from One of Airbnb's Earliest Hustles," *Inc.*, accessed September 2, 2020, https://www.inc.com/alex-moazed/cereal-obama-denver-the-recipe-these-airbnb-hustlers-used-to-launch-a-unicorn.html.

158 C. Clifford, "How the Co-Founder of Airbnb Went from $25,000 in Credit Card Debt to Running His $30 Billion Company," CNBC Make It, 2017, accessed September 2, 2020, https://www.cnbc.com/2017/06/30/airbnb-ceo-went-from-25000-in-debt-to-running-a-30-billion-company.html.

159 A. H. Monroe, *Principles and Types of Speech* (Chicago: Scott Foresman, 1935).

160 "Chapter 17.3 Organizing Persuasive Speeches," University of Minnesota Libraries, accessed September 3, 2020, https://open.lib.umn.edu/publicspeaking/chapter/17-3-organizing-persuasive-speeches/.

161 "Social Theory at HBS: McGinnis' Two FOs," *The Harbus,* New York, 2004, accessed September 2, 2020, https://harbus.org/2004/social-theory-at-hbs-2749/.

162 D. Ariely, *Predictably Irrational: The Hidden Forces That Shape Our Decisions* (New York: HarperCollins, 2009).

163 "Richard H. Thaler, Facts," The Nobel Prize, accessed September 2, 2020, https://www.nobelprize.org/prizes/economic-sciences/2017/thaler/facts/.

164 D. Kahneman and A. Tversky, "Prospect Theory: An Analysis of Decision Under Risk," *Econometrica* 47, no. 2 (1979): 263–91, DOI: 10.2307/191418.

165 G. Lucas, dir., *Star Wars Episode VI: A New Hope* (CA: Lucasfilm, 1977), DVD.

Chapter 7

166 C. Melore, "Ill manners: Many Employees Will Still Go to Work Sick after COVID-19 Outbreak Ends," Study Finds, 2020, accessed September 8, 2020, https://www.studyfinds.org/many-employees-still-go-to-work-sick-after-covid-19-outbreak-ends/.

167 R. Travis, "Without Sick Pay Benefits, COVID-Infected Healthcare Workers Feel Pressure to Return to Work," Fox 5 Atlanta, 2020, accessed September 8, 2020, https://www.fox5atlanta.com/news/without-sick-pay-benefits-covid-infected-healthcare-workers-feel-pressure-to-return-to-work.

168 "COVID-19 Pandemic Won't Stop Some People from Going to Work Sick, Survey Shows," *Safety and Health Magazine,* 2020, accessed September 8, 2020, https://www.safetyandhealthmagazine.com/articles/20136-covid-19-pandemic-wont-stop-some-people-from-going-to-work-sick-survey-shows.

169 J. Adamy, "Families File First Wave of Covid-19 Lawsuits against Companies over Worker Deaths," *Wall Street Journal,* 2020, accessed September 8, 2020, https://www.wsj.com/articles/families-file-first-wave-of-covid-19-lawsuits-against-companies-over-worker-deaths-11596137454.

170 "What You Should Know about COVID-19 and the ADA, the Rehabilitation Act, and Other EEO Laws," U.S. Equal Employment Opportunity Commission, 2020, accessed September 8, 2020, https://www.eeoc.gov/wysk/what-you-should-know-about-covid-19-and-ada-rehabilitation-act-and-other-eeo-laws.

171 "Age and Tenure in the C-Suite," Korn Ferry, 2020, accessed September 8, 2020, https://www.kornferry.com/about-us/press/age-and-tenure-in-the-c-suite.

172 "Fish Rots from the Head Down," The Idioms, accessed September 8, 2020, https://www.theidioms.com/fish-rots-from-the-head-down/.

173 "'Culture Eats Strategy for Breakfast'—What Does It Mean?," *The Alternative Board* (blog), February 26, 2020, accessed September 8, 2020, https://www.thealternative-board.com/blog/culture-eats-strategy.

174 K. Stevens, "The Glint of Light on a Broken Glass," *Word Press* (blog), January 4, 2015, accessed September 9, 2020, https://wordpress.com/dailypost/2015/01/04/the-glint-of-light-on-broken-glass/.

175 S. Lazzaro, "Is This Soap Dispenser Racist? Controversy as a Video of Machine That Only Responds to White Skin," *NZ Herald,* 2017, accessed September 9, 2020, https://www.nzherald.co.nz/technology/news/article.cfm?c_id=5&objectid=11908554.

176 "MBO Programs Help Employees Reach Maximum Potential," *Xactly* (blog), September 23, 2014, accessed October 29, 2020, https://www.xactlycorp.com/blog/mbo-programs#:~:text=Culture%20Shock,Fostering%20a%20great%20company%20culture.&text=Managers%20can%20create%20individual%20and,their%20workforces%20and%20their%20businesses.

177 "America's Most Innovative Leaders," *Forbes*, 2019, accessed September 9, 2020, https://www.forbes.com/lists/innovative-leaders/#425895b926aa.

178 R. Cialdini, *Pre-Suasion: A Revolutionary Way to Influence and Persuade* (New York: Simon & Schuster, 2016), 163.

179 A. Lewis, "It's Time to Believe the Research: Wellness Isn't Working," *Employee Benefit News*, 2019, accessed September 9, 2020, https://www.benefitnews.com/opinion/time-to-believe-why-wellness-isnt-lowering-healthcare-costs.

180 "Much-Touted Workplace Wellness Programs Don't Live Up to Hype in Sweeping Study That Could Put Doubts to Rest," Kaiser Health News, April 17, 2019, accessed September 9, 2020, https://khn.org/morning-breakout/much-touted-workplace-wellness-programs-dont-live-up-to-hype-in-sweeping-study-that-could-put-doubts-to-rest/.

181 K. Baicker and Z. Song, "Effect of a Workplace Wellness Program on Employee Health and Economic Outcomes: A Randomized Clinical Trial," *JAMA* 321, no.15 (2019): 1491–1501, https://doi.org/10.1001/jama.2019.3307.

182 L. Lovlie, A. Polaine, and B. Reason, *Service Design: From Insight to Implementation* (New York: Rosenfield Media, 2013),163.

183 R. Hill, "How to Get Honest Answers on Employee Surveys," Bright Horizons, accessed July 7, 2020, https://www.brighthorizons.com/employer-resources/employee-surveys.

184 "Role of race with the suffrage movement", Susan B. Anthony Birthplace Museum, accessed December 1 2020, http://www.susanbanthonybirthplace.com/racism.html.

Chapter 8

185 W. Littlefield, *Top of the Rock: Inside the Rise and Fall of Must-See TV* (New York: Doubleday, 2012), 6.

186 *1st Must See TV Promo? 1993, Seinfeld, Frasier, Larroquette*, online video, NBC, 1993, accessed October 14, 2020, https://www.youtube.com/watch?v=GwOlQpld-Haw&list=PLnHs7SDcQstcW-DGVNilZ9URAMInaEW5Y&index=1.

187 *Lexico*, US Dictionary, accessed October 14, 2020, https://www.lexico.com/en/definition/cyborg.

188 S. O'Dea, "Smartphone Penetration in the United States as Share of Population 2018–2024," Statista, 2020, accessed October 14, 2020, https://www.statista.com/statistics/201184/percentage-of-mobile-phone-users-who-use-a-smartphone-in-the-us/.

189 A. Smith, "Nearly Half of American Adults Are Smartphone Owners," Pew Research Center, 2012, accessed October 14, 2020, https://www.pewresearch.org/internet/2012/03/01/nearly-half-of-american-adults-are-smartphone-owners/#:~:text=Nearly%20half%20(46%25)%20of,owned%20a%20smartphone%20last%20May.

190 J. Dunn, "Here's How Huge Netflix Has Gotten in the Past Decade," *Business Insider*,

2017, accessed October 14, 2020, https://www.businessinsider.com/netflix-subscribers-chart-2017-1.

191 Z. Honig, "Hulu Announces 2012 Results: $695M Revenue, 3 Million Hulu Plus Subscribers," Engadget, 2012, accessed October 14, 2020, https://www.engadget.com/2012-12-17-hulu-2012-results.html#:~:text=Hulu%20announces%202012%20results%3A%20%24695,million%20Hulu%20Plus%20subscribers%20%7C%20Engadget.

192 A. Watson, "Number of Netflix Paid streaming Subscribers in the U.S. 2011–2020," Statista, 2020, accessed October 14, 2020, https://www.statista.com/statistics/250937/quarterly-number-of-netflix-streaming-subscribers-in-the-us/#:~:text=In%20the%20second%20quarter%20of,2019%20stood%20at%20167%20million.

193 A. Watson, "Number of Hulu's Paying Subscribers in the U.S. 2010–2020, by Quarter," Statista, 2020, accessed October 14, 2020, https://www.statista.com/statistics/258014/number-of-hulus-paying-subscribers/.

194 Q3 2013 Global Video Index, Ooyala 2013, 4, accessed October 15, 2020, http://go.ooyala.com/rs/OOYALA/images/Ooyala-Global-Video-Index-Q3-2013.pdf.

195 Q2 2020 Global Video Index, Brightcove, 2020, 11, accessed October 15, 2020, https://files.brightcove.com/en/video-index/GVI_2020_Q2_Report_Media_Entertainment.pdf.

196 A. Watson, "Disney+ Number of Subscribers Worldwide from 1st Quarter 2020 to August 2020," Statista, 2020, accessed October 15, 2020, https://www.statista.com/statistics/1095372/disney-plus-number-of-subscribers-us/#:~:text=In%20a%20call%20discussing%20its,the%20end%20of%20Q2%202020.

197 Q2 2013 Global Video Index, 3.

198 D. Moschetti, "Wellness Incentives: Can the Use of Financial Incentives and Penalties Be Effective for Motivating Participation in Wellness Programs and Sustaining Health Behavior Modification?," Seminar Research Paper Series, Paper 30, 2013, 23, accessed October 30, 2020, https://digitalcommons.uri.edu/cgi/viewcontent.cgi?article=1037&context=lrc_paper_series.

199 S. Miller, "Employers Boost Benefits to Win and Keep Top Talent," SHRM, 2019, accessed October 30, 2020, https://www.shrm.org/resourcesandtools/hr-topics/benefits/pages/employers-boost-benefits-to-win-and-keep-talent.aspx.

200 National Sleep Foundation, "The Connection between Sleep and Overeating," Sleep Foundation, accessed October 15, 2020, https://www.sleepfoundation.org/articles/connection-between-sleep-and-overeating#:~:text=The%20Connection%20Between%20Sleep%20and%20Overeating&text=Two%20hormones%20that%20help%20regulate,to%20an%20increase%20in%20hunger.

201 Touré Tillery, Maferima, and Ayelet Fishbach. "Three Sources of Motivation." Consumer Psychology Review 1, no. 1 (2018): 123–34.

202 M. Nelson, "Soviet and American Precursors to the Gamification of Work," MindTrek '12: Proceeding of the 16th International Academic MindTrek Conference, Association for Computing Machinery, 2012, 23–26, accessed November 25, 2020, https://doi.org/10.1145/2393132.2393138.

203 Nelson, "Soviet and American Precursors," 23–26.

204 C. Coonradt, The Game of Work: How to Enjoy Work as Much as Play (Kaysville, UT, Gibbs Smith, 2007).

205 D. Newman, "How to Drive Employee Engagement with Workplace Gamification," *Forbes*, 2017, accessed October 16, 2020, https://www.forbes.com/sites/danielnewman/2017/11/28/how-to-drive-employee-engagement-with-workplace-gamification/#454a07de3cf0.

206 R. Hunicke, M. LeBlanc, and R. Zubek, "MDA: A Formal Approach to Game Design and Game Research," Northwestern University, accessed October 16, 2020, https://users.cs.northwestern.edu/~hunicke/pubs/MDA.pdf.

207 Hunicke, LeBlanc, and Zubek, "MDA."

208 *Future of Fitness: Understanding the Growth of Mobile Video*, Penthera and Apptopia, 2020, 10, accessed October 16, 2020, https://info.penthera.com/fitnessreport?utm_campaign=fitness%20report&utm_source=linkedin&utm_medium=Penthera&utm_content=we%E2%80%99re_excited_to_announce.

Chapter 9

209 L. Minsky, *How to Succeed in Advertising When All You Have Is Talent*, 2nd ed. (Chicago: Copy Workshop, 2007), 336.

210 *Keeping Your Customers Engaged: Research Insights*, online video, presenter Rima Touré-Tillery, Marketing Science Institute, 2020, accessed October 19, 2020, https://www.msi.org/videos/keeping-your-customers-engaged-research-insights/.

211 *Keeping Your Customers Engaged.*

212 Personal conversation, March 5, 2020.

213 N. Karlinsky and J. Stead, "How a Door Became a Desk, and a Symbol of Amazon," *Amazon Blog* (blog), January 17, 2018, accessed October 29, 2020, https://blog.aboutamazon.com/working-at-amazon/how-a-door-became-a-desk-and-a-symbol-of-amazon.

214 Minsky, *How to Succeed*, 186.

215 L. Minsky, *Advertising under One Hour*, Under One Hour LLC, 2018, 65.

Chapter 10

216 "About Motorola University: The Inventors of Six Sigma," Wayback Machine, 2005, accessed October 19, 2020, https://web.archive.org/web/20051106025733/https://www.motorola.com/content/0%2C%2C3079%2C00.html.

217 D. Wilkie, "Is the Annual Performance Review Dead?," SHRM, 2015, accessed October 19, 2020, https://www.shrm.org/resourcesandtools/hr-topics/employee-relations/pages/performance-reviews-are-dead.aspx.

218 M. Quartz, "How Millennials Forced GE to Scrap Performance Reviews," *The Atlantic*, 2015, accessed October 19, 2020, https://www.theatlantic.com/politics/archive/2015/08/how-millennials-forced-ge-to-scrap-performance-reviews/432585/.

219 MAX NISEN, QUARTZ AUGUST 18, 2015, https://www.theatlantic.com/politics/ar-

chive/2015/08/how-millennials-forced-ge-to-scrap-performance-reviews/432585/

220 Quartz, "How Millennials Forced."

221 "U.S. Army Adopting Lean Six Sigma," Six Sigma, 2016, accessed October 19, 2020, https://www.6sigma.us/six-sigma-articles/us-army-adopting-lean-six-sigma/.

222 "Lean Six Sigma in the US Army—Toward Efficiency," Six Sigma, 2017, accessed October 19, 2020, https://www.6sigma.us/armed-forces/lean-six-sigma-in-the-us-army-to-improve-efficiency/.

223 M. Pollan, *How to Change Your Mind: What the New Science of Psychedelics Teaches Us about Consciousness, Dying, Addiction, Depression, and Transcendence* (New York: Penguin, 2018).

224 S. McLeod, "Albert Bandura—Social Learning Theory," Simply Psychology, 2016, accessed October 20, 2020, https://www.simplypsychology.org/bandura.html.

225 A. Bandura, *Social Learning Theory* (New York: Prentice-Hall, 1976).

226 D. Mielach, "We Can't Solve Problems by Using the Same Kind of Thinking We Used When We Created Them," *Business Insider*, 2012, accessed November 3, 2020, https://www.businessinsider.com/we-cant-solve-problems-by-using-the-same-kind-of-thinking-we-used-when-we-created-them-2012-4.

Afterword

227 *Navigating Together: Supporting Employee Wellbeing in Uncertain Times*, MetLife, 2020, 39, accessed October 30, 2020, https://www.metlife.com/content/dam/metlifecom/us/ebts/pdf/MetLife-Employee-Benefit-Trends-Study-2020.pdf.

228 K. Greenwood and N. Krol, "8 Ways Managers Can Support Employees' Mental Health," *Harvard Business Review*, 2020, accessed October 30, 2020, https://hbr.org/2020/08/8-ways-managers-can-support-employees-mental-health.

229 C. Boyle, "Clients Do Not Come First. Employees Come First. If You Take Care of Your Employees, They Will Take Care of Your Clients," LinkedIn, 2018, accessed November 4, 2020, https://www.linkedin.com/pulse/clients-do-come-first-employees-you-take-care-your-charlie-boyle/.

230 "Working at Virgin," The Virgin Group, accessed November 4, 2020, https://www.virgin.com/about-virgin/virgin-careers.

231 Personal conversation, April 15, 2020.

INDEX